FUNDAMENTALS OF

Sales and Distribution Management

TEXT & CASES

FUNDAMENTALS OF
Sales and Distribution Management

Bholanath Dutta
Asst. Professor
Dept. of Management Studies
CMR Institute of Technology
Bangalore

NEW DELHI

Published by
Techsar Pvt. Ltd.
4435–36/7, Ansari Road, Daryaganj
New Delhi-110 002 (India)
E-mail: tech_info@techsarworld.com
Website: www.techsarworld.com

ISBN 978-93-80578-91-0

Reprint 2024

To
My Parents
Shri Jatindranath Dutta
Smt. Jharna Dutta
and
My loving wife and best friend
Paramita

PREFACE

Importance of sales management is critical for any commercial organization. Expanding business is not possible without increasing sales volumes, and effective sales management goal is to organize sales team work in such a manner that ensures a growing flow of regular customers and increasing amount of sales.

There is no need to explain the importance of sales management and its role in any commercial organization. All companies in the world aim to sell more products and make more profit because expanding business in not possible without increasing sales volumes. However, when sales start to grow, companies understand that it is very hard to manage enlarged sales workflow as effectively as they did before.

Managing increased sales volumes is more difficult because sales management process becomes more complicated and sales department has to deal with all aspects of the process. Not only the number of sales tasks grows but also grows the number of regions, customers and products. It is almost impossible for salespersons to handle with sales grows without a special system for planning, tracking, analyzing, reporting, and controlling all aspects of sales activity, projects and tasks.

As sales management is an important function, similarly distribution management is another function which is very commonly known as life-blood of any organization. The distribution management generally refers efficient transfer of goods from the place where they are manufactured to the place where they are sold or used and it involves such activities as warehousing, materials handling, packaging, stock control, order processing, and transport.

This book covers fundamental concepts of sales and distribution management. It also includes a detail insight on supply chain management and retail management. It covers the MBA syllabus of Devi Ahilya University, Indore, Kannur University Kerala, Uttarakhand Technical University, UP Technological University, Jodhpur University, IP University, Maharshi Dayanad University, Punjab Technological University, Gujarat Technological University, Bangalore University, Visvesvaraya Technological University, JNTU, West Bengal Technological University and all other Indian Universities.

The author will be highly grateful to those who will find out the various ways to improve the book further. The author will feel himself amply satisfied if this book can meet the demand of the students.

The author requests teachers and students to send their comments and valuable suggestion for improvement of this book in the coming years. Please post your suggestions to: *bhola_dutta@yahoo.com.*

Bholanath Dutta

ACKNOWLEDGEMENTS

While preparing the manuscript, the author takes the help from some foreign books and inserts the idea, opinion and data, etc. in order to create attractions to the students and clarify critical concepts. The author expresses his heartiest thanks and gratitude as well as indebtedness to the authors and publishers of those books.

In order to get the book ready for the students, all employees of IK International Publishing House have performed such a tremendous job for which no thanks for their contribution will be enough. My special thanks to Mr. Krishan Makhijani-Managing Director and Mr. VR Babu- DGM (Southern Region) of IK International Publishing House for their all help in bringing out this book.

I feel great pleasure in expressing my profound gratitude to Dr. KC Sabita Ramamurthy – President, CMR Jananadhara Trust (CMRJT) , Shri KC Ramamurthy (IPS – Retd) –Chairman- CMRJT, Shri Jayadeep (CEO- CMRJT), Ms. Tristha Ramamurthy(Vice-President- CMRJT), Dr. KVS Anand Babu – Principal, CMRIT, Dr. L Sudarshan Reddy – Vice-Principal, CMRIT, Dr. Col (Retd.) Mukesh Kumar V – Director- MBA , Prof. K Ravi – Director, Career Guidance & Placement Bureau, CMRIT, Prof. Sundar Raj Vijaynagar, Prof. MB Lobo and all my esteemed colleagues in CMRIT for their incessant guidance, stimulation and encouragement in my academic endeavor.

Last but not the least, the silent support received from Mrs. Paramita Dutta, my wife, my parents (Shri Jatindranath Dutta & Smt. Jharna Dutta), in-laws (Shri Dipak Chaudhri & Smt. Keya Chaudhuri), who stand behind all of my even or odd situations to convert any distress into delight, desire unconditional recognition.

Bholanath Dutta

CONTENTS

THE AUTHOR

Bholanath Dutta, is an Accredited Management Teacher by All India Management Association-New Delhi, holds an M.Phil (Entrepreneurship), MBA (Marketing), Post Graduate Diploma in Tourism Management, Diploma in Electronics & Telecom Engg., Diploma in Advanced Accountancy, and couple of courses in specific areas (CRS, Ticketing, Tours & Travels & Airlines Mgmt.) of tourism industry from Indian Institute of Tourism and Travel Management, Ministry of Tourism.

He is currently working as Asst. Professor, Dept. of Management Studies, in CMR Institute of Technology. He has over 20 years of experience as varied as industry, academic, teaching, administration, research and consulting.

He has received two awards: "Best Professor 2009"—a national level event constituted by 24/7—a leading MNC and "Arch of Excellence (Education)"—a national award for his contribution in education. He is an accredited trainer & motivator for developing entrepreneurship in college campus by Visvesvarya Technological University.

Dutta is a prolific writer. He has authored 15 books in the area of marketing, entrepreneurship and general management. His more than dozen articles are selected and published in derivative reference books. He has published more than 70 papers till date including articles/research paper/case study in the area of general management, marketing and entrepreneurship in the leading national and international management magazine/journal and still counting. He presented many papers in national and international conferences. He is a Resource Person in Management education and has delivered lectures at various institutes. He is a guest editor to www.mybigeconomy.com & www.mybigstartup.com. He is the Coordinator of "Center for Research & Publication" and Founder Chief-Editor for a national level research journal-"Jnanatapsa". He has chaired many sessions in national and international conferences.

He is a fellow member of Institute of Marketing Management, member of AIMA, AIMS-International, NEN Network, Indian Society for Training and Development, BMA and life member of Institution of Homoeopathic Practitioners.

1

CHAPTER

Introduction and Basic Concepts

"You don't get paid for the hour. You get paid for the value you bring to the hour."

—Jim Rohn

The nature of personal selling – personal selling in marketing mix – features – fundamentals of successful personal selling – pros and cons of personal selling – disadvantages of personal selling – objectives – scope of personal selling – new dimension of personal selling – sales management environment – sales forecasting techniques – sales planning process – sales management planning – selling strategies – selling methods.

LEARNING OBJECTIVES

After going through this chapter, students will be able to understand

- The meaning of personal selling
- Importance of personal selling
- Nature of personal selling
- Different dimensions of sales management
- Importance of sales management environment
- Various sales forecasting techniques
- Personal selling process
- Process of sales management planning
- Different selling strategies
- Methods of selling.

INTRODUCTION

The spirit of salesmanship being ethical from movie "Rocket Singh–Salesman of the year".

You are well aware that marketing does not mean only offering the goods and services produced to the consumers for price and distributing them. Consumer satisfaction is the core of marketing. Goods and services are produced after studying the requirements of the consumers. Once these are produced, the consumers are informed and convinced that the products in question can satisfy their needs. Advertisement serves the purpose of keeping the customers informed about the products available in the market besides this; consumers also need to be informed about the new products likely to be introduced. Consumers are to be convinced about the quality of the products and the benefits thereof. They need to be persuaded to buy the products. This can best be done by personally contacting the prospective buyers. It is called personal selling.

Marketing and sales are different, but have the same goal. Marketing improves the selling environment and plays an important role in sales. If the marketing department

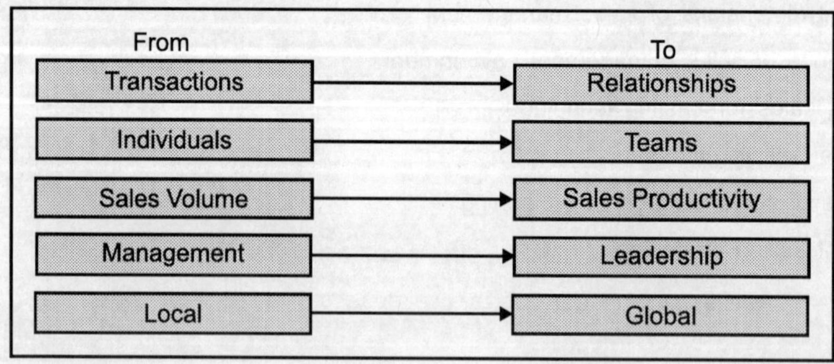

Fig. 1.1. Sales management trends.

generates a potential customers' list, it can be beneficial for sales. The marketing department's goal is to increase the number of interactions between potential customers and the sales team using promotional techniques such as advertising, sales promotion, publicity, and public relations, creating new sales channels, or creating new products (new product development), among other things.

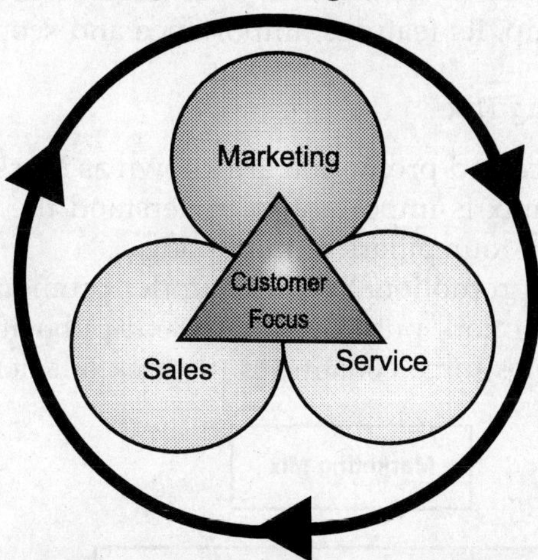

Fig. 1.2. Customer focus is the mantra.

Table 1.1. Difference between marketing and selling

Basis of Difference	Marketing	Selling
1. Origin	Marketing is a new approach	Selling is a classical word
2. Activities	It includes the entire process of discovering and satisfying the consumer needs	It includes only the physical distribution of goods and services
3. Scope	Marketing includes the performance of many allied activities also.	Selling is limited only to the physical distribution
4. Product-orientation vs. Customer-orientation	Marketing is customer-oriented	Selling is product oriented
5. Target	The aim of marketing is to satisfy the consumer needs	The aim of sale is to earn the maximum profit
6. Approach to Profit	It stresses upon maximization of profit through maximum social satisfaction	It stresses upon maximization of profits through maximization of sales
7. Nature	Marketing has long-term objectives with certain philosophical implications	Selling is a routine activity with short-term objectives
8. Views Business	Views business as a 'customer satisfying process'	Views business as a 'good producing process'
9. Product Determination	What should be offered as a 'product' is determined by the buyer	The seller determines what 'product' is to be offered
10. Determination of Price	Consumer determines price; price determines costs	Cost determines price
11. View the Customer	Marketing views the customer as the king	'Selling' views the customer as the last link in the business
12. Emphasis	The emphasis is on an integrated approach; through an integrated strategy covering product, promotion, pricing and distribution	The emphasis is on 'somehow selling'; there is no coordination among the different functions of the total marketing tasks

Salesmanship today covers a wide range of activities and constitutes an integral part of management. It also offers wide scope for development in future. In fact, modern salesmanship is growing on scientific lines, day by day. Time is not far when a salesman will be in a position to dictate to the producers of goods and services, what, when and how much to produce for sale in the market. This lesson will help you to understand the meaning of salesmanship, its features, importance and scope.

Personal Selling in Marketing Mix

4Ps, i.e., product, price, place and promotion are known as Marketing Mix in marketing. Understanding marketing mix is important to understand the marketing management subject. These are known as four pillars of marketing.

There are five different promotional vehicles under promotion (4th P): Advertising, personal selling, sales promotion, public relations and publicity and direct marketing. Personal selling through sales force constitutes the area of sales management.

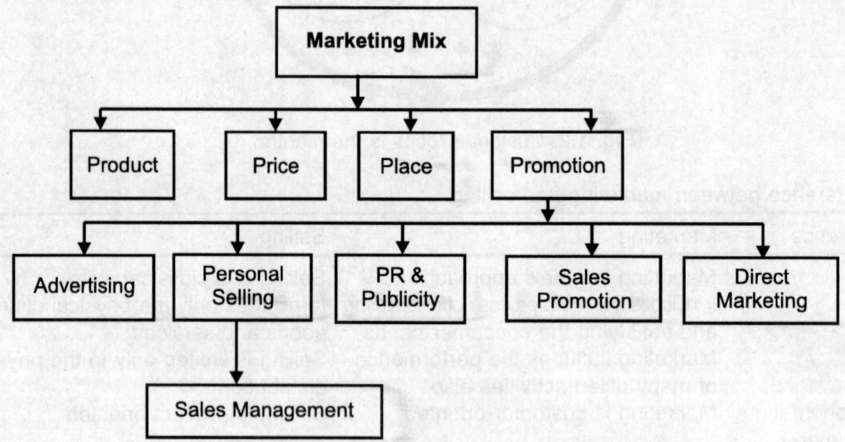

Fig 1.3. Personal selling in marketing mix.

The concept of personal selling in marketing mix can be explained as follows:

(i) ***Personal Selling with respect to Product Strategy:*** Since sales people are in direct liaison with prospective customers, their input is valuable during product development. Their inputs help designing the product based on customer preferences and needs. Old products are being replaced by new products. Some new products achieve acceptance from the customer, while some are forgotten and result in total loss to the manufacturer.

(ii) ***Personal Selling and Pricing Decisions:*** Sales personnel undergo requisite interaction with prospective customers to gauge their mood with respect to different price levels. Hence, their inputs are considered useful in formulating pricing strategies. The sales personnel are also well aware of the competitors' price and, based on the market reaction and customers' sentiments, they can advise a more prudent price policy to the management.

(iii) ***Personal Selling and Distribution:*** Whether the channel of distribution is direct or indirect, sales force has a significant role to play. The end result of any distribution effort is the availability of the product to the customer, in the right quantity and at the right place. If the product is not available when it is actually required by the customer, then the whole business activity and all related efforts are rendered useless. In view of this, the sales force plays an important role in coordinating, liaisoning and advocating the product's utility to the end user.

(iv) ***Personal Selling and Product Promotion:*** The sales force actually stimulates and generates enough interest in the customer and helps him in making the final decision to buy the product. Sharing the same values that the customer does, a salesperson provides motivation and generates interest and confidence in the customer for the product. Without this effort, the whole exercise of advertising and public relations would be futile. And thus, personal selling promotes a product.

PERSONAL SELLING

Personal selling is a promotional method in which one party (e.g., salesperson) uses skills and techniques for building personal relationships with another party (e.g., those involved in purchase decision) that results in both parties obtaining value. In most cases the "value" for the salesperson is realized through the financial rewards of the sale while the customer's "value" is realized from the benefits obtained by consuming the product. However, getting a customer to purchase a product is not always the objective of personal selling. For instance, selling may be used for the purpose of simply delivering information.

Because selling involves personal contact, this promotional method often occurs through face-to-face meetings or via a telephonic conversation, though newer technologies allow contact to take place over the Internet using videoconferencing or text messaging (e.g., online chat).

Concept

The elementary concepts associated with personal selling can be listed as follows:

- It is a part of product mix
- It is a personal (face-to-face, telephone, or Internet chat) presentation for the purpose of making sales and building relationships
- Oral presentation
- Salesmanship
- Perceive and persuade buyers

The effort of sales people go far beyond simply making transactions, they also include the following:

- Explaining product benefits
- Demonstrating the proper operation of the product

- Educating customers about the new product
- Answering questions and responding to the objections
- Organizing and implementing point of purchase promotion
- Arranging the terms of purchase
- Following up the purchase to ensure that customers are satisfied
- Developing the relationship with the buyers
- Collecting market and competitive information to improve marketing strategies

Personal selling is mostly used when

- The market is concentrated either geographically, in a few industries or a few large customers.
- The product has a high unit value, quite technical in nature or requires demonstration.
- The product must be suitable to the individual customer's needs as in case of insurance or investments.
- The product is in the introductory stage of its life cycle.
- The organization does not have enough money for adequate advertising.

Features

Some of the features of personal selling, which makes it more effective than other promotional tools:

- More specific communication aimed at one or more persons.
- Effective at buyers' preferences, conviction and actions.
- Cost per person is high, the most expensive promotional tool.
- Greater impact on the consumers.
- Provides immediate feedback.
- Allow the marketer to adjust message quickly to improve communication.
- Buyer feels a great need to listen and respond.
- Long-term commitments are needed to develop a sales force.

Nature of Personal Selling

Personal selling is a distinct form of promotion. It involves direct face-to-face contact between the salesman and the prospect:

(i) *Face-to-face contact:* Salesmanship or personal selling is most effective because it is direct and face-to-face.

(ii) *Highly flexible:* The personal selling efforts are highly flexible as it can be matched perfectly to the needs and moods of the customers or prospect or prospects.

Success Factors in Selling	**Mean**	**S.D.**
Highest level of importance		
Listening skills	6.502	0.683
Follow-up skills	6.358	0.772
Ability to adapt sales style from situation to situation	6.321	0.687
Tenacity-sticking with a task	6.107	0.924
Well organized	6.084	0.889
Verbal communication skills	6.047	0.808
Proficiency in interacting with people at all levels of a customer's organization	6.000	0.991
Demonstrated ability to overcome objections	5.981	1.085
Closing skills	5.944	1.109
Personal planning and time management skills	5.944	0.946
Proficieny in interacting with people at all levels of your organization	5.912	0.994
Negotiation skills	5.827	0.975
Dresses in appropriate attire	5.791	1.063
Empathy with the customer	5.723	1.074
Planning skills	5.005	0.900
Prospecting skills	5.673	1.209
Creativity	5.670	0.936
Ability to empathize with others	5.549	1.105
Skills in preparing for a sales call	5.526	1.219
Decision-making ability	5.502	1.023

Note: All items were scaled as follows: 1 = of no importance at all in hiring decisions, 7 = of the utmost importance in hiring decisions. S.D. = standard deviation.
Importance ratings of success factors for professional salespeople

Source: Greg W. Marshall, Daniel J. Coebèl, and William C. Moncrief, "Hiring for Success at the Buyer-Seller Interface," Journal of Business Research 56 (2003), pp. 247-255.

Exhibit 1.1. Success factors in selling.

(iii) ***Psychological work:*** Though a salesman's work consists of physical tasks of approaching the prospect or prospects, his major tasks are psychological where he uses AIDA formula whereby he converts desire into demand. It is the most difficult task.

(iv) ***Productive way:*** Salesman has the special ability of demonstrating the product that he wants to sell which creates strong trust.

(v) ***Educative process:*** Personal selling is an educative process where the salesman shares his perfect ideas about products. He is not only informing but also entertaining.

(vi) ***Both science and art:*** It is a science because the theories and principles can be learnt and practised and it is an art as it involves selling skills, presentation, negotiating and tactical skills.

Fundamentals of Successful Personal Selling

- Salesperson must have greater flexibility; he must tailor sales presentations to fit the needs and behaviour of the individual customers
- He must have the potential of explaining the benefits of the product, answer questions of his customers
- He must be truthful
- He must behave in a reliable manner
- Must seek similarity of personality between you and the customer and the commodity interest and goals
- Salesperson must see whether the person or his prospect has the potential to pay for the product or not.

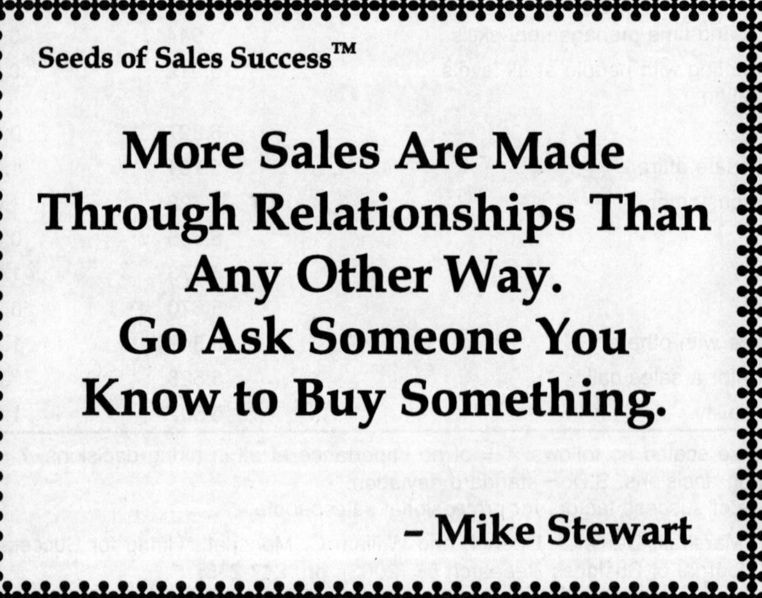

Advantages of Personal Selling

- Personal selling is a face-to-face activity; customers therefore obtain relatively a high degree of personal attention.
- The sales message can be customized to meet the needs of the customer.
- The two-way nature of the sales process allows the sales team to respond directly and promptly to customer's questions and concerns.
- Personal selling is a good way of getting across large amounts of technical or other complex product information.
- Face-to-face sales meeting gives the sales force opportunity to demonstrate the product.
- Frequent meetings between sales force and customer provide an opportunity to build long-term relationships.

Disadvantages of Personal Selling

Possibly the biggest disadvantage of selling is the degree to which this promotional method is misunderstood. Most people have had some bad experience with salespeople who they perceived were overly aggressive or even downright annoying. While there are certainly many salespeople who fall into this category, the truth is salespeople are most successful when they focus their efforts on satisfying the customers over the long term and not focusing on their own selfish interests.

A second disadvantage of personal selling is the high cost in maintaining this type of promotional effort. Costs incurred in personal selling include:

High Cost-per-action : Since personal selling involves person-to-person contact, the money spent to support a sales staff (i.e., sales force) can be high. For instance, in some industries it costs well over (US) $300 each time a salesperson contacts a potential customer. This cost is incurred whether a sale is made or not! These costs include compensation (e.g., salary, commission, and bonus), providing sales support materials, allowances for entertainment spending, office supplies, telecommunication and much more. With such high cost for maintaining a sales force, selling is often not a practical option for selling products that do not generate a large amount of revenue.

Training Costs : Most forms of personal selling require the sales staff be extensively trained on product knowledge, industry information and selling skills. For companies that require their salespeople attend formal training programmes, the cost of training can be quite high and includes such expenses as travel, hotel, meals, and training equipment while also paying the trainees' salaries while they attend the training programme.

The third disadvantage is that personal selling is not for everyone. Job turnover in sales is often much higher than other marketing positions. For companies that assign salespeople to handle certain customer groups (e.g., geographic territory), turnover may leave a company without representation in a customer group for an extended period of time while the company recruits and trains a replacement.

Objectives

Personal selling is used to meet the five objectives of promotion in the following ways:

Building Product Awareness : A common task of salespeople, especially when selling in business markets, is to educate customers on new product offerings. But building awareness using personal selling is also important in consumer markets. Word-of-mouth marketing leads the personnel a useful mechanism for introducing consumers to new products.

Creating Interest : The fact that personal selling involves person-to-person communication makes it a natural method for getting customers to experience a product for the first time. In fact, creating interest goes hand-in-hand with building product awareness as sales professionals can often accomplish both objectives during the first encounter with a potential customer.

Providing Information : When salespeople engage customers a large part of the conversation focuses on product information. Marketing organizations provide their sales staff with large amounts of sales support including brochures, research reports, computer programs and many other forms of information material.

Stimulating Demand : By far, the most important objective of personal selling is to convince customers to make a purchase. Salespeople accomplish this when they offer detailed coverage of the selling process used to gain customer orders.

Reinforcing the Brand : Most personal selling is intended to build long-term relationships with customers. A strong relationship can only be built over time and requires regular communication with a customer. Meeting with customers on a regular basis allows salespeople to repeatedly discuss their company's products and by doing so helps strengthen customers' knowledge of what the company has to offer.

Scope of Personal Selling

In the business there are two types of personal selling activities

- Inside selling
- Outside selling

Inside Selling

It involves retail stores. In this group we include the salesperson in the stores and the salespeople at the catalogue retailers who take orders on telephone. Also included are telephone orders takes by manufacturers and wholesalers, most of whom taking existing customers' routine orders over the telephone.

Outside Selling

Salespeople go to the consumer. They make contact by telephone or in person. Most outside sales force usually represents producers or wholesaling, middleman, selling to the business users and not to the household consumers. In outside selling, we also include:

1. Producers whose representatives sell directly to the household consumers, e.g., insurance companies.
2. Representatives of retail organizations who go to the consumer's house to demonstrate a product, give advice, or provide an estimate such as salespeople for some furniture stores and home heating and air-conditioning retailers.
3. Representatives of non-profitable organizations, e.g., charity funds raisers, workers for political candidate.

Dimensions of Personal Selling

(i) ***Customer relationship management:*** Getting new customers costs more than increasing sales with existing customers. Therefore, it is necessary to establish long-term relationship with the existing customers. This would lead to better understanding of customers' needs and to develop and design products to satisfy the needs of these customers. This also helps in creating new demands for the existing customers.

(ii) ***Sales force diversity:*** The workforce is changing in many ways. More women and minorities are taking up carriers in personal selling and are advancing into

sales management positions. To remain competitive, sales managers need to capitalize on the strengths of women and minorities in selling and to be aware of what these individuals want in a sales job.

(iii) ***Electronic communication system:*** In today's world of customers' expectations and complex competition, information search is a vital factor. The internet, intranets and extranets and other electronic technologies enable salespeople and sales managers to improve their productivity.

(iv) ***Selling team:*** It is necessary to implement the concept of selling team to respond to the changes in customers' buying patterns. A selling team is a group of people representing the sales department and other functional areas in the organization, such as finance, production and research and development.

(v) ***Complex channels of distribution:*** In order to capture the market share, the organization needs to develop and maintain suitable distribution channels. Modern distribution channel is characterized by rapid change and complexity which should be adapted by the sales managers to be competitive.

(vi) ***An international perspective:*** With the firms going global and many global players entering into the market, the competition is intensified. Different cultures and ways of doing business in foreign countries pose real challenges. Keeping these aspects in mind, business organizations need to be well equipped to face the emerging forces.

(vii) ***Ethical behaviour and social responsibility:*** It is necessary that the sales managers establish a clear ethical dimension of the salesman's role. Sales managers need to achieve a stronger level of ethical awareness during sales meetings, in training sessions, etc. It is vital that the organization should inculcate ethical business practices to serve customers better, to maintain long-lasting relationship with the customers and to remain a professional entity in the society.

New Dimension of Personal Selling

Personal selling today is quite different from what it was years ago. Today selling is a respectable profession and one can earn huge amount apart from salary as commission/ incentives. Today's salesmen are highly professional and are also called marketing consultants. This new breed works to relay consumer wants back to the firm so that appropriate products may be developed. Today's sales professionals are expected to solve customers' problems, not just take orders. They are not just selling they are also into relationship selling.

The new-type reps also serve as territorial profit managers. They have the autonomy to take independent decisions that affect their own territory's profitability. Many decisions that would have been made by the sales manager in the past are today made by the sales people. Sales people are empowered to act in the best interest of their firms. Technological advancement has empowered salespeople to increase the quality of contact and service they provide to their customers by allowing them to tap into huge data banks.

DEFINITION OF SALE AND SALESMANSHIP

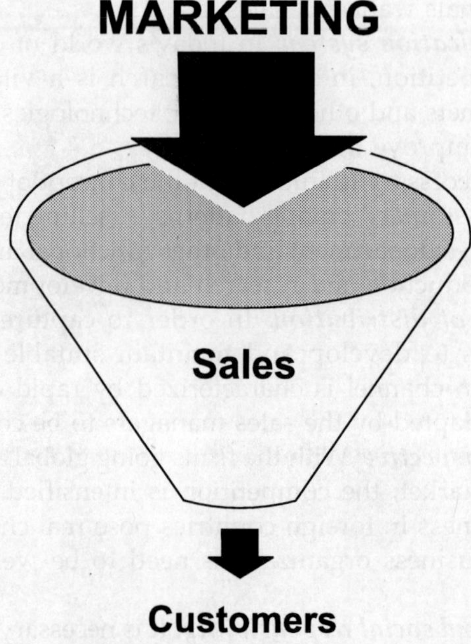

Legally, a sale is a transaction in which one person persuades another to purchase something at an agreed price. From a business point of view, the sale should result in a profit to the seller. As a legitimate phase of commerce, it should convey an advantage or a profit to the buyer.

Salesmanship has been defined by different people in different ways: Some people say salesmanship is: "Practice of investigating and satisfying customer needs through a process that is efficient, fair, sincere, mutually beneficial, and aimed at long-term productive relationship."

"The art of successfully persuading prospects or customers to buy products or services from which they can derive suitable benefits, thereby increasing their total satisfaction."

— I.J. Sapiro

Professor Stephenson defines salesmanship as: "a concise effort on the part of the seller to induce a prospective buyer to buy even if he had not thought of it favourably."

Gauss, Weightman and Bates observe: "Salesmanship consists of persuading people to buy what you have for sale, in making them want it, in helping to make their minds."

E.F. Schumaker defined selling as "the process affecting the transfer with a profit to buyer and seller of goods and services that give them lasting satisfaction that the buyer is predisposed to come back to the seller for more of the same."

According to American Marketing Association, "Salesmanship is an oral presentation in a conversation with one or more prospective customers for the purpose of making sales."

According to C.A. Paderson, "Salesmanship is the process whereby a seller ascertains and activates the needs or wants of the buyer and satisfies these needs and wants to the mutual continuous advantage of both the buyer and seller."

According to National Association of Marketing Teachers of America, "Salesmanship is the ability to persuade people to buy goods or services at a profit to the seller and benefit to the buyers."

Hence, salesmanship can be defined as an art of influencing another person for the object of persuading him to buy a specific product. It may be regarded as the process of winning the confidence of consumer. According to Whitehead, "It is a method regard to the desirability of some article, service of idea." Salesmanship may also refer to convincing a customer by certain technique and he is really persuaded for buying the particular product.

If we closely observe the above definitions, we find certain essential features of salesmanship. They can be summarized as follows:

(i) Salesmanship is the ability to persuade.
(ii) Salesmanship benefits both the buyer and seller.
(iii) Salesmanship stands for commercial honesty.
(iv) Salesmanship aims at winning the buyers' confidence.
(v) Ideal salesmanship aims at serving the producer, distributor and consumer.
(vi) Salesman acts as a link between the seller and the consumer.
(vii) Salesmanship is an educative process.
(viii) Salesmanship creates satisfied customers.

MARKETING ENVIRONMENT

An organization operates within the larger framework of the external environment that shapes opportunities and poses threats to it. The external environment is a set of complex, rapidly changing and significant interacting institutions and forces that affect the organization's ability to serve its customers. External forces are not controlled by an organization, but they may be influenced or affected by that organization. It is necessary for organizations to understand the environmental conditions because they interact with strategy decisions. The external environment has a major impact on the determination of marketing decisions. Successful organizations scan their external environment so that they can respond profitably to unmet needs and trends in the targeted markets.

According to Kotler, there are four types of environment pertaining to any company:

i) **Organizational environment:** Company department, company division, company's organizational structure and company channels.
ii) **Market environment**: It consists of actual and potential consumers or purchasers of the product.
iii) **Macro environment**: PEST
iv) **Extra-environment:** It forms that part of the environment which the organization usually does not scan because it seems to be of negligible or zero relevance to the organization.

Kinds of Marketing Environment

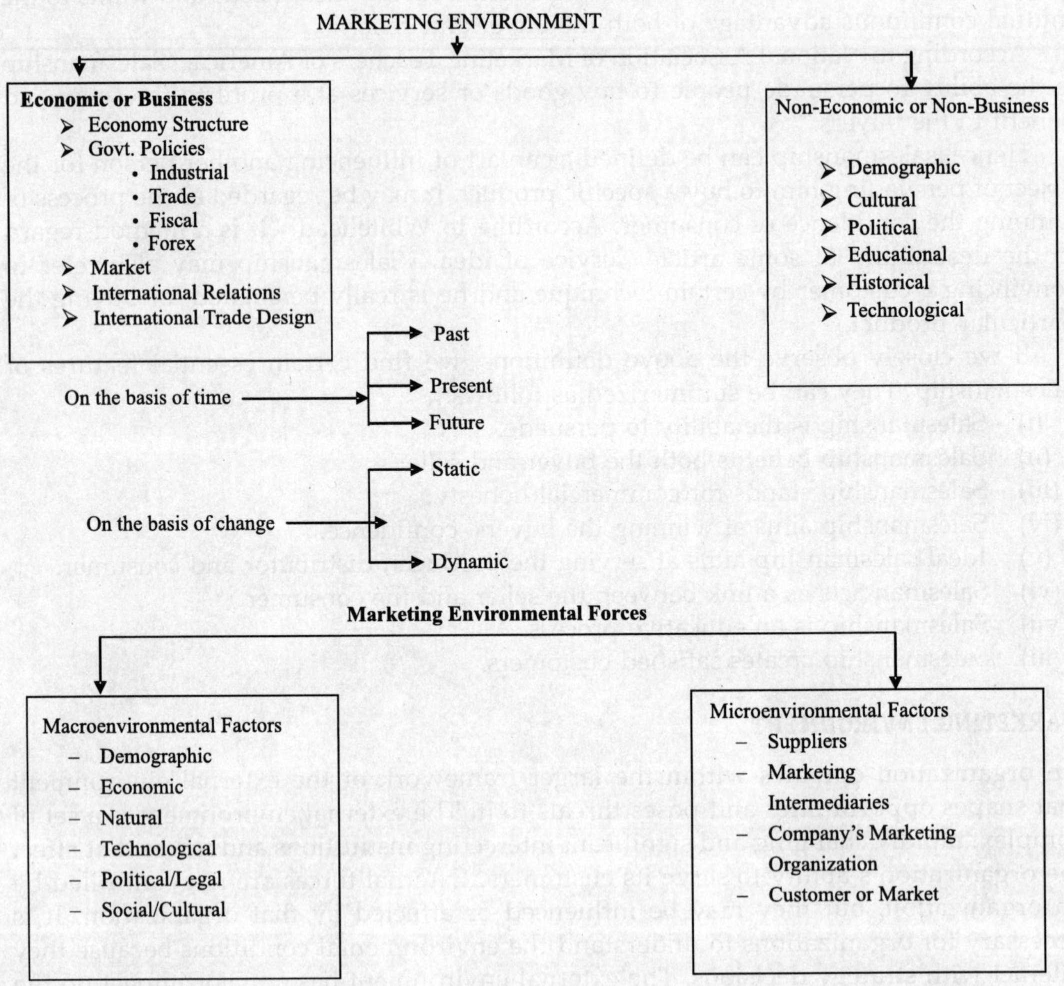

Macroenvironment

The macroenvironment consists of all the outside institutions and forces that have an actual or potential interest or impact on the organization's ability to achieve its objectives: competitive, economic, technological, political, legal, demographic, cultural, and ecosystem. Though non-controllable, these forces require a response in order to keep positive actions with the targeted markets. An organization with an environmental management perspective takes aggressive actions to affect the forces in its marketing environment rather than simply watching and reacting to it.

Competitive Environment

Adopting the marketing concept means that an organization must provide greater customer value than its competitors. Being good is not good enough if a competitor is better. It is impossible for an organization to develop strong competitive positioning strategies without a good understanding of its competitors and the strengths and weaknesses of the competitors.

Economic Environment

The economic environment consists of factors that affect consumer's purchasing power and spending patterns. Economic factors include business cycles, inflation, unemployment, interest rates, and income. Changes in major economic variables have a significant impact on the marketplace. For example, income affects consumer's spending capacity which affects sales for organizations. According to *Engel's Laws,* as income rises, the percentage of income spent on food decreases, while the percentage spent on housing remains constant.

People spend, save, invest and try to create personal wealth with differing amounts of money. How people deal with their money is important to marketers. Trends in the economic environment show an emphasis on global income distribution issues, low savings and high debt, and changing consumer's expenditure patterns. If you consider access to telephones, washing machine, dryers, microwaves, etc., there is little visible difference between the poor and non-poor. Indeed, recent figures indicate that the affluent are shopping at discount stores, having adopted some of the shopping habits of those with less income.

Marketers can't control the problems that have cropped up, and that may continue to develop, at various hotspots across the global economy. But they can—and should—take proactive steps to shelter their organizations from unwanted consequences of a worldwide downturn. When an organization's underlying financials are strong, it is able to capitalize on competitors' weaknesses, prosper, and continue to grow, even in adverse economic situations.

Technological Environment

The technological environment refers to new technologies, which create new products and market opportunities. Technological developments are the most manageable uncontrollable forces faced by marketers. Organizations need to be aware of new technologies in order to turn these advances into opportunities and a competitive edge. Technology has a tremendous effect on lifestyles, consumption patterns, and the economy. Advances in technology can start new industries, radically alter or destroy existing industries, and stimulate entirely separate markets. The rapid rate at which technology changes has forced organizations to quickly adapt in terms of how they develop, price, distribute, and promote their products.

Political and Legal Environment

Organizations must operate within a framework of governmental regulation and legislation. Government relationships with organizations encompass subsidies, tariffs, import quotas, and deregulation of industries.

The political environment includes governmental and special interest groups that influence and limit various organizations and individuals in a given society. Organizations hire lobbyists to influence legislation and run advocacy ads that state their point of view on public issues. Special interest groups have grown in number and power over the last three decades, putting more constraints on marketers. The public expects organizations to be ethical and responsible. An example of response by marketers to special interests is *green marketing*, the use of recyclable or biodegradable packing materials as part of marketing strategy.

The major purposes of business legislation include protection of companies from unfair competition, protection of consumers from unfair business practices and protection of the interests of society from unbridled business behaviour. The legal environment becomes more complicated as organizations expand globally and face governmental structures quite different from those within the United States.

Demographic Environment

Demographics tell marketers who are the current and potential customers are; where they are; and how many are likely to buy what the marketer is selling. Demography is the study of human populations in terms of size, density, location, age, sex, race, occupation, and other statistics. Changes in the demographic environment can result in significant opportunities and threats presenting themselves to the organization. Major trends for marketers in the demographic environment include worldwide explosive population growth; age, ethnic and educational mix; new types of households; and geographical shifts in population.

Cultural Environment

Social/cultural forces are the most difficult and uncontrollable variables to predict. It is important for marketers to understand and appreciate the cultural values of the environment in which they operate. The cultural environment is made up of forces that affect society's basic values, perceptions, preferences, and behaviours. U.S. values and beliefs include equality, achievement, youthfulness, efficiency, practicality, self-actualization, freedom, humanitarianism, mastery over the environment, patriotism, individualism, religious and moral orientation, progress, materialism, social interaction, conformity, courage, and acceptance of responsibility. Changes in social/cultural environment affect customer behaviour, which affects sales of products. Trends in the cultural environment include individuals changing their views of themselves, others, and the world around them and movement toward self-fulfilment, immediate gratification, and secularism.

Ecosystem Environment

The ecosystem refers to natural systems and its resources that are needed as inputs by marketers or that are affected by marketing activities. Green marketing (the greening of America) or environmental concern about the physical environment has intensified in recent years. Environmental consciousness has a strong presence in Western Europe and Japan, as well as in the United States. To avoid shortages in raw materials, organizations can use renewable resources (such as forests) and alternatives (such as solar and wind energy) for non-renewable resources (such as oil and coal). Organizations can limit their energy usage by increasing efficiency. Goodwill can be built by voluntarily engaging in pollution prevention activities and natural resource.

Microenvironment

The external microenvironment consists of forces that are part of an organization's marketing process but are external to the organization. These microenvironmental forces include the organization's market, its producers, suppliers, and its marketing intermediaries. While these are external, the organization is capable of exerting more influence over these than forces in the microenvironment.

The Market

Organizations closely monitor their markets in order to adjust to changing tastes and preferences. A market is people or organizations with wants to satisfy, money to spend, and the willingness to spend it. Each target market has distinct needs, which need to be monitored. It is imperative for an organization to know their customers, how to reach them and when customers' needs change in order to adjust its marketing efforts accordingly. The market is the focal point for all marketing decisions in an organization.

Consumer markets are individuals and households that buy goods and services for personal consumption. Business markets buy goods and services for further processing or for use in their production process. Reseller markets buy goods and services in order to resell them at a profit. Government markets are agencies that buy goods and services in order to produce public services or transfer them to those that need them. The federal government is the largest buyer in the United States. International markets consist of buyers in other countries.

Suppliers

Suppliers are organizations and individuals that provide the resources needed to produce goods and services. They are critical to an organization's marketing success and an important link in its value delivery system. Marketers must watch supply availability and monitor price trends of key inputs. If there is a breakdown in the link between the organization and its suppliers, the result will be delays and shortages that can negatively impact the organization's marketing plans. On the other hand, positive and cooperative relationships between the organization and its suppliers can lead to enhanced service and customer satisfaction.

Marketing Intermediaries

Like suppliers, marketing intermediaries are an important part of the system used to deliver value to customers. Marketing intermediaries are independent organizations that aid in the flow of products from the marketing organization to its markets. The intermediaries between an organization and its markets constitute a channel of distribution. These include middlemen (wholesalers and retailers who buy and resell merchandise). Physical distribution firms help the organization to stock and move products from their points of origin to their destinations. Warehouses store and protect the goods before they move to the next destination. Marketing service agencies help the organization target and promote its products and include marketing research firms, advertising agencies, and media firms. Financial intermediaries help finance transactions and insure against risks and include banks, credit unions, and insurance companies.

SALES MANAGEMENT ENVIRONMENT

Without understanding the environmental factors and its influence on business, a company cannot develop its strategy. No business can operate in an isolated environment. The environmental factors consistently impact on firm's operations. Hence, it is a must for the company to understand the environment. Environmental forces constrain the ability to pursue certain marketing strategies or activities and determine the ultimate success or failure of marketing strategies. Any changes in the environment create new marketing opportunities and at the same time environmental variables are affected by marketing activities.

Macroenvironmental Factors

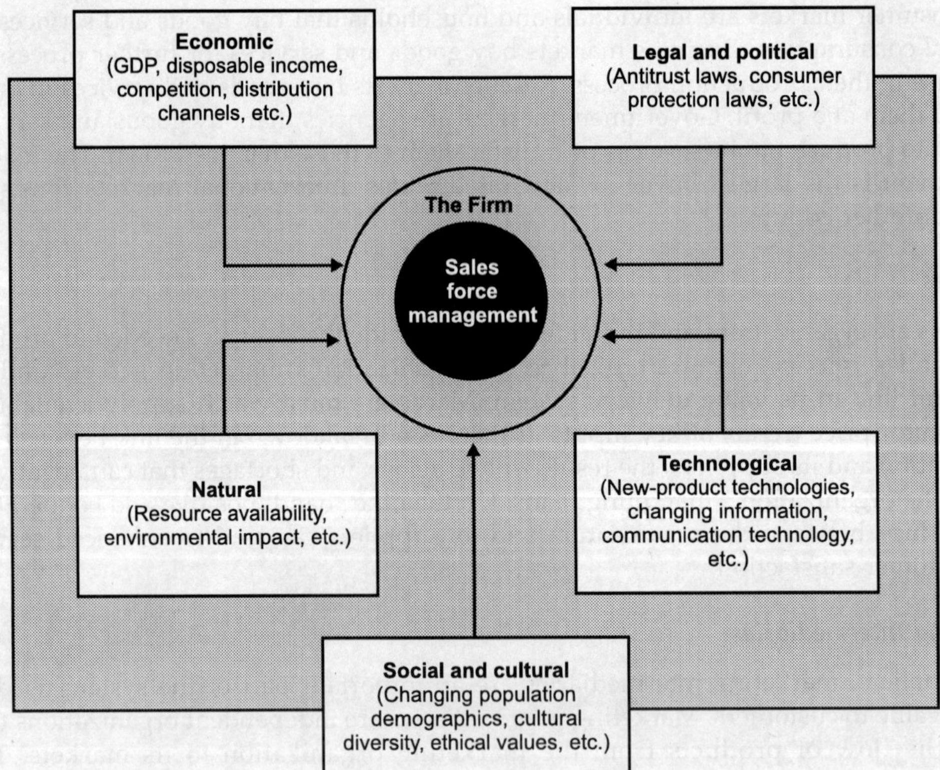

Fig. 1.4. Sales environmental factors: Macroenvironment.

Economic Environment

- Buyer-seller interactions take place within the context of current economic conditions.
- The economy impacts real potential demand.
- Global economic conditions are important.
- Competitive structure affects selling success.

Legal-Political Environment

- Many of the changes in society's values reflect new laws and new government regulations.
- Three broad categories of laws are relevant:
  - Antitrust
  - Consumer Protection
  - Equal Employment Opportunity

Technological Environment

- Changing the way salespeople and sales managers do their jobs
- Influences sales strategies
- Provides increased opportunities for product development
- Transportation, communications, and data processing technologies change sales territories, sales rep deployment and sales performance evaluation

Social and Cultural Environment

- Ethics concerned with development of moral standards by which actions and situations can be judged.
- Of concern to sales managers:
  - Their relationships with salespeople
  - Interactions between salespeople and their customers
- Managers must influence ethical performance by example
- Ethical standards reflect integrity of the firm

Natural Environment

- Nature influences demand for products
  - Weather
  - Natural disasters
  - Availability of raw materials
  - Energy resources
- Demarketing may result from shortages caused by nature
- Growing social concern about the possible negative impact of product and production have important implications for marketing and sales programmes

Microenvironmental Factors

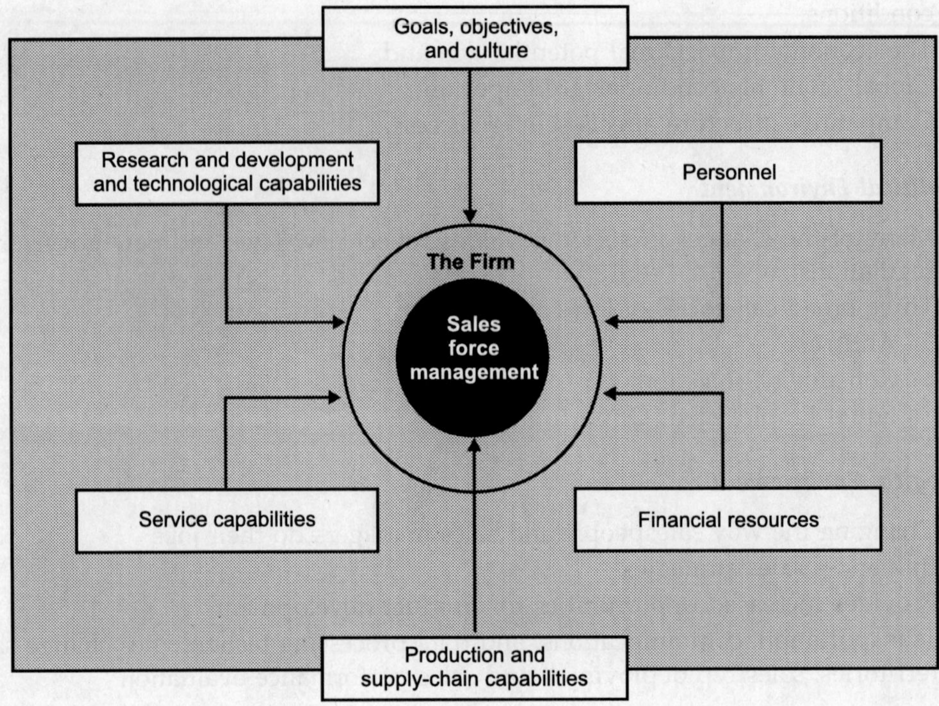

Fig. 1.5. Microenvironmental factors.

Goals/Objectives/Culture

- Mission and objectives drive customer management approaches
- A well-defined mission + successful corporate history + top management values = strong corporate culture

Personnel

- Modern sales organizations are highly complex and dynamic
- Often difficult to expand to take advantage of growing markets
- Utilizing outside specialists can help firms meet need to expand

Financial Resources

- Lack of financial resources can:
  - constrain ability to develop new products
  - limit promotional budget
  - limit size of sales force

Production and Supply Chain Capabilities

- Production capacity
- Location of production facilities
- Transportation costs
- Ability to ensure seamless distribution and service after the sale.

Service Capabilities

- Opportunity for strong competitive advantage.
- Difficult for other firms to compete for same customers.
- Customers reluctant to switch regardless of price.

R&D and Technological Capabilities

- Excellence in design and engineering provide major promotional appeal.
- Ability to communicate technological sophistication as value-add helps prevent over-reliance on price to get sales.

SALES FORECASTING

Sales forecasting is a difficult area of management. Most managers believe they are good at forecasting. However, forecasts made usually turn out to be wrong! Marketers argue about whether sales forecasting is a science or an art. The short answer is that it is a bit of both.

Reasons for Undertaking Sales Forecasts

Businesses are forced to look well ahead in order to plan their investments, launch new products, and decide when to close or withdraw products, and so on. The sales forecasting process is a critical one for most businesses. Key decisions that are derived from a sales forecast include:

- Employment levels required
- Promotional mix
- Investment in production capacity

Types of Forecasting

There are two major types of forecasting, which can be broadly described as **macro** and **micro**:

- **Macroforecasting** is concerned with forecasting markets in total. This is about determining the existing level of market demand and considering what will happen to the market demand in the future.
- **Microforecasting** is concerned with detailed unit sales forecasts. This is about determining a product's market share in a particular industry and considering what will happen to that market share in the future.

The selection of which type of forecasting to use depends on several factors as under.

(1) **The degree of accuracy required:** If the decisions that are to be made on the basis of the sales forecast have high risks attached to them, then it stands to reason that the forecast should be prepared as accurately as possible. However, this involves more cost.

(2) **The availability of data and information:** In some markets there is a wealth of available sales information (e.g. clothing retail, food retailing, holidays); in others it is hard to find reliable up-to-date information.

(3) **The time horizon that the sales forecast is intended to cover**. For example, are we forecasting next week's sales, or are we trying to forecast what will happen to the overall size of the market in the next five years?

(4) **The position of the products in its life cycle.** For example, for products at the "introductory" stage of the product life cycle, less sales data and information may be available than for products at the "maturity" stage when time series can be a useful forecasting method.

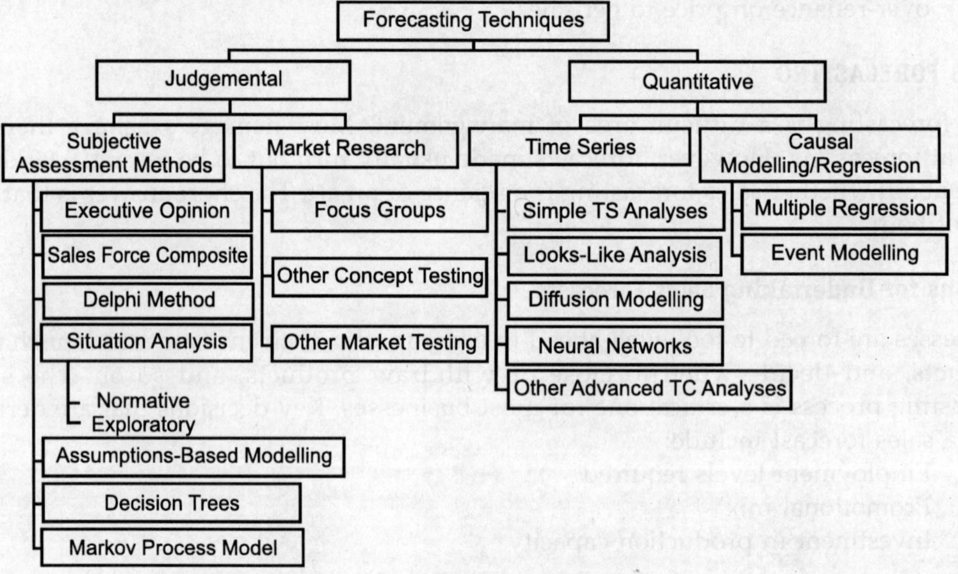

Fig 1.6. Various sales forecasting techniques.

Criteria for Selection of a Suitable Forecasting Method

Comprehensibility: Basic method must be thoroughly understood by the forecaster to have sufficient confidence in the estimates to use them. Complicated techniques that can be understood by statistician never find credibility among sales executive.

Accuracy: The forecasting method must provide sufficiently accurate results. An accuracy within the limits of 10% is considered acceptable by most of the sales forecasters.

Timeliness: It must generate forecast in time to be useful. Complex techniques take long time to get prepared. So, the managers who require results quickly can resort to quicker, perhaps less accurate estimates.

Availability of information: All forecasting methods primarily depend on amount and quality of information available to the organization.

Qualified personnel: Personnel to participate in any aspect of forecast must be fully qualified for the job. Highly skilled people are advisable to develop an accurate forecast.

Flexibility: The sales forecasting method should be flexible enough to adopt the changing conditions. Flexibility can be achieved by monitoring the actual sales and comparing them with forecasted sales. Deviations indicated by the results guide for the revised forecast.

Costs and benefits: Benefits arrived at from these forecast must be more than the cost incurred on making these forecasts.

Sales Forecasting Concept

There are five levels of concern in sales forecasting:

(a) Market potential
(b) Sales potential
(c) Actual sales forecasts
(d) Sales quotas
(e) Sales budgets

Market Potential: It is the highest possible expected industry sales of a good or service in a specified market segment for a given time period. For example, the market potential for the sales of antifreeze in New England might be 20 million gallons annually. (Based on buyers ability to buy and willingness to buy).

Sales Potential: It refers to an individual firms market share of the market potential, where market share is defined as the percentage of market controlled by a particular company or product. It is the maximum sales a firm can hope to obtain.

Sales Forecasts: It is the sales estimate the company actually expects to obtain, based on the market conditions, company resources, and the firms marketing plan. The sales forecast is less than the sales potential since it is based on realistic circumstances.

Sales Quota: It is a sales goal assigned to a salesperson, region or a team. They are usually derived from the sales forecasts, sales goals and objectives sought by management.

Sales Budgets: It is a management plan for the expenditure to accomplish sales goals.

Sales Forecasting Procedures

There are basically three steps in sales forecasting process:

(i) Preparing a forecast for general economic conditions
(ii) Preparing a forecast of industry sales
(iii) Preparing a forecast of the product or company sales

(i) Forecasting the General Economic Conditions

It is measuring the GDP, which is the value of goods and services produced within a country during a given year. Some of the others factors are; stock market fluctuation, personal income, level of employment, consumer price index, etc. These data are usually available from government or trade associations.

(ii) Estimating Industry Sales

Small firms often rely on industry estimates available from trade associations and government sources.

In other cases more sophisticated quantitative techniques are used to determine sales. Large organizations have economists and analysts to provide support and information for sales forecasts.

(iii) Estimating Company and Product Sales

Forecasting methods can be classified as either qualitative or quantitative. *Qualitative methods* rely upon subjective opinions or judgements, whereas *quantitative technique* applies statistical methods.

Qualitative Methods

(i) Jury of Executive Opinion

Panel charged with developing a sales forecast. The group has executives from different departments like marketing, sales, marketing research, finance, production, operations, etc.

Each member is asked to provide an estimate of future sales with written justification. The opinions are then pooled and analyzed at group meetings. The advantage is its simplicity, but might take too much time of the executives involved.

(ii) Delphi Technique

- Group of experts used to make long-range projections.
- Issues like future direction of business conditions, business activities, technology, new product development, and market conditions.
- These experts are kept apart from each other so that their opinions are established independently.
- They prepare individual forecasts, which are then compiled and then given back to them for a second round of projections.
- This process continues until a consensus on forecast of the future emerges. The Delphi technique has the advantage of eliminating the group pressures of a typical committee meeting.

(iii) Sales Force Composite

- Forecasts arrived at by combining salespersons estimates of expected sales for their respective territories.
- Field sales people should be motivated to accept sales quotas when they know that the information they supplied played a major role in forecasting.

- A major disadvantage is that salespeople might be a poor judge of future sales level or market conditions. They can have biased opinions as well.

(iv) Survey of Buyer's Intention

Forecast survey of a limited and well-defined group of buyers. This is when the potential customers are well defined and limited in number, such as industrial products.

Disadvantage is that a customer might not always do what they say and they plan to do. Secondly customer-buying behaviour might alter in response to change in the operational environment.

Quantitative Methods

(i) ***Continuity extrapolation:*** Technique that attempts to project the last increment of sales change into the future.

(ii) ***Time series analysis:*** Projection of the average increment of sales change into the future. A time data series is determined by four basic elements of sales variations (a) trends or long-run changes (b) cyclical changes (c) seasonal variations (d) unexpected factors. Most form of times series analysis use a moving average to analyze and project sales.

(iii) ***Exponential smoothing:*** A weighted average time series analysis. Actual sales of recent periods are weighted more heavily than the average sales of earlier periods.

(iv) ***Regression and correlation analysis:*** Aim of regression analysis is to identify factors that influence, or are closely associated with changes in sales. A simple regression is a forecasting technique using only one independent variable while multiple regressions use two or more independent variables.

SALES PLANNING PROCESS

The sales plan consists of the following stages:

(i) ***Evaluation of the current situation:*** An evaluation and analysis needs to be done of where the organization is today and where it will be if no changes are made. Perspectives can be obtained by reviewing the organization's past performance and by judging it progress against that of competitors and its success in accomplishing objectives and goals.

(ii) ***Setting objectives:*** An environmental study helps in setting the objectives. The internal as well as external factors of environment are properly evaluated to find out how far they would assist in the achievement of objectives. The strengths and weaknesses of the company are assessed to formulate feasible and useful plans. The objectives should be specific and framed within the limits of the corporate objectives.

(iii) ***Determining market potentials:*** Both market and sales potentials are usually estimated for a specified time under the most favourable assumptions about the market environment and marketing expenditures. Sometimes, three estimated, namely, optimistic, expected and pessimistic are developed to determine market potential and sales potential under different scenarios.

(iv) ***Forecasting sales:*** It involves determining the volume of sales, the quality, and design of the product are forecast for the total market and for each market. The sales forecast is made on the basis of records of past year's sales records by territory, local conditions in each market, information on one's strengths and weaknesses. The data are compiled at the head office and specific forecasting is done about the sales volume expected. The probable effects of all the factors are assessed to determine their influence on the sales volume in each territory.

(v) ***Selecting strategies:*** Once the goals are set and sales forecasts are made, the next step is to determine the way to achieve these goals. Strategic decisions give the organization a total plan of action to serve customers better, to take advantage of competitor's weaknesses, and to capitalize on the firm's strengths.

(vi) ***Budgeting:*** The term budgeting refers to the inflows and outflows of resources estimated by planners. It includes money, materials and manpower. Sales expenses are also budgeted to rationalize the fund allocation. Periodical estimates of the sales performance of the budget should be made. Overall, the budget's purpose is to coordinate and control company's resources during the period covered by the sales forecast.

(vii) ***Implementation:*** This refers to the specific activities to be performed in future. It also determines the sequence in which specific activities will be performed by salespersons. It decides on the resources to be allocated between the sales force and branch offices. Each salesman decides how to achieve the predetermined objectives. The implementation may consider customer classification, product line emphasis, sales approach and new designs of sales function.

(viii) ***Sales control:*** A sound planning process demands a built-in monitoring device that will aid management in controlling the plan's operations. This control device should consist of a series of regular measurements that will check progress toward specific objectives and signal deviations in time to take corrective actions and get back on tract. Whenever possible, these measurements should be quantitative.

SALES MANAGEMENT PROCESS

The sales management process monitors and measures each staff member's ability to either support sales or do the actual selling to customers. An effective sales management strategy includes setting goals, providing sales support and training, creating or updating the sales strategy, and monitoring results.

The sales management process can include goals for individual staff members, departments, and the entire company. These standards must be discussed with staff. This includes communicating updated goals based on performance, the economy, and the competitive environment.

Once goals have been established, the sales management process continues by providing tools and training to reach those goals. This can include in-depth information about the company's products, target audience, and sales strategy. Effective training is not a one-time occurrence. Ongoing training is needed to ensure success.

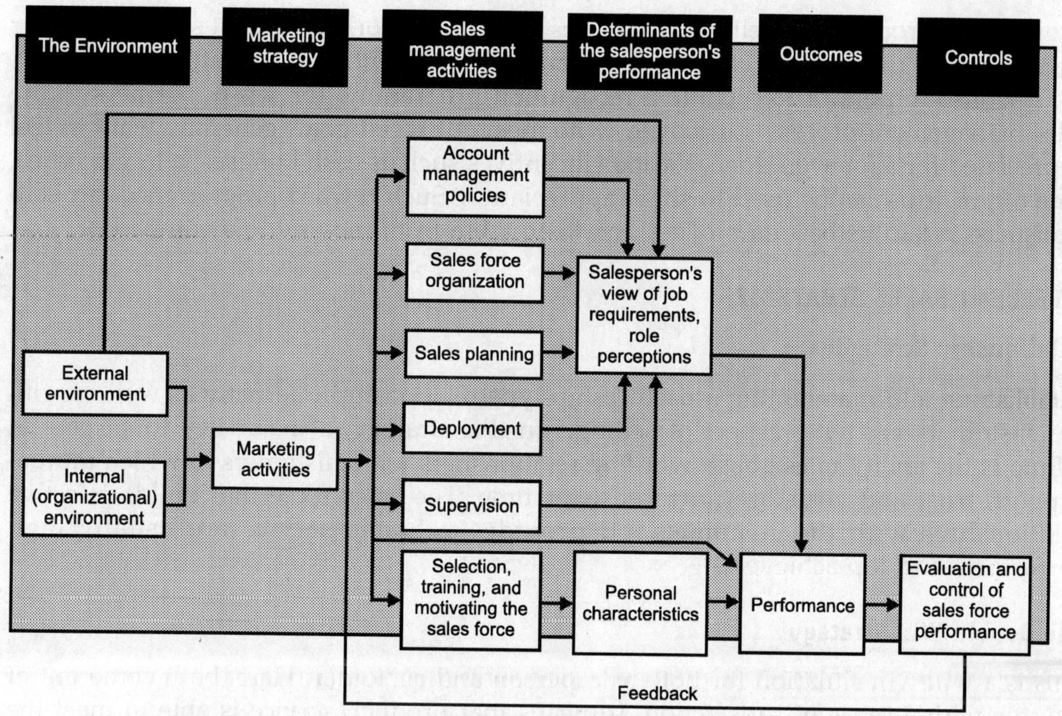

Fig 1.7. Sales management process.

Sales managers typically monitor results to determine if the current sales process is working. This review should include the entire sales process, from taking the order to delivery to follow-up service. Accountability must be included in any successful sales management process.

If goals are not being met, the sales manager needs to determine where any problems lie and offer a solution. Poor sales can be the result of an inferior product, non-competitive pricing, and manufacturing or delivery delays, customer service issues, or employee issues. The sales manager usually relies on several departments, including production, customer service, and marketing, to find the root of any problems.

Along with other department managers, the sales manager must review whether the product is competitive and is delivered on schedule. If the product is not the issue, the manager must ensure that proper support and training were provided during the sales management process. The sales manager also can work closely with the marketing department to be sure the product is being advertised effectively to the correct target audience.

If all product, training, and marketing issues are ruled out as the source of a problem, the sales manager must review the salesperson's personal ability to do the job. The manager can provide more training or personal coaching to help the salesperson achieve stated goals. If additional training or coaching is not effective, the sales manager may decide to terminate the employee.

Conversely, sales managers must also be keenly aware of what is working in the sales management process so that successes can be duplicated. Sales managers need to know which products are selling, what sales techniques work, and must solicit customer feedback. This information can then be shared with the entire sales staff.

It is also important to include a recognition programme for top performers in the sales management process. Employees who meet or exceed goals generally want to feel appreciated for a job well done. Various incentives such as cash bonuses, a larger office, time off, or trips can be used to show appreciation. Such reward programmes can help a business retain its best employees and keep them from moving to a competitor.

DIFFERENT SALES STRATEGIES

Relationship Strategies

Establishing and maintaining a partnership-type relationship internally as well as with the customers is a vital aspect of selling. In this strategy, a major key to success in selling is the ability to establish working relationships with customers in which mutual support, trust and goals are nurtured over time. The sales force that builds effective relationships with the customer and provides valuable service are usually high performers and top achievers.

The Double-Win Strategy

This is a win-win situation for both salesperson and customer. Here, both come out of the sale with a sense of satisfaction. It means that product/service is able to meet the requirement of the customer and salesperson is able to clarify the customer and the customer is also convinced. This kind of sales strategy is highly desirable.

Instant Service

The philosophy behind this strategy is even the product/service is of high quality but if it is not delivered at the quickest possible time to customer otherwise the whole efforts are failed. Sales people take every possible care to deliver the products fast and make the customers delighted.

Hard Sell Vs Soft Sell Strategy

Hard sell strategies are aggressive and usually put a high amount of pressure on the client. The clerk who sold me the shovel is a simple example. Other tactics include cold calls, forceful sales letters, and unsolicited pitches. You're there to sell, they know it, and you know it—there's no grey area.

The main advantage of hard selling is that it gets straight to the point. This is especially important for clients who are ready to buy and aren't looking around to do a few more meetings. The decision should be made now, and you want to step up and offer yourself as a part of their team.

The problem with the hard sell is that when it's done too aggressively, attempt to help will be seen as an annoyance. This plays a big role, especially if the salesperson is working with small businesses that are savvy to such sales techniques. No matter how genuine the offer is, it might come off sounding like a scam.

Soft selling focuses on the relationship-building aspect of sales. Salesperson should not put psychological pressure on potential buyers, instead should show them the solutions they are looking for.

Integrated Sales Strategy

Sales and distribution management constitutes one of the most important areas for customer satisfaction. Sales management has been defined as the management of a firm's personal selling function while distribution is an indirect function. Therefore, integration is required between sales and distribution functions.

Client-centred Selling Strategy

It focuses the entire selling process and efforts are put on the clients' needs, problems and successes. It considers everything about the client—who he/she is, what he/she does and where, when, how he/she does it. It demands sound knowledge about the client. This strategy shifts the emphasis of the selling process away from the product and focuses, instead, on the client, whose wants and needs become the most important factor driving any selling process.

METHODS OF SELLING

Telemarketing

Telemarketing (known as telesales in the UK and Ireland) is a method of direct marketing in which a salesperson solicits to prospective customers to buy products or services, either over the phone or through a subsequent face-to-face or Web conferencing appointment scheduled during the call.

Telemarketing can also include recorded sales pitches programmed to be played over the phone via automatic dialing. Telemarketing has come under fire in recent years, being viewed as an annoyance by many.

Sales on the Internet

Electronic commerce, commonly known as e-commerce or ecommerce, or e-business consists of the buying and selling of products or services over electronic systems such as the Internet and other computer networks. The amount of trade conducted electronically has grown extraordinarily with widespread Internet usage. The use of commerce is conducted in this way, spurring and drawing on innovations in electronic funds transfer, supply chain management, Internet marketing, online transaction processing, electronic data interchange (EDI), inventory management systems, and automated data collection systems. Modern electronic commerce typically uses the World Wide Web at least at some point in the transaction's life cycle, although it can encompass a wider range of technologies such as e-mail as well.

A large percentage of electronic commerce is conducted entirely electronically for virtual items such as access to premium content on a website, but most electronic commerce involves the transportation of physical items in some way. Online retailers are sometimes known as e-tailers and online retail is sometimes known as e-tail. Almost all big retailers have electronic commerce presence on the World Wide Web.

Electronic commerce that is conducted between businesses is referred to as business-to-business or B2B. B2B can be open to all interested parties (e.g., commodity exchange) or limited to specific, pre-qualified participants (private electronic market). Electronic commerce that is conducted between businesses and consumers, on the other hand, is referred to as business-to-consumer or B2C. This is the type of electronic commerce conducted by companies such as Amazon.com. Online shopping is a form of electronic commerce where the buyer is directly online to the seller's computer usually via the internet. There is no intermediary service. The sale and purchase transaction is completed electronically and interactively in real-time such as Amazon.com for new books. If an intermediary is present, then the sale and purchase transaction is called electronic commerce such as eBay.com.

Electronic commerce is generally considered to be the sales aspect of e-business. It also consists of the exchange of data to facilitate the financing and payment aspects of the business transactions.

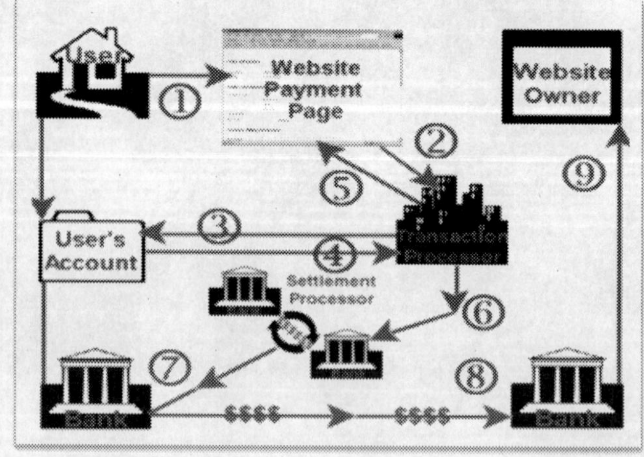

Mail-Order Sales

Mail-order sales continue to flourish, in part because companies can attract customers without incurring overhead costs such as retail space and related expenses. Specialty cataloguers—particularly those that sell niche items like hand-made apparel, kitchen equipment, luxury items, and organic foods—have enjoyed considerable success. This section looks at the advantages and disadvantages of direct mail selling and also points out a few regulations that affect operations.

Mail-order selling is increasingly popular, and there are good reasons for that. Operating a mail-order business is good for cash flow, because credit cards make it possible to routinely receive payment in advance for goods that a business may not even need to stock. What's more, a company typically has 30 or 60 days to arrange payment for the goods it then sells to consumers. That's a boon to cash flow, if managed properly, of course. Other costs can be controlled or avoided outright: There is no need to rent or buy retail space, for instance, and little or no need to maintain stocks. Flexible working hours can be the norm, which can help attract customer service personnel, and staffing usually can be adjusted in line with demand. For a specialty retailer or manufacturer, setting up a mail-order operation is a good way of expanding market reach. Mail-order also appeals to almost every income level.

There are few disadvantages as well. First-time customers may be wary about sending money or providing credit card information to an unknown firm at a distant address. Mail-order houses must also continually send brochures or catalogues via direct mail to attract more sales, and the response rate can be less than 1%. As postal rates keep climbing, this expense can mount. There's also the cost of purchasing lists of prospective customers, which are essential to generating new sales. To a degree, there's also a limit on what can be sold by mail order, although limits keep being stretched. Finally, mail-order houses must rely on delivery firms like UPS and Fedex; in turn, customer satisfaction is unusually dependent on these third-party firms over whom your business has no direct control.

Direct Marketing

Direct marketing is sometimes a controversial sales method by which advertisers approach potential customers directly with products or services. The most common forms of direct marketing are telephone sales, solicited or unsolicited emails, catalogues, leaflets, brochures and coupons. Successful direct marketing also involves compiling and maintaining a large database of personal information about potential customers and clients. These databases are often sold or shared with other direct marketing companies.

For many companies or service providers with a specific market, the traditional forms of advertising (radio, newspapers, television, etc.) may not be the best use of their promotional budgets. For example, a company which sells a hair loss prevention product would have to find a radio station whose format appealed to older male listeners who might be experiencing this problem. There would be no guarantee that this group would be listening to that particular station at the exact time the company's ads were broadcast. Money spent on a radio spot (or television commercial or newspaper ad) may or may not reach the type of consumer who would be interested in a hair restoring product.

This is where direct marketing becomes appealing. Instead of investing in a scattershot means of advertising, companies with a specific type of potential customer can send out literature directly to a list of pre-screened individuals. Direct marketing firms may also keep e-mail addresses of those who match a certain age group or income level or special interest. Manufacturers of a new dog shampoo might benefit from having the phone numbers and mailing addresses of pet store owners or dog show participants. Direct marketing works best when the recipients accept the fact that their personal information might be used for this purpose. Some customers prefer to receive targeted catalogs which offer more variety than a general mailing.

Fig 1.8. Direct marketing process.

Sales Through Wholesalers and Retailers

An intermediary is one who buys in bulk from manufacturers for resale to retailers or other traders. Some wholesalers sell directly to the public. One type of wholesaler is a cash and carry, which offers discounted prices for bulk purchases that are paid for and taken away at the time of sale. Cash and carries traditionally serve the business community, but many now allow the general public to buy from them.

A business which sells goods to the consumer, as opposed to a wholesaler or supplier which normally sell their goods to another business. Retailers include large businesses such as Wal-Mart, and also smaller, non-chain locations run independently such as a family-run bookstore.

Let Us Sum Up

Salesmanship can be defined as an art of influencing another person for the object of persuading him to buy specific product. It may be regarded as the process of winning the confidence of consumer. According to Whitehead "It is a method regard to the desirability of some article, service of idea." Salesmanship may also refer to convincing a customer by certain technique and he is really persuaded for buying the particular product.

Without understanding the environmental factors and its influence on business, a company cannot develop its strategy. No business can operate in isolated environment. The environmental factors consistently impact on firm's operations. Hence, it is a must for the company to understand the environment. Environmental forces constrain the ability to pursue certain marketing strategies or activities and determine the ultimate success or failure of marketing strategies. Any changes in the environment creale new marketing opportunities and at the same time environmental variables are affected by marketing activities.

Sales forecasting is a difficult area of management. Most managers believe they are good at forecasting. However, forecasts made usually turn out to be wrong! Marketers argue about whether sales forecasting is a science or an art. The short answer is that it is a bit of both. Businesses are forced to look well ahead in order to plan their investments, launch new products, and decide when to close or withdraw products, and so on. The sales forecasting process is a critical one for most businesses.

Another important area is sales budgeting. Sale budgeting is estimating future levels of revenue, selling expenses, and profit contributions of the sales function.

The sales management process monitors and measures each staff member's ability to either support sales or do the actual selling to customers. An effective sales management strategy includes setting goals, providing sales support and training, creating or updating the sales strategy, and monitoring results.

Questions for Discussion

1. What do you understand by marketing mix and promotional mix? Explain the importance of personal selling.
2. What is personal selling? Explain the situations when personal selling is highly effective.
3. List out the features of personal selling. What are the advantages and disadvantages of personal selling?

4. Explain the objectives of personal selling. Explain briefly the dimension of sales management.
5. What is the scope of personal selling? What are the new dimensions to personal selling?
6. Define sales management environment. Explain various macro and micro sales environmental factions in a nutshell.
7. Define sales forecasting. What are the different types of sales forecasting and explain the criteria for selection of a particular sales forecasting type?
8. Write short notes on (i) Market Potential (ii) Sale Potential (iii) Sales Forecast (iv) Sales Quota (v) Sales Budget.
9. Explain in detail the sales forecasting procedure.
10. What are the different sales forecasting methodologies? Explain briefly.
11. Write short notes on (i) Delphi Technique (ii) Executive Opinion (iii) Sales Force Composite (iv) Time Series Analysis (v) Exponential Smoothing, and (vi) Regression Analysis.
12. Explain the concept of sales budget. What are the different sales budget techniques?
13. Explain the sales budgeting procedure.
14. Explain the sales management planning process in detail with diagram.
15. Write short notes on (i) Sale (ii) Salesmanship (iii) Marketing Mix, and (iv) Promotional Mix.
16. Write short notes on (i) Sales Environment (ii) Sales Forecasting, and (iii) Personal Selling.
17. Explain various selling strategies.
18. What are the different methods of selling? Write in brief about every method.
19. Write short notes on (i) Direct Marketing (ii) Tele Marketing (iii) Internet Marketing (iv) Mail-Order Sales (v) Wholesaler, and (vi) Retailer.
20. Explain the sales planning process.

2

CHAPTER

Organizing and Executing the Sales

"To speak and to speak well are two things. A fool may talk, but a wise man speaks."

—Ben Jonson

Introduction – Sales organization – Managerial position in sales organization – functions – different types of sales organization – sales department relations – distributive network relations – the selling process – sales personality traits – different types of sales people.

LEARNING OBJECTIVES

After going through this chapter, students will be able to understand

- The concept of sales organization
- Nature of sales management position
- Different types of sales organization
- Sales department relations with other departments
- Sales relationship with distributive outlets
- Various steps in selling process
- Different types of sales people
- Sales personality traits

INTRODUCTION

Organization means the systematic coordination of the functions essential for achieving organizational objectives. The objectives of a sales organization, therefore, are the performance of various activities necessary to promote sales. A sales organization is both an orienting point for cooperative endeavour and a structure of human relationships. It is a group of individuals striving jointly to reach qualitative and quantitative objectives, and bearing informal and formal relations to one another. Implicit in the concept of a sales organization is the notion that individual members cooperate to attain ends. The sales organization is not an end in itself but rather the vehicle by which individuals achieve the given ends. Existence of a sales organization implies the existence of patterns of relationships among subgroups and individuals established for purposes of facilitating the group's aims.

Definition

An organization of individuals either working together for the marketing of products and services manufactured by an enterprise or for products that are procured by the firm for the purpose of reselling.

A sales organization defines duties, roles, rights, and responsibilities of salespeople engaged in selling activities meant for the effective execution of the sales function.

Nature of the Sales Management Position

The nature of the sales management position is described as under:

(i) ***Technician:*** Positions where the major emphasis is on technical knowledge, namely, engineering salesperson who is primarily a consultant to the client companies, comes under this category.

(ii) ***Deliverer:*** Positions where the job of the salesman is mainly to deliver the product like milk, brand, fuel, ice cream, etc. comes under this category.

(iii) ***Order taker:*** Positions where the job of the salesman is mainly an order taker at the sales counter or an outside order taker, comes under this category.

(iv) ***Missionary:*** Positions where the salesman is not expected to take an order but is called only to build goodwill or to educate the actual or the potential user.

(v) ***Demand Creator:*** Positions that demand the creative sale or tangible products such as vacuum cleaners, refrigerators or intangible such as insurance, advertising services or education; comes under this category.

Functions of Sales Organization

The functions of sales organization can be classified as:

(i) Planning Function: Sales forecasting, sales budgeting, selling policy.

(ii) Administrative Function: Selecting salesmen, training salesmen, control of salesmen,

(iii) Executive Function: Sales promotion, selling routine – executive of customers' orders.

Scope and Importance of Sales Organization

The scope and importance of sales organization are:

(i) ***Reduction of risk:*** A good sales organization reduces the risk element of sales of the enterprise. When sales organization are efficient, the flow of purchase, sales, finance and production will be absolute.

(ii) ***Efficiency of management:*** A successful sales organization makes sure that the efficiency of work reduces sales cost, mutual friction, red tapism and all above rapid increase in sales efficiency of the sales free which helps the management to be more efficient.

(iii) ***Division:*** In a large seal of sales, one man is not able to work smoothly, for these a good sales organization provides subdivision and division to control. By functioning all the work smoothly the salesmen can be specialized in specific field.

(iv) ***Increase in sales:*** A good sales organization helps to increase the sale of goods of the organization. These help the enterprise to increase the production, advertising and selling of goods which indicate the mass production and mass distribution.

(v) ***Market creation:*** Sales department of sales organization can create a good market of the product by the creation of demand of product through market.

(vi) ***Coordination and controlling:*** A better sales organization can coordinate and control all of the sales force, which lead to control and coordination of all individual efforts and thus motivate them to work.

(vii) ***Other functions of management:*** Sales organization performs works like market research, sales forecasting, sales budgeting, product planning, consumer, etc. which lead to the efficiency and profitability of the organization.

(viii) ***Sales organization ensures effective coverage of the sales territory.***

(ix) ***Reduces the repetition of activities.***

(x) ***Helps proper distribution of goods.***

Factors Influencing Sales Organization Structure

There are various factors which affect the structure of the organization. These factors are as follows:

(i) ***Nature of market:*** The nature of market helps to determine the sales organization. If the product is for local people and short period, the organization structure will be simple but if the product is for international market, the organization structure will be vast and complex.

(ii) ***Price of product:*** Price affects the organization to determine its structure because if the price of the product is more and not basic required good for all, then the organization will be small like motor car, air cooler, etc. But if the price is less and on the basic required goods like vegetable and rice, etc. then its organization is big and complex for sale.

(iii) ***Nature of product:*** Nature of product affects in determining the sales organization structure because if the products are perishable like vegetable, fish, meat which have short duration, for these sales organization is big for more supervision and support.

(iv) ***Size of the enterprise:*** For big enterprise big sales are required and automatically big sales organization will be required and vice versa. Example: Tata, Wipro and other big companies have big sales organization.

(v) ***Selling policy of enterprise:*** Selling policy of the organization also helps to determine the structure of sales organization in such a way that if the enterprise adopts aggressive sales policies then the sales organization will be difficult, complex.

(vi) ***Number of products:*** If the company produces products of different varieties, then automatically sales organization will be bigger and complex.

(vii) ***Financing facilities:*** If the company has large capital, then the company can sell the product directly to customer and consumer and for the sales organization will be big. But if the company has small amount of capital then it has to sell the product through wholesaler and other agencies for that small sales organization is required.

Different Types of Sales Organizations

The various types of sales organizations are:

(i) ***Formal and Informal Organization:*** Every firm has a formal and an informal organization. The formal organization is that of the management whereas the informal organization is often developed from the informal relationships existing within the organization. Also called the grapevine, informal organization is basically a communication pattern that emerges to facilitate the operation of its formal counterpart. Most formal organizations would be totally ineffective if it were not for a supportive informal organization.

The development of an effective sales organization requires that informal relationships and communication patterns be recognized as being equally useful in accomplishing sales objectives. They should be encouraged to the extent that they improve organizational efficiency.

(ii) ***Horizontal and Vertical Organization:*** A sales force can have either a horizontal or a vertical organizational format. This arrangement varies among companies even within the same industry.

A vertical sales organization has several layers of sales management - all of which report vertically.

The other extreme is a horizontal organization. Here the number of management levels is reduced appreciably, but the number of managers at any particular level is increased. Instead of two or three district sales managers, there may be seven or eight.

The factor that determines whether a vertical or horizontal organizational structure should be employed is the effective span of control. The span of control refers to the number of employees who report to the next higher level in the organization. Horizontal structures tend to exist where larger spans of control are acceptable, while vertical organization characterize cases in which closer managerial supervision is required.

(iii) ***Centralized and Decentralized Organizations:*** In a highly centralized organization, the sales function and its related tasks are managed from corporate

headquarters. In a decentralized organization, field sales managers do the recruitment, training, evaluation and compensation of sales force. The degree of centralization and decentralization depends upon the size of operation, effectiveness and competitive necessity.

	Centralized (concentrated)	Decentralized (dispersed)
Plant, Personnel, Equipment (Facilities)	Product, service and business functions concentrated in one building or in several buildings within a localized area.	Products, services and business functions scattered in many areas; multi-plant operation; each subunit is a separate entity; may be autonomous self-sufficient entity performing most major business functions.
Authority (Decision-making)	High degree of concentration and retention of decision-making at upper levels of management; subordinates highly dependent.	High degree of delegation and dispersion of decision-making horizontally or vertically downward to lower levels of management; subordinates relatively independent; "Profit Centre" concept.

(iv) ***Line and Staff Components:*** Marketing organization also features line and staff components. A line function is a primary activity and a staff function is a supporting activity. In a marketing organization, the selling function is the line component whereas advertising, marketing research, marketing planning, sales training and distributor relations are usually considered staff roles.

Although the use of terms—line and staff—has been criticized in many quarters, the basic premise behind them remains applicable to marketing organizations. A modern sales force has to receive various types of support in order to accomplish its objectives.

If the needs of the marketplace become more complex, or if the company expands, then there is usually a need to add specialists prepared to deal with these problems. Over time, these specialists become the staff departments found in most large organizations. Line executives are in command and have power. Staff does not enjoy the power to command. They may become backroom boys.

Tall (Vertical) & Flat (Horizontal) Organization Structures

Tall Structures

In this structure numbers of hierarchical levels are more and span of control is narrow. As numbers of levels are more, communication gets difficult. Decision-making is highly centralized.

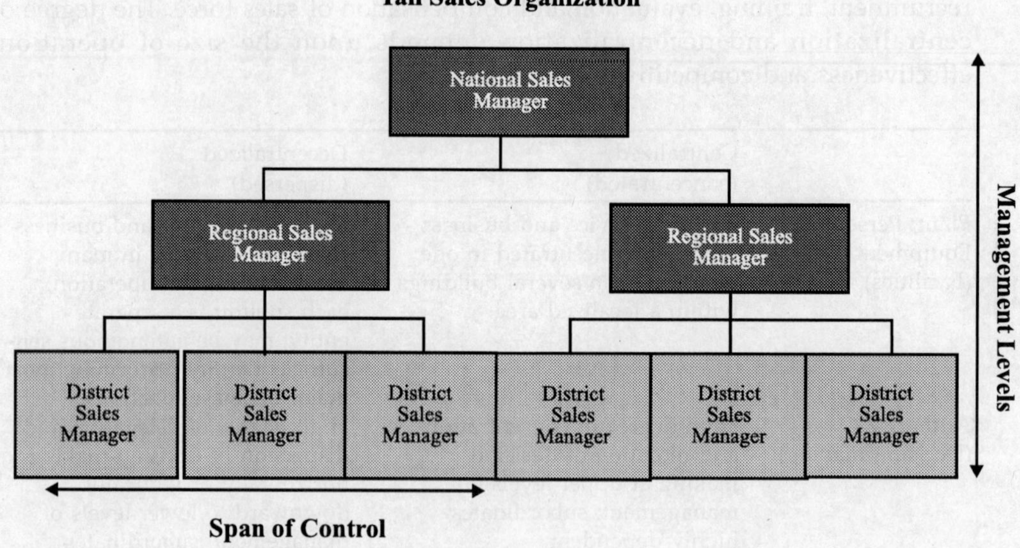

Fig. 2.1. Span of control vs. management levels.

Flat Structure

In flat organization structure authority is delegated and span of control is wide. It reduces the levels of management. Decision-making capacity is more decentralized.

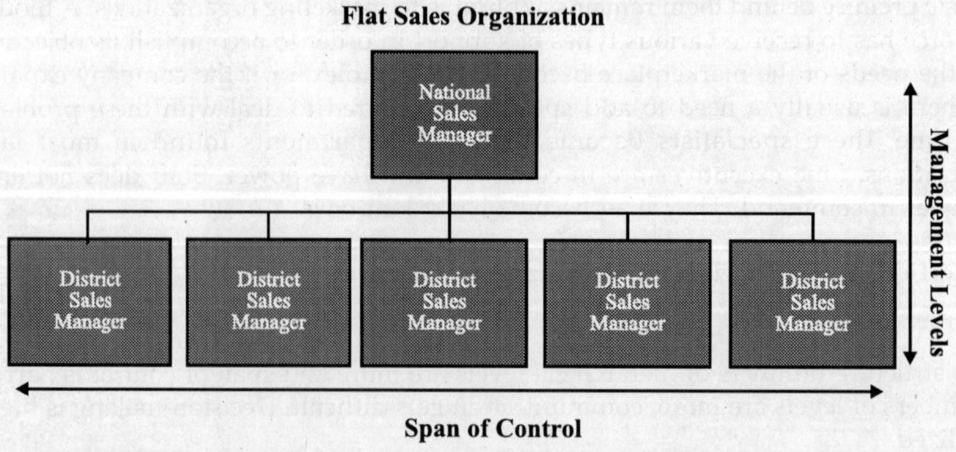

Fig. 2.2. Span of control vs. management levels.

Basic Types of Sales Organization Structure

The grouping of activities into positions and the charting of relationships of positions causes the organization to take on structural form. The most common structures are line & line and staff. Functional organizational structures are rare. Most sales departments have hybrid organizational structures, with variations to adjust for personalities and to fit specific operating conditions.

Line Sales Organization

In this kind of sales organization lines of authority and instructions are vertical, i.e., they flow from the top to the bottom. The unity of command is maintained in a straight and unbroken line. It implies that each subordinate receives instructions from his immediate superior alone and is responsible to him only.

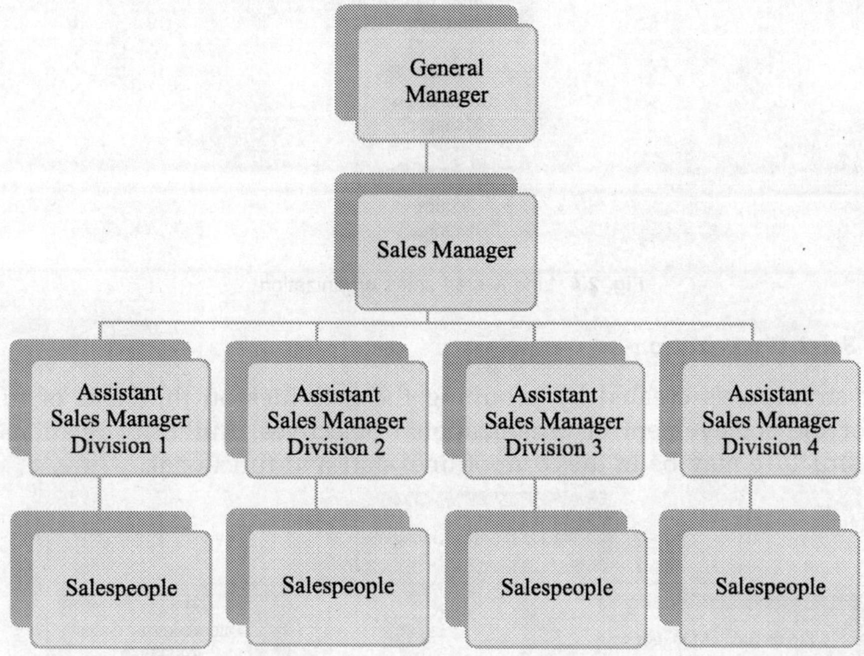

Fig. 2.3. Line sales organization.

Line & Staff Sales Organization

Refers to a pattern in which staff specialists advise managers to perform their duties. Here, staff managers provide advice to the line managers who are generally specialists in the field.

Staff positions are purely advisory in nature. They have a right to recommend but have no authority to enforce their preference on other dept. The line executives are the "DOERS" or commanders, whereas, the specialists are the "THINKERS" or advisors.

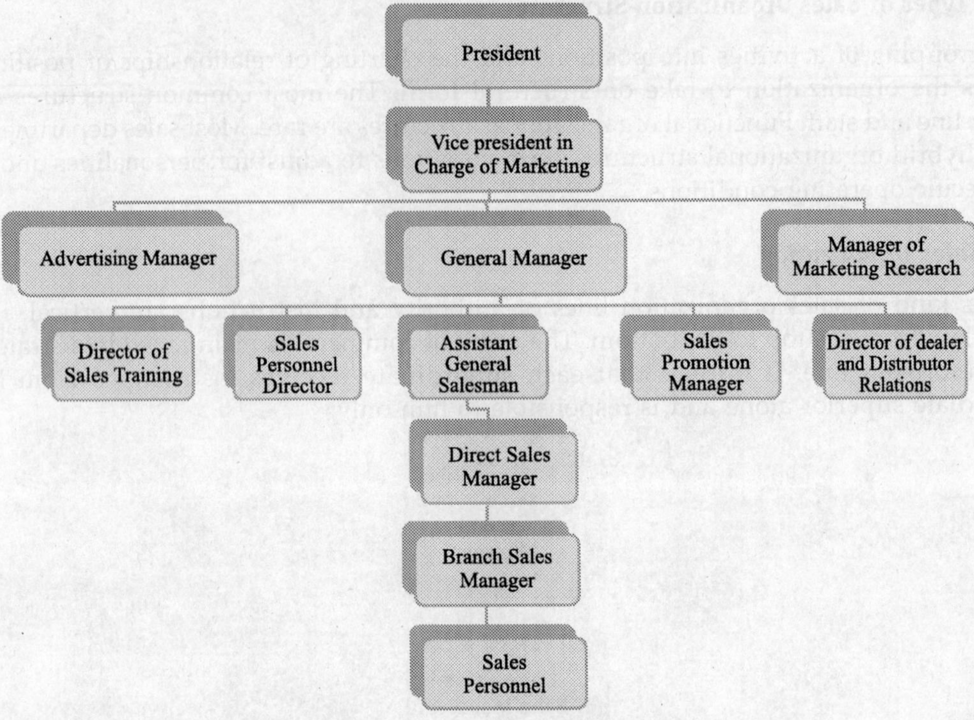

Fig. 2.4. Line & staff sales organization

Functional Sales Organization

Functional structure is created by grouping the activities on the basis of functions required for the achievement of organizational objectives. Authority relationships in functional structure may be in the form of line, staff and functional.

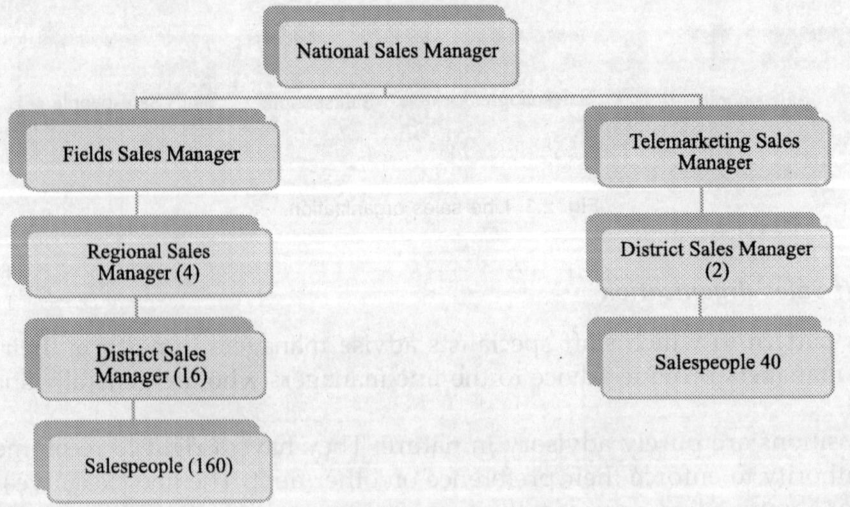

Fig. 2.5. Functional sales organization.

Schemes for Dividing Line Authority in the Sales Organization

As marketing operations expand, line authority and responsibility eventually become excessively burdensome for the top sales executive. There is an increasing number of people to supervise. Ordinarily, the first remedial step taken is to add a general line assistant, for example an assistant sales manager. As the burden of line administrative work continues to grow, it is necessary to provide additional assistants. These new subordinates are given line responsibilities narrower than those of the assistant general sales manager. Although they work with a variety of matters, their assignments cover a limited area of operations. Tasks of line administration are subdivided among these new assistants in one of three ways: (i) by geographic area, (ii) by-products or, (iii) by customers or marketing channels.

Product Sales Organization

Product based organizations are useful for complex products because they require the sales force to concentrate on a limited product line. Product specialization is generally combined with geographical specialization at the higher levels, while at the level of field operators, different salesmen may be assigned to specific product lines.

Organization includes duplication of calls and buyer frustration. This duplication of coverage can lead to increased selling costs.

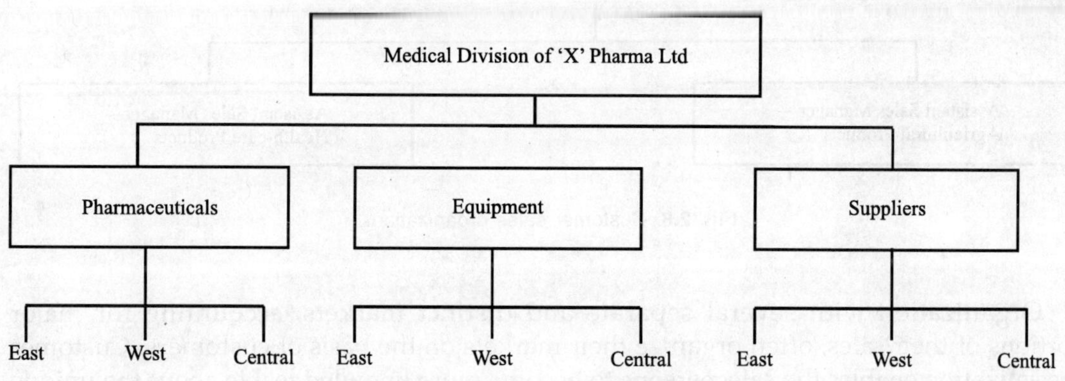

Fig. 2.6. Product sales organization.

Geographic Sales Organization

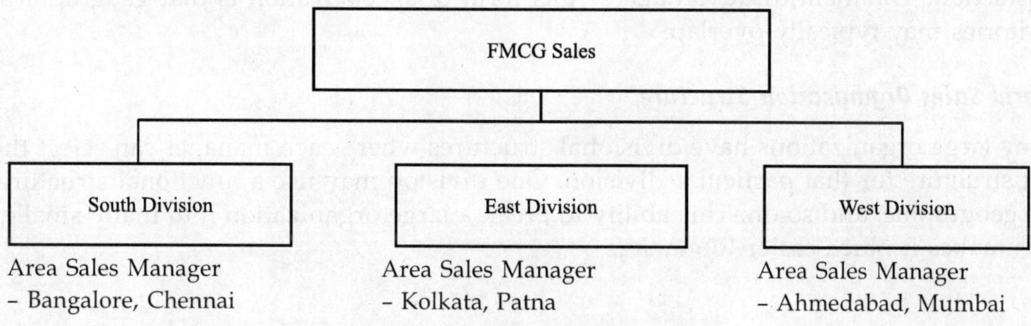

Fig. 2.7. Geographic sales organization.

The most common means of specialization of the sales force is by geographic region. In a geographically based sales force, a salesperson has to visit all current and potential customers in a given geographic territory. Some advantages of geographic organizations are like proper coverage of territory, defining the responsibility, familiarity with local economic and competitive conditions, etc. making them better able to serve local customers.

The disadvantages of this kind of structure is that the salespersons need to be responsible for the entire product line in their territory even though they may not be having uniform knowledge about all products. Further, within their territory, they may choose to concentrate on products and customers that are easy prospects.

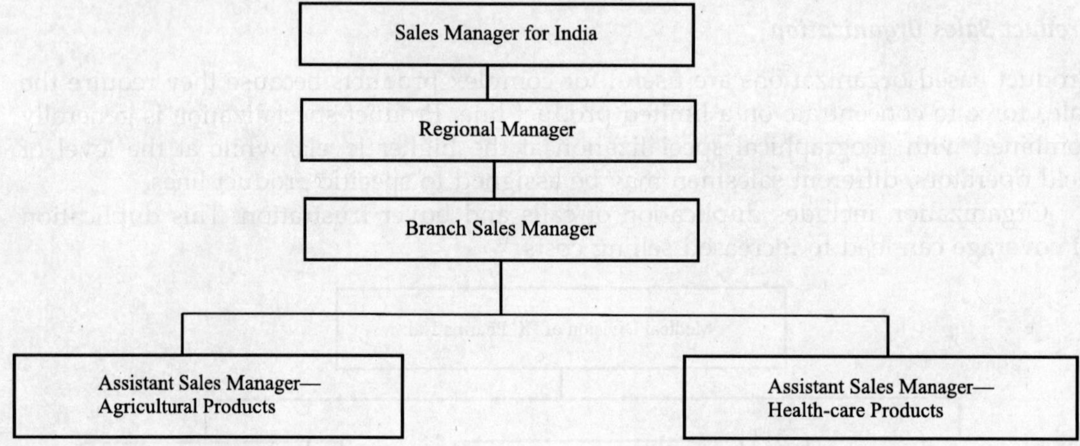

Fig. 2.8. Customer sales organization.

Organization with several separate and distinct markets, accounting for major portions of their sales, often organize their markets on the basis of customers. Customer specialization enables the salespersons to become more knowledgeable about the unique problems and needs of each group of customers. A customer-oriented sales force is consistent with the marketing concept with its increased emphasis on consumer satisfaction. The main disadvantage of this form of specialization is that geographical territories may typically overlap.

Hybrid Sales Organization Structure

Many large organizations have divisional structures where each manager can select the best structure for that particular division. One division may use a functional structure, one geographic, and so on. This ability to break a large organization into many smaller ones makes it much easier to manage.

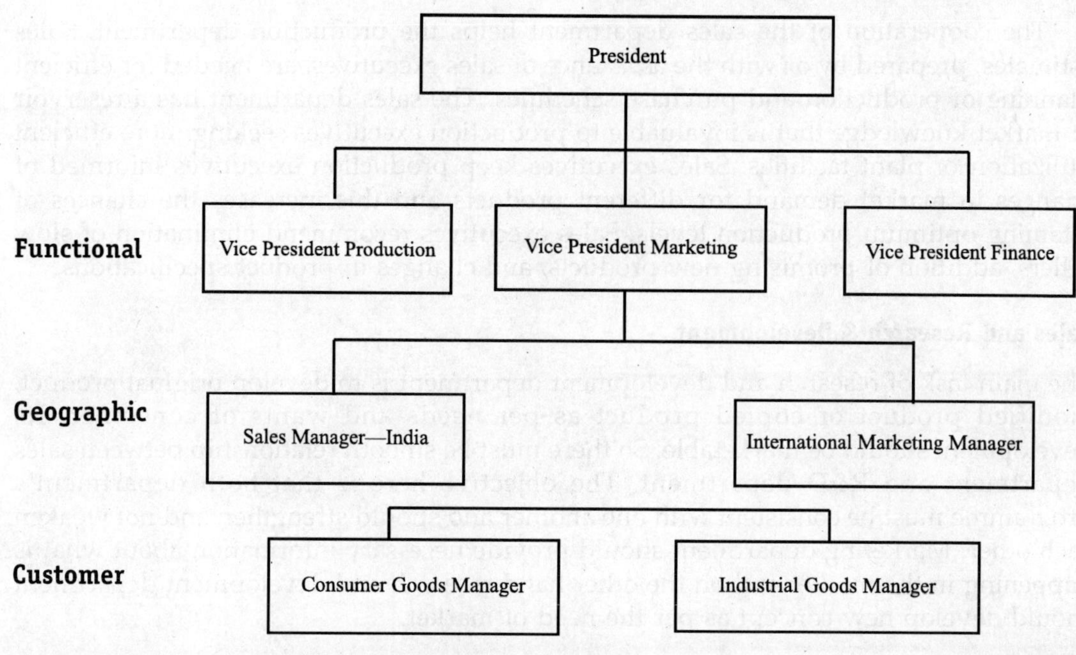

Fig. 2.9. Hybrid sales organization structure.

In this type of organization structure there are two or more different types of organization types are combined. This structure is designed to overcome the problems of individual sales organizations. Its main advantage is the ability to offer customers the service they need using the most efficient method. The primary disadvantage of hybrid sales organization is the difficulty of managing multiple sales forces, whether they are serving the same or different customers.

SALES DEPARTMENT RELATIONS

The success of an organization largely depends on effective marketing department and in turn on the performance of the sales department. It must gear its activities in terms of satisfaction of customer needs and desires. For this sales department must establish good relationship with other functions departments such as research and development department, production and operation department, finance and accounting department and human resource department, legal departments, public relations department, etc.

Sales and Production

Coordination of sales and production activities is essential. Whereas at one time production was started only after orders were on hand, today most production is in anticipation of future sales. Similarly, although some products, such as defence materials for the armed forces, are manufactured to specifications established by buyers, most products today are manufactured according to specifications set within the company itself.

The cooperation of the sales department helps the production department. Sales estimates, prepared by or with the assistance of sales executives, are needed for efficient planning of production and purchase schedules. The sales department has a reservoir of market knowledge that is invaluable to production executives seeking more efficient utilization of plant facilities. Sales executives keep production executives informed of changes in market demand for different products and this increases the chances of attaining optimum production levels. Sales executives recommend elimination of slow sellers, addition of promising new products, and changes in product specifications.

Sales and Research & Development

The main task of research and development department is to develop original product, modified product or copied product as per needs and wants of consumer. Its development should be marketable. So there must be smooth relationship between sales department and R&D department. The objective here is that both department's programme must be consistent with one another and should strengthen and not weaken each other. Marketing department should provide necessary information about what is happening in the market and on the other hand research and development department should develop new concept as per the need of market.

Sales and HR Department

Human resource department should cooperate with the sales department to provide a strong marketing team. Human resource department is to help the marketing department with its specialized knowledge. This department can help introduce a proper training programme for personnel in the marketing department. So, cooperation between these two can considerably help in getting the right personnel and utilizing it for maximum benefit.

Sales and Finance

The sales department assists the finance department by furnishing sales estimates for the company budget, by developing the sales department's budget, and by assisting in control of selling cost. The finance department assists the sales department by providing rapid credit checks on prospective accounts, keeping sales people informed of customers' credit standing, helping locate prospective accounts, and providing credit information on candidates for sales position. In some firms, salespersons represent the financial department in making collections and securing credit information. These interdepartmental activities require good communications, consistent policies and close working relationships. Most organizational plans provide for formal coordination through budget and executive committees.

Sales and Purchasing

The sales and purchasing departments cooperate in three main ways. First, the sales department provides purchasing with sales estimates so that adequate stocks of raw materials, fabricating parts and other items can be procured in advance of scheduled production runs. Sometimes these data are furnished through an intermediary such as the production department or data-processing unit. Second, the purchasing department informs the sales department, again sometimes through an intermediary, of material surpluses and shortages so sales emphasis can be changed with regard to products made from these materials. Third, data on sales department needs are furnished to the purchasing department so that purchases can be made on advantageous terms.

Sales and Legal

Legislation regulating and effective marketing activities make effective coordination of the sales and legal departments imperative. Every sales department activity has, or can have, legal implications. Sales executives require legal advice on contracts with sales personnel, pricing, relations with competitors and trade associations, salesperson recruiting policy and practice and disputes with customers. Sales executives and legal officers are in continuing communication to avoid costly litigation and unfavourable publicity. Formal coordination of the sales and legal departments is achieved through top management, but interdepartmental coordination on legal matters in informal.

Sales and Public Relations

The sales department works closely with the public relations (PR) department. PR department is consulted on any contemplated moves that might have public relations repercussions, and the sales department assists public relations personnel by relaying information, secured through its contacts with various PR departments, that has public relations significance. Relations between the two departments are normally informal and with frequent personal contacts, with formal coordination being the responsibility of top management.

Distributive Network Relations

Developing and maintaining good relations with the channel partners is an important function of the sales department. Distribution channels are the conduits through which goods of a company flow to the final buyer. Any hindrance in smooth flow of goods to the buyers is bad for the health of any company. Even companies like HUL, who have a strong consumer pull for their products pay due importance to relations with the distribution partners. Since sales personnel are dealing directly with the distributor, they are the face of the company to the distributors. Hence, relation of sales department with the distributor is crucial for the smooth flow of goods to the final buyers.

Need for Setting up Cooperative Programmes with Distribution Network

The role of distribution outlets is crucial for a company in implementing its marketing programme. When a company plans an aggressive advertising campaign to launch a product, it is very important that adequate stocks of the product are available at the retail outlets. If there is no coordination between the advertising campaign and the availability of the product at the retail outlets, the whole advertising campaign will go waste. Influenced by the advertising campaign, the consumer will ask for that product at the retail outlet, and on not finding the product at the retail outlet will most likely not ask for it again unless there is another campaign. Similarly, the display of the product at the retailer's point is equally important. If a product is visible at a retail counter, the chances of sales increase manifold. This is more true in case of products where impulse buying by the consumer is a prominent feature.

A modern-day retailer has a lot of choice. He is bombarded daily by a number of sales persons, and with scores of products. In a particular product category, a retailer has a choice of selling around 5-6 equally popular brands. Hence, it is the responsibility of the company to build relations with the retailers so that they cooperate with them in the sale of their products. Also , in most marketing situations, the company's organization is larger, more experienced, and better equipped to plan and administer cooperative programmes, and the distributive outlet usually look to the manufacturer to set up and manager any cooperative efforts.

Some companies enjoy a strong consumer pull, for instance, HUL, P&G. They enjoy an upper hand in their relationship with the distributors. Still, they know the importance of retailers and distributors in their marketing programme. One finds the maximum point of purchase displays by these strong companies, who know well that a good display at the selling point increases the chances of selling.

Objectives of Cooperation with the Distributive Network

According to Still, Cundiff and Govoni, companies undertake cooperative programmes with distributors

(i) To build distributive network loyalty
(ii) To stimulate distributive outlet to greater selling effort and
(iii) To develop managerial efficiency in distributive organizations.

Selling Process

The actual selling process can be likened to a chain, each link of which must be closed successfully or the seller will fail to get the order. However, each step overlaps the other, and their sequence may be altered to meet the situation at hand.

The eight steps of the sales process are:

1. Prospecting
2. Preapproach—planning the sale
3. Approaches
4. Need assessment
5. Presentations
6. Meeting objections
7. Gaining commitment
8. Follow-up

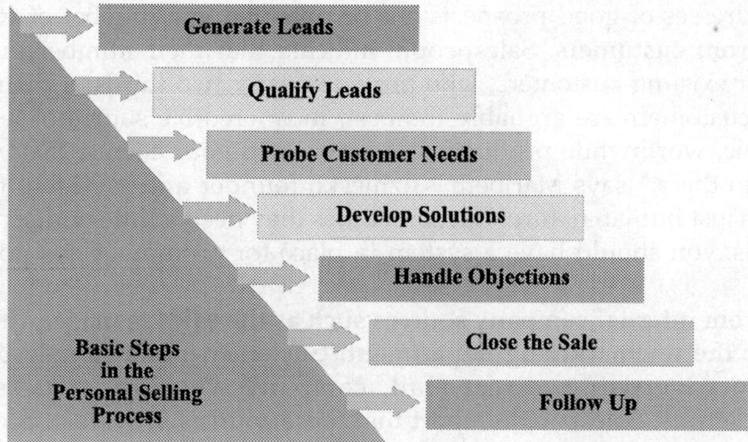

Fig. 2.10. Selling process.

PROSPECTING

Succeeding in today's competitive environment means that a company must constantly find new customers. A salesperson's basic strategy should be to spend as much time as possible with excellent prospects – people who recognize their need and are ready to buy. As Phil Clark, an IBM regional sales manager in Dallas, succinctly told his sales force, "The idea is that through our advertising and promotional efforts, we stand on a ladder shouting loudly all over Dallas, 'Everyone who is ready to buy a computer please raise their hands.' Then we go and sell one computer to each person who responds."

Prospecting is the method or system by which salespeople learn the names of people who need the product and can afford it. There are two steps in successful prospecting. The first step is identifying leads – generating potential customers. The second step is qualifying leads according to which – who is most likely to buy.

Identifying Leads

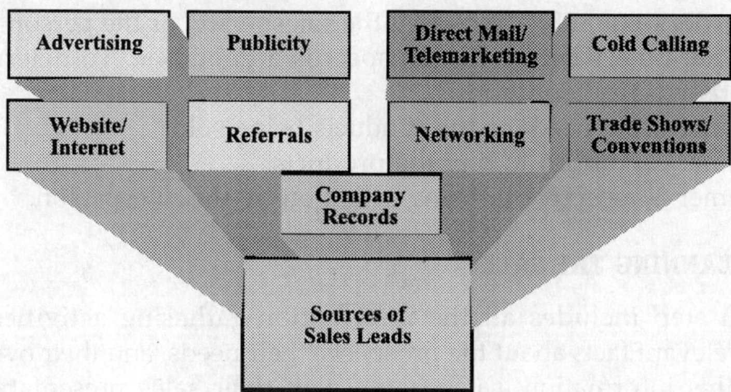

Fig. 2.11. Generating leads.

Names and addresses of good prospects can be obtained in a number of ways:

Referrals from customers: Salespeople indicate that their number one source of referrals is their existing customers, who provide nearly two-thirds of their leads. Two referrals from customers are arguably the best, most credible source of leads. "If you provide valuable, worthwhile products and services to your clients, they will want to share you with others," says Maribeth Kuzmeski, founder and president of Red Zone Marketing. "It's just human nature! But sometimes they need a little nudge. So whatever your business is, you should have a system in place for promoting this positive 'word of mouth.'"!

Referrals from internal company sources such as the sales manager, the marketing department, or the telemarketing department: Customer inquiries may be generated from company advertising, direct mail, company websites, trade shows, and teleprospecting efforts. Salespeople report that these sources provide approximately 23 per cent of their leads.

Referrals from external referral agencies: Some companies turn to outside agencies for the generation and qualification of leads. This trend is on the upswing due to an increasing number of dot-com businesses, which typically provide a list of leads for reasonable fees.

Published directories: Trade associations, the government, local chambers of commerce, and the yellow pages all are good sources of prospects. Many of the directories are available on the Internet.

Networking by the salesperson: Salespeople often use their friends and acquaintances to make new contacts. Many salespeople join professional and civic organizations in part to meet new people who may be potential customers or who may be able to provide leads.

Qualifying Leads

Whatever the source of the lead, it is important that the lead be qualified. Philosophically, professional salespeople do not want to bother people who have no need for their products. Moreover, it is very expensive for salespeople to make calls that have little chance of success because the customer does not need, does not want, or cannot afford the products. In order to qualify a prospect, the salesperson or the person providing the referral should determine whether the prospect is a good one. To determine this, the prospect must satisfy three conditions:

1. The customer has a need for the products being sold.
2. The customer can afford to buy the products.
3. The customer is receptive to being called on by the salesperson.

PREAPPROACH: PLANNING THE SALE

The preapproach step includes all the information-gathering activities salespeople perform to learn relevant facts about the prospects, their needs, and their overall situation. Then, based on this information, salespeople plan their sales presentations, selecting the most appropriate objective for each call.

Fig. 2.12. Qualifying leads.

Customer Research

The sales rep should learn everything possible about the prospective customer's business—its size; its present purchasing practices; the location of its plants; the names of its executives; and, most important, the names of people who make the buying decision as well as those who influence the purchase. It is also helpful to learn something about the buyers' background, such as their education, social affiliations, or personality. If the prospective buyer has been having problems, the seller should, if possible, become familiar with those problems.

When researching a current customer or one that has been called on previously by a salesperson from your company, start by reading the company files. They should provide a wealth of background information on the company and possibly on the buyers as well—sales records, correspondence, past sales, call reports, and other relevant information. Many companies store information about their customers in a database to which their salespeople have easy access using laptop or notebook computers.

For new customers, you can easily obtain a great deal of information by using the Internet or online information services such as LexisNexis, Dialog, and Dow Jones News/Retrieval. Other sources include trade magazines, industrial directories, magazine and newspaper articles, chambers of commerce, and government publications, as well as the annual reports of companies. Sometimes the company's current suppliers, customers, and certain employees can provide information.

Planning the Sales Presentation

The most important part of planning the sales presentation is defining the objective or goal for the particular call. The goal is not necessarily to close or complete the sale on each call. In fact, salespeople report that, on average, it takes four calls to close a sale. However, on each call the salesperson does want to obtain from the buyer some type of commitment for action that moves the sale forward. For example, the salesperson may try to obtain a list of the customer's vendor selection criteria or get the buyer to set up a meeting with some of the other people who will be involved in the decision. The objective may be any agreement on an action that moves the sales forward.

Salespeople may also plan how they are going to approach the buyer and what kind of questions they want to ask. It is important that salespeople recognize differences across selling situations and adapt their presentations accordingly. Based on their precall customer research, they will make a tentative judgement as to which of their products best meet their customers' needs and then formulate a tentative plan for presenting the features and benefits of those products. Of course, the information gained by salespeople during the actual call may often cause them to alter their initial objectives or plans. This is called adaptive selling.

THE APPROACH

Once the sales rep has the name of a prospect and adequate preapproach information, the next step is the actual approach. Making an appointment to see the buyer increases the chances that the salesperson will have the buyer's attention during their meeting.

A good approach makes a favourable impression and establishes some degree of rapport between the salesperson and the buyer. In order to make a favourable impression with customers in the United States, the salesperson should have a firm handshake, be professionally attired, and make good eye contact. Usually each call starts with an introduction (unless the salesperson has called on this customer before) and a limited amount of small talk. Sometimes salespeople will draw attention to their products by handing the buyer a sample or by highlighting some benefit in which the buyer will likely be interested.

The approach usually takes up only the first minute or so of a call, but it can make or break the entire presentation. If the approach fails, the salesperson often does not get a chance to give a presentation. At the end of the approach, the salesperson must gain the buyer's agreement to move into the need assessment stage of the call.

NEED ASSESSMENT

Companies and consumers purchase products and services to satisfy needs or to solve problems. In a business situation, the company's purchases are always related to the need to improve performance—to become more efficient and effective at fulfilling

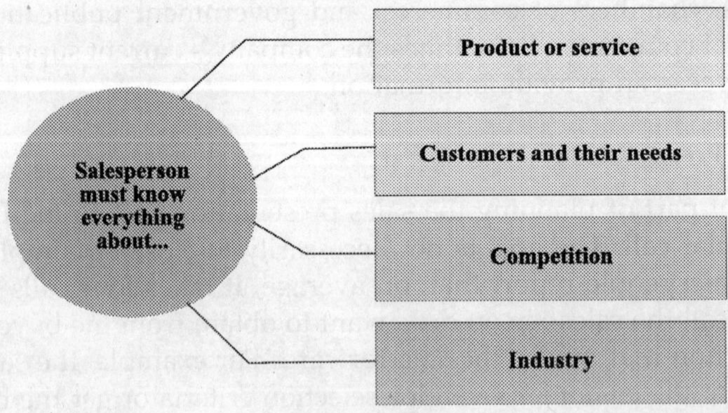

Fig. 2.13. Probing needs.

customer's needs. Need assessment is the stage in which the salesperson must discover, clarify, and understand the buyer's needs. The best way to uncover and understand needs is by asking questions. In fact, research has determined that the more questions salespeople ask, the more likely it is that they will be successful.

Salespeople ask these questions in the logical order just presented. The situational questions should be asked first, followed by the problem discovery questions, the problem impact questions, the solution value questions, and then the confirmatory questions. Each type naturally leads to the following type, and each one helps build the buyer's interest in hearing about the solutions the salesperson has to offer. It should be noted that studies by Neil Rackham of 35,000 sales calls demonstrate that the most successful salespeople are those who use fewer situational questions and more problem discovery, impact, and solution value questions.

THE PRESENTATION

After assessing the needs and desires of the customer, the salesperson moves into the main body of the sale, the presentation. The presentation is primarily a discussion of those products and/or service features, advantages, and benefits that the customer has indicated are important. While most presentations are oral, they often include written proposals and supporting material as well as visual aids. The goal of the presentation is to convince the customer that the product or service being sold will satisfy the customer's needs better than that of a competitor.

Features describe the characteristics of the product or service, advantages describe how the feature changes the performance of the product or service, and benefits describe how the advantage will help the buyer. For each feature and advantage that a salesperson presents, he or she should also present one or more benefits of that feature to the buyer. In fact, the benefits should be those that address specific needs mentioned by the customer.

Prepared Sales Presentations

The advisability of using a prepared sales presentation, better known as a canned sales talk, is debatable. Without doubt, a prepared presentation done poorly and without feeling is a dismal experience. However, many firms do use canned talks successfully. The prepared presentation has several advantages:

- It gives new salespeople confidence.
- It can use tested sales techniques that have proven effective.
- It gives some assurance that the complete story will be told.
- It greatly simplifies sales training.

The use of a prepared presentation does not mean that sales reps must use someone else's words. Above all, the salesperson's own feelings and personality should be evident in the presentation.

Developing Effective Presentations

The task of developing a presentation is not an easy one. Some simple advice may be helpful here:

Keep the presentation simple. The temptation to tell everything is overwhelming. Don't do it. The prospect can absorb only a limited amount of information at any one time. Don't overload the system.

Talk the prospect's language. Don't build the presentation around industry jargon or product model numbers. If customers don't understand what the rep is talking about, they seldom say so. That would be an admission of ignorance. They usually pretend to understand and then say, "I'll have to think it over for a while."

Stress the application of the product or service to the prospect's situation. Tailor the presentation to the application or person at hand. Even within the same firm, different individuals place different priorities on what is important about the product. You must adapt your presentation to the situation and person.

Above all, seek credibility at every turn. The entire presentation is nothing if it is not believed. Each statement must be credible. Prove points one by one. A critical point is not complete until the prospect believes it. The real key to successful selling lies in this credibility.

MEETING OBJECTIONS

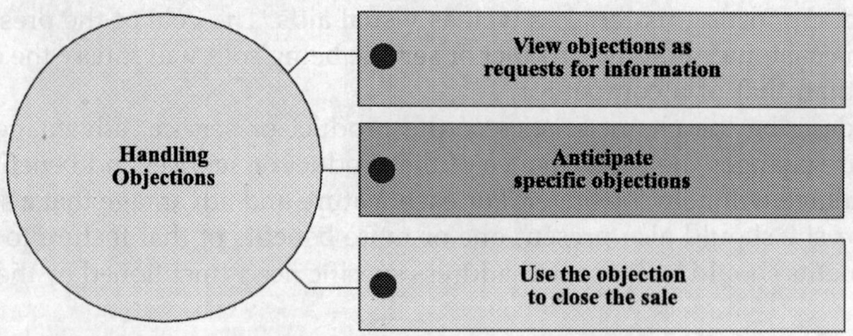

Fig. 2.14. Handling objections.

Objections are encountered in practically every presentation. They should be welcomed because they indicate that the prospect has some interest in the proposition. A prospect who is not interested in buying seldom raises any objections, silently going along with the presentation but saying at the end, "I'm not interested in your deal." There are several important techniques that should be used in responding to a buyer's objection:

Listen to the buyer. It is important that you listen actively. "Learn as much as you can about the objection," says certified professional sales trainer and speaker Rick Grosso. "Encourage your prospect to expand and tell you more." Do not assume that you know what the buyer is going to say, and never interrupt—nothing annoys a buyer more!

Clarify the objection. Repeat and clarify the objection by asking for more information, using questions such as "Let me see if I understand you correctly, (repeating the objection as you understand it). Is that correct?" The buyer may confirm that you are correct in your understanding or provide additional information. Sometimes this step can uncover a misunderstanding that the buyer has about your product and/or service.

Respect the buyer's concern. Acknowledge that you understand and appreciate the concerns. Remember that the buyer is not attacking you personally, so you should not become defensive.

Respond to the objection. It is important that you respond to the buyer's concern. The specific response to the objection depends on the type of objection it is.

The most common types of objections and specific strategies for handling them are discussed next.

Price or Value Objections

Buyers who say "I don't need it" or "It costs too much" are indicating that they don't think the value of solving the problem or meeting the need is worth the cost. In this case, the salesperson must convince the buyer of the importance of the problem and of the value of the solution. It may be necessary to go back to the need assessment part of the call to ask some additional problem impact and solution value types of questions to increase the buyer's perception of the seriousness of the problem and the importance of a solution. If the buyer acknowledges the importance of the problem but still feels that the company can't afford the product/service or that it is not a price-competitive solution, then the salesperson can offer some price value comparisons of alternative solutions.

Product/Service Objections

Sometimes the buyer acknowledges the importance of a problem but doubts whether the product or service can solve his problem or improve his operations. The buyer may disagree with the salesperson's assessment or, in some cases, even doubt the genuineness of the salesperson. In this case the salesperson needs to convince the buyer that her/his product will do what she/he says. She/he must demonstrate or prove that the product has the capability to fulfil the need.

Hidden Objections

Prospects may state their objections to a proposition openly and give the salesperson a chance to answer them. This is an ideal situation, because everything is out in the open and the salesperson does not need to read the prospect's mind. Unfortunately, prospects often hide their real reasons for not buying. Further, stated objections may be phony. A prospect may say she does not like the looks of a product, when she really thinks the price is too high. The rep must determine the real barrier to the sale to be able to overcome it.

GAINING COMMITMENT

At some point after the salesperson has convinced the buyer that his or her products at least warrant further attention, the salesperson must ask the buyer to commit to some

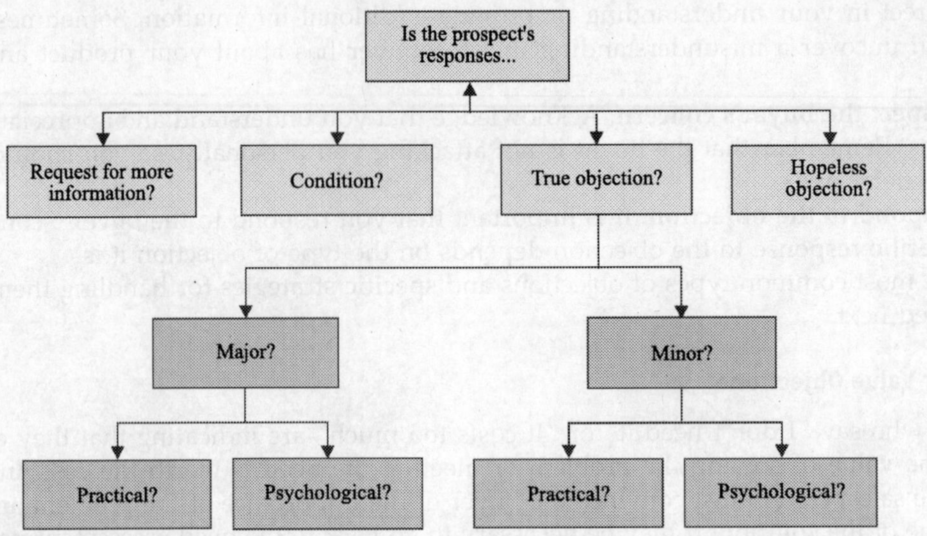

Fig. 2.15. What does a prospect mean by objection.

action that moves the sale forward. This is called gaining commitment. In a relatively simple sale, it is important for the salesperson to get a commitment from the buyer to purchase the product on the first call (usually the only call) or he/she will have lost the sale. Some of the techniques frequently used to close these transaction sales are highlighted in the box titled "Common Sales Closes."

However, sales of complex business products usually require more than one call. In fact, some large sales may take several years to complete. To get the buyer to agree to some action that moves the buyer closer to the sale, the salesperson may suggest a demonstration, review the specifications, or offer a sample. The keys to obtaining commitment are, first, to plan realistic objectives for each sales call and, second, to ask for a commitment. If the salesperson doesn't ask, then he or she won't move the sale forward. To ask for an action that in effect finalizes the sale, the salesperson may simply say, "Can I place an order for you today?"

Sometimes the buyer may volunteer to take an action that moves the sale forward or even finalizes the sale. For example, the buyer may say, "We've decided that we need to make a change and we think your company is in the best position to serve our needs." But often it does not happen this way, and the salesperson must ask for the commitment.

CLOSING THE SALES AND FOLLOW-UP

Sales Resistance

Prospects show sales resistance by pointing out real or imagined obstacles, and by voicing objections, sincere or insincere. In analyzing sales resistance, the salesperson need skill in accurate and rapid appraisal of people and their motivations. A prospect's expressed sales resistance is either an obstacle or an objection. An obstacle is real or unreal; an objection is sincere or insincere.

Obstacles to Sales

Obstacles are real or apparent reasons that the prospect has for not buying. If the obstacle is real, it precludes the consummation of the sale. But it is apparent; there are ways to circumvent it. A prospect says a temporary shortage of cash prevents buying an obstacle, not an objection and the salesperson helps the prospect to circumvent it by explaining a method for financing the purchase. Some obstacles can be circumvented, some cannot, when an obstacle arises, the salesperson determines whether or not there is a way to get around it. If the salesperson recognizes the specific obstacle and knows a way to circumvent it, the next move is to present the solution to the prospect.

Sales Objection

Objections are never good reasons for failing to complete the sale, but they nearly always divert the salesperson's presentation from its main course. At best, an objection requires a satisfactory answer; at worst, it blocks the sale. Adroitness in handling objection is a difference between effective and ineffective salespeople. Sincere objections trace to incompleteness, inaccuracy, or vagueness in the sales presentation. Prospects may not recognize the nature of their needs, or they may have doubt about the appropriateness of the product to fulfil those needs.

Prospects may be confused in some respect, or may react unfavourably to the salesperson's personality. Except when personality conflict cannot be resolved (a real obstacle, not an objection), sincere objections are overcome by patient and thorough explanations. Prospects raise insincere objections to discourage salespersons, to get rid of them, to test their competence, and as false excuses for not buying. When salespersons sense that an objection is insincere, they seek to regain the offensive as soon as possible.

They do not permit an insincere objection to provoke an argument—one of the surest ways to lose a sale. Some sales executives say that every objection, no matter how insincere, should be treated with the utmost courtesy. Others say that insincere objections should be ignored. The best defensive strategy often is the strong counterattack, and the salesperson should seek to regain the initiative as soon as he or she can gracefully do so.

CLOSING SALES

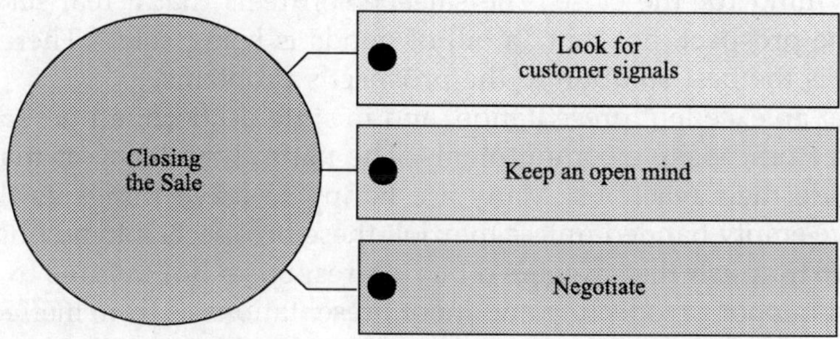

Fig. 2.16. Closing the sale.

The selling tactics followed affect the ease of closing the sale. Low pressure sales are closed more easily than the high pressure ones. On low pressure sales, prospects feel that they are reaching the buying decisions themselves, and primarily through rational processes of thought, so there is no need for extra push just before the sales are consummated. In high pressure sales, the main thrust is to the prospect's emotions, so salespersons attempt to propel prospects into buying decisions. Often, the prospect regains normal perspective as the sale nears its climax, and, if this happens, the salesperson needs unusually effective persuasion to close the sale.

Every salesperson approaches certain closings with apprehension.

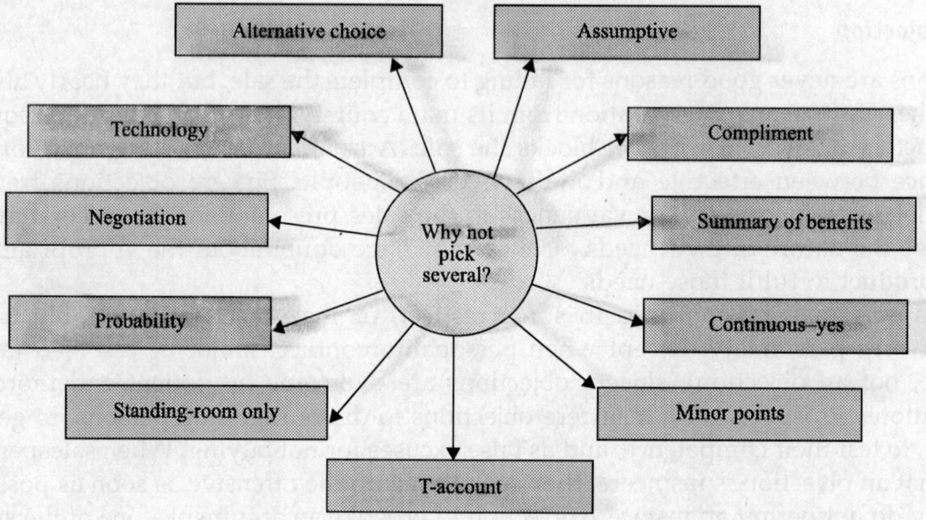

Fig. 2.17. Techniques for closing the sale: Which close should be used?

At closing time, either the salesperson sells the prospect an order or the prospect sells the salesperson on a "no sale." Closing time provides an opportunity to register tangible proof of selling skill. Occasionally even the best salesperson must rely upon closing skill to make the sale. Prospecting, if well done, puts the salesperson in the proper frame of mind for the close. The salesperson feels that a real service is being performed for the prospect, not that "a bill of goods is being sold." There is no doubt that the product is the best solution to the prospect's problems.

But even after an excellent presentation, and in spite of thorough prospecting, some prospects refrain from positive commitments. The natural tendency of many people is to let inertia guide their reactions. Many are happy to leave things as they are, and salespersons leave empty handed unless they jolt these prospects into buying. The skilled closer gives the extra push that triggers a buying response. But failures to get an order result as much from poor prospecting and inept presentations as from ineffective closing.

When an attempted close fails, the salesperson should normally try another. The refusal does not necessarily imply an unwillingness to buy; it may indicate the prospect's need for additional information or for clarification of some point. Some executives recommend that sales personnel attempt as many as five closes before giving up. Early closing attempt should be so expressed that a refusal will not cut off the presentation. A salesperson judges the sincerity of a prospect's refusal, surrendering gracefully when it is clear that no sale will be made.

The salesperson first uses an indirect close, that is, attempts to get the order without actually asking for it. The salesperson may ask the prospect to state a preference from among a limited number of choice (as to models, delivery dates, order size, or the like), so phrasing the question that all possible responses are in the salesperson's favour except for one: "none at all." Or the salesperson may summarize, emphasizing features that visibly impress the prospect, showing how the reasons for the purchase outweigh those opposed to it. Then the salesperson pauses for the prospect's response, which is expected to be, "Go ahead and write the order." Sometimes, the extra push may be a concession that makes the sale. Or the salesperson may assume that the sale is made, write out the order, and hand it to the prospect for approval if the prospect balks, the issue is clearer. Perhaps one last objection is voiced, but after it is answered, the sale is made. Many indirect closes are in common use, and books on selling contain numerous examples.

When open or more attempts at a indirect close fail, the salesperson uses the direct approach. Few prospects respond negatively to a frank request for the order in fact, many people, especially those who are themselves engaged in selling, do not buy unless the order is asked for outright.

Reps must learn that the sale is not over when they get the order. Good sales reps follow up in various ways. They make certain that they have answered all the buyer's questions and that the buyer understands the details of the contract. If the merchandise is delivered at a later date, the reps are present at the time of delivery or call soon afterward to ensure that everything is in order.

The follow-up step of the sales process has become critical to the success of contemporary sales organizations. This is especially true given recent sales management trends toward the concepts of relationship marketing and consultative selling. That is, instead of focusing on one-time, transactional sales, today's salespeople work to build and maintain long-term, mutually beneficial partnerships with their customers. Of course, customers would never form partnerships with organizations whose salespeople forget about them after the sale!

Indeed, the concepts of relationship marketing have made sales organizations rethink the steps of the sales process. Organizations realize that it is much more expensive to acquire new customers than it is to retain the existing customers. So, although generating new accounts is still important, salespeople must be careful not to sacrifice effective follow-up for prospecting. Further, effective follow-up essentially consists of asking questions to customers in an ongoing attempt to monitor their needs. Thus, when dealing with loyal customers, salespeople must continually revisit the need assessment step of the sales process.

THEORIES OF SELLING

Selling is both an art and a science. Many consider it an art evolving into a science. Selling is viewed differently by those who consider it an art and those who treat it as a science. This gives rise to two contrasting theories of selling.

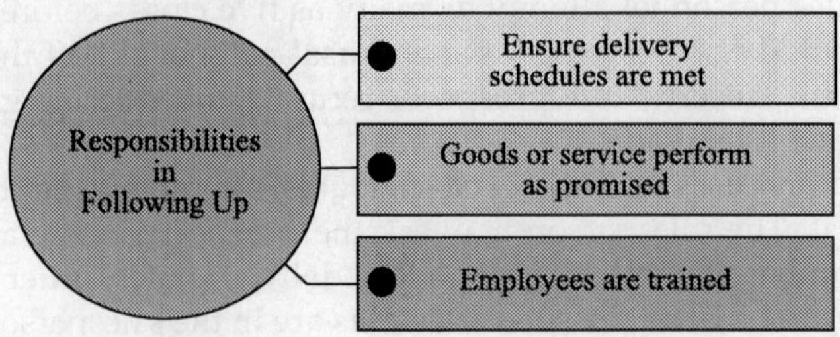

Fig. 2.18. Following up.

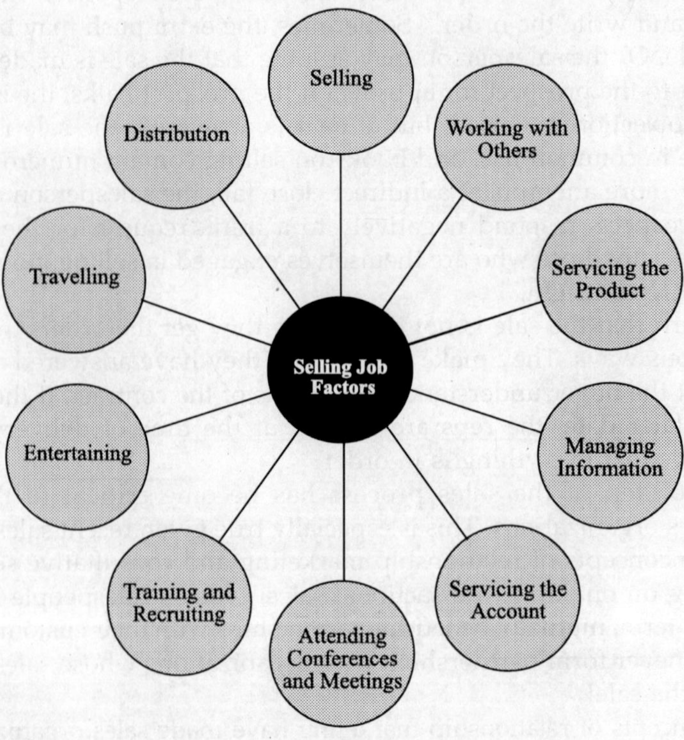

Fig. 2.19. Selling job factors.

Selling is studied as the cumulative experience of salespersons and advertising professionals. It distils knowledge from practice, and psychology learnt through experience. It teaches how all this can be put into practice. The emphasis is on 'how to' rather than 'why'. Empirical evidence is considered more valuable than a systematic body of knowledge. But such knowledge can never be foolproof.

In the second approach, theories of behavioural sciences are applied to selling.

The seller-oriented theories are AIDAS theory and right set of circumstance theory. The buyer-oriented theory is 'buying-formula' theory. The behavioural equation considers the mutual influences of the buyers and sellers.

(i) AIDAS Theory of Selling

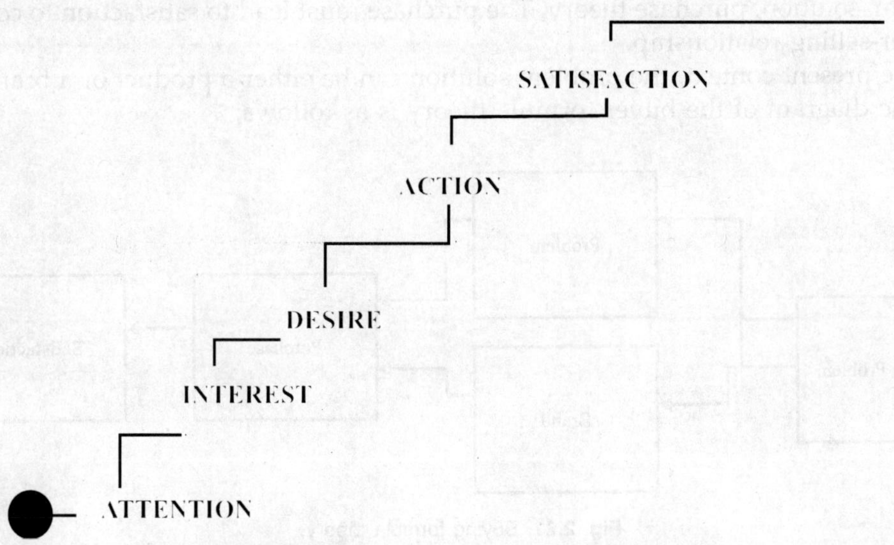

Fig. 2.20. AIDA model.

The salesman, in order to affect a sale, must persuade the customer to buy his products. This act of persuasion needs proper planning of strategy and tactics. The customer must be taken through certain stages of the mind. These stages are very effectively summarized by what is known as the AIDAS model:

'A' Attention: It is the starting point in the sales process. The attention of the customer must be attracted to the product, and the want that the product is able to satisfy.

'I' Interest: The salesman must create an interest in the mind of the customers. The customers must be made to realize how the product will benefit them, and must feel curious to know more about the product, its features and its merits.

'D' Desire: The salesman must ignite the desire of the prospect after securing his attention and after arousing his interest in the product. The salesman must use all his powers for persuasion and conviction to create an urge to buy.

'A' Action: It means gaining an order. The culmination of the first three stages should be into the actual purchase of the product. The customer must be induced to buy the product or place an order for the product. The want must be converted into demand.

'S' Satisfaction: Follow-up or post-sale contact is necessary to ensure customer satisfaction and to remove any post-sale problems. It is also a source of feedback from the customer. Satisfaction leads to repeat orders.

(ii) Buying Formula Theory

This is a buyer-oriented theory which seeks answers to why a consumer buys what he does. It emphasizes the problem-solving job of a salesman. This theory takes into account the internal factors, and does not place all the importance on external factors. It is simply a problem, solution, purchase theory. The purchase must lead to satisfaction to continue the buyer-selling relationship.

In the present context, the problem solution can be either a product or a brand. The schematic diagram of the buyer formula theory is as follows:

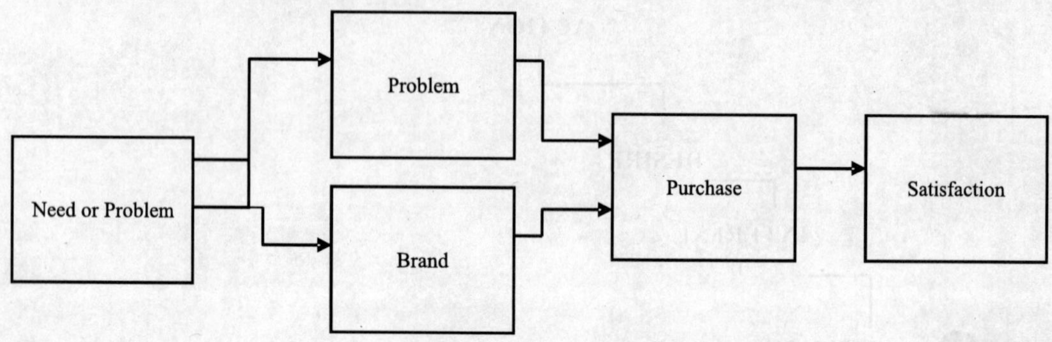

Fig. 2.21. Buying formula theory.

Product or brands must be considered adequate in solution and must induce pleasant feelings. Both adequacy and pleasant feelings can be simultaneously present. Sometimes it is either-or situation. The buying formula in its modified form looks as follows:

A buyer should be aware why the product/brand is an adequate solution and should have pleasant feeling towards it. This establishes his buying habit. There is an assault on this habit by rival ads, competing salesperson's presentation and a friend's remark. He defends his decision on the strength of adequacy and pleasant feelings. These act as good defence mechanism. In most purchases, this defence mechanism is not at work. Just there is a direct association of a problem and solution.

Each selling problem has its answers in the above formula, and the variations in the answers are in effect the variations of emphasis on the elements constituting this formula.

(iii) Behavioural Equation Theory

Howard explains buying behaviour as phases of the learning process resulting into purchasing. Basically, this is modified stimulus-response (SR) model. Drives, cues, response and re-inforcement are the four elements of the learning process. Drives are strong internal stimuli which can be innate like hunger, thirst, pain, sex, etc. or can be learnt like recognition, prestige, approval, etc. cues are weak stimuli which decide when the buyer will respond. They can trigger the decision-making or may not trigger it. Product cues are directly received from the product. Information cues provide information of a symbolic nature about the product. Response is what a buyer does. Any event that strengthens this response is called reinforcement. Howard puts forward this as an equation.

$$B = P \times D \times K \times V$$

B = Response or purchasing
P = Force or habit
D = Drive level or motivation
K = Value of the product to provide satisfaction
V = Intensity of all cues.

It is a multiplicative relationship. B is dependent variable and the rest are independent variables. If these independent variables have a zero value, B will also be zero. P increases if K increases. A salesperson influences P directly. The use of the product affects P much more. Sales affect D to exercise influence.

SALES PERSONALITY

There are 7 key traits that we see time and again that produce a star sales employee. These are:

1. Sociability
2. Self-confidence
3. Composure
4. Tough-mindedness
5. Endurance
6. Ambition
7. Control

Sociability

Extrovert, outgoing, friendly, gregarious, neighbourly, congenial. Warm hearted individuals who enjoy interacting and participating with others. They greet strangers openly, are quick to form friendship, and enjoy careers dealing with people rather than things. They are rarely content in solitary work. People that are highly rated in sociability are happier people overall in life.

Self-Confidence

Self-assured, certain, secure, brave, fulfilled, poised, self-reliant, believe they have the knowledge and ability to be successful at whatever they attempt. They cope successfully with challenges and are not easily discouraged. They handle unexpected situations well, make decisions with assurance, and are quick to express ideas and opinions.

Composure

Calm, emotionally mature, tranquil, peaceful, serene, unperturbed, placid, composed, can control their emotions and function effectively in stressful situations. Have the capability to maintain composure and deal with stress in a calm, objective manner.

Rarely allow their feelings to negatively affect performance, and are not easily discouraged or frustrated by problems. Will not become upset over mistakes or misfortune.

Tough-Minded

Resilient, realistic, unsentimental, tough-minded, durable, hard, possibly insensitive and callous can function normally in difficult and unpleasant situations. Not deterred by obstacles, disappointments or setbacks. Can accept strong criticism, do not become easily upset, and recover quickly when things go wrong. Do not need excessive praise or encouragement from others.

Endurance

Industrious, energetic, determined, vigorous, diligent, enduring, persevering. Willing to put forth the physical effort necessary to be successful. Will exert sustained effort and persistence to accomplish their tasks and goals. Unrelenting in work habits, will practice long and hard, and will not give up easily on problems.

Ambition

Competitive, aspiring, enthusiastic, enterprising, industrious, goal-oriented, eager, striving. Strong desire to reach higher levels of achievement and to respond positively to competitive situations. Aspire to accomplish difficult tasks and set and maintain high goals. Tend to approach most situations competitively

Control

Deliberate, calculating, analytical, designing, possibly indecisive and prone to procrastinate. Highly disciplined, maintain control over their behavior and do not act impulsively. It would be unusual for them to speak or act without considering the consequences. May be slow to act or hesitant to make decisions in some situations.

Let Us Sum Up

A sales organization defines duties, roles, rights, and responsibilities of sales people engaged in selling activities meant for the effective execution of the sales function. There are two types of organization structure: tall and flat. There are various factors which decide the structure of the organization like product and service related factors, marketing mix related factors, the speed of market change, customer relationship management, etc.

Basically there are three types of organization structure: line sales, line & staff sales and functional sales organization structure. There are three schemes for dividing line authority in sales organization: product sales, geographic sales and customer sales organization. There is another type of sales organization known as hybrid sales organization.

Sales department is a very important function in the organization and maintains good relationships with R&D department, finance department, production department, legal department, etc. Sales department also needs to maintain the distribution networks.

There are eight steps in the selling process: Prospecting, Pre-approach – planning the sale, Approaches, Need assessment, Presentations, Meeting objections, Gaining commitment and Follow-up.

Question for Discussion

1. What do you understand by organization structure? Define a sales organization.
2. Explain the relationship between sales executive and other professional in the company.
3. Differentiate between tall and flat structure. List out the advantages and disadvantages.
4. Write short notes on (i) Line sales organization (ii) Line and staff sales organization (iii) Functional sales organization.
5. Write notes on (with diagrams) (i) Product sales organization (ii) Geographic sales organization (iii) Customer sales organization.
6. What do you understand by hybrid sales organization? Explain with a diagram.
7. Explain in detail sales department relations with other department in the organization.
8. Explain the requirements of maintaining sound distribution network relationships.
9. Explain the selling process with diagram.
10. Write short notes on (i) Sales resistance (ii) Closing a sale (iii) Hidden objection in selling process.
11. Write short notes on (i) AIDAS model (ii) Buying formula theory (iii) Behavioural equation theory.
12. Write down the different personality traits of sales people.
13. What are the different types of sales people? Explain briefly.
14. Explain the functions of sales organization.
15. Explain different types of sales organization.

3

CHAPTER

Sales Force Management

"Pearls lie not on the seashore. If thou desirest one thou must dive for it."

– Chinese Proverb

Recruitment sources – process – selection of sales personnel – training – motivating – compensating and controlling sales personnel – controlling the sales effort – sales budget – sales quotas – sales territories – sales control and cost analysis – sales force management system.

LEARNING OBJECTIVES

After going through this chapter, students will be able to understand

- Recruitment process of sales personnel
- Selection of sales personnel
- Training of sales people
- Motivating techniques for sales people
- Compensation mechanism
- Controlling the sales effort
- Sales budget, sales quotas, sales territories
- Cost analysis
- Sales force automation

INTRODUCTION

Effective management of the sales force is needed to implement the company's chosen sales force design and achieve its sales objectives. Sales force management covers the steps in recruiting and selecting, training, supervising, motivating, and evaluating representatives.

Recruiting and Selecting Sales Representatives

At the heart of a successful sales force is the selection of effective representatives. One survey revealed that the top 27 per cent of the sales force brought in over 52 per cent of the sales. Beyond differences in productivity is the great waste in hiring the wrong people. The average annual turnover rate for all industries is almost 20 per cent.

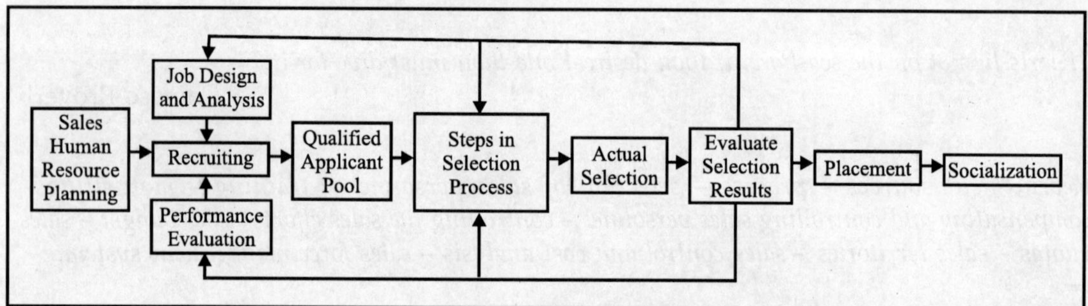

Fig. 3.1. Major influences and components of sales force selection.

When a representative quits, the costs of ending and training a new rep, plus the cost of lost sales, can run into the high five figures—and a sales force with many new hires is less productive.

In selecting sales reps, the company can start by asking customers what traits they prefer in salespeople. Most customers want honest, reliable, knowledgeable, and helpful reps. Another approach is to look for traits that are common to successful salespeople. Charles Garfield concluded that super sales performers exhibit risk taking, a powerful sense of mission, a problem-solving bent, care for the customer, and careful planning.

Mayer and Greenberg noted that the effective salesperson has empathy, the ability to feel as the customer does, and ego drive, a strong personal need to make the sale. After the management develops suitable selection criteria, the next step is to recruit applicants by various means, including soliciting names from current sales reps, using employment agencies, placing print and on-line job ads, and contacting graduating college students. Selection procedures can vary from an informal interview to prolonged testing and interviewing. Although test scores are only one information element in a set that includes personal characteristics, references, past employment history, and interviewer reactions, they are weighted quite heavily by such companies as IBM, Prudential, Procter & Gamble, and Gillette. Gillette claims that tests have reduced turnover by 42 per cent and have correlated well with the subsequent progress of new reps in the sales organization.

RECRUITMENT SOURCES

There are five main sources of recruitment

(i) Advertisement
(ii) From inside - the company's own staff
(iii) Recruitment agencies
(iv) Educational institutes
(v) Competitors and other industries.

RECRUITMENT PROCESS

After the management develops its selection criteria, it must recruit.

(i) ***Job Analysis:*** The company must be clear about the job to be filled. Thus, a job analysis should be conducted to establish the duties, requirements, responsibilities and conditions involved in the job.

(ii) ***Job Description:*** Job description follows job analysis. The description should be in writing so that it can be referred to as and when the need arises. The written job description will give an idea of what the duties and responsibilities of the position are and on what criteria the new employee will be evaluated.

(iii) ***Job Qualifications:*** The duties and responsibilities set forth in the job description should be converted into a set of qualifications that the recruit should have in order to perform the job satisfactorily.

(iv) ***Personality Traits:*** There is no ideal list covering all qualities which are most important for a sales position. However, Mayer and Greenberg offered one of the shortest lists of traits. They concluded that the effective salesperson has two basic qualities: empathy—the ability to feel as the customer does and ego drive—a strong personal need to make the sale.

(v) ***Attracting a Pool of Applicants:*** The personnel department seeks applicants by various means, including soliciting names from current sales representatives, using employment agencies, placing job ads and contacting college students.

SELECTION PROCESS

Selection systems for sales personnel range from simple one-step systems consisting of nothing more than an informal personal interview, to complex multiple-step systems incorporating diverse mechanisms designed to gather information about applicants for sales jobs.

A selection system is a set of successive "screens", at any of which an applicant may be dropped for further consideration. A selection system fulfils its main mission if it improves management's ability to estimate success and failure probabilities. Management, in other words, has the information gathered through the selection system, makes more accurate estimates of the chances that a particular applicant will succeed.

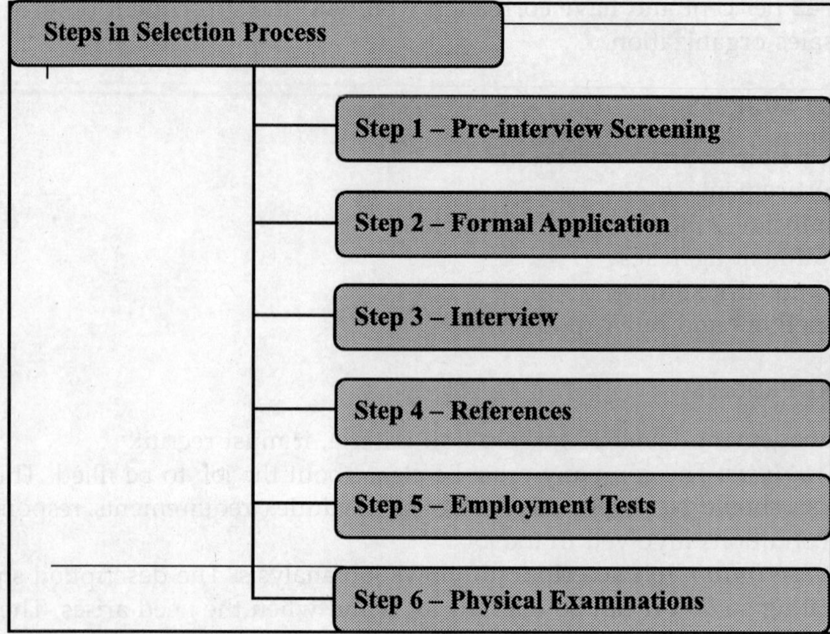

Fig. 3.2. Selection process.

(i) ***Pre-Interview Screening:*** Pre-interview screening is for the purpose of eliminating obviously unqualified applicants, thus saving the time of interviewers and applicants. The applicant is provided information about the company and general details about selling positions in it. A well-prepared recruiting brochure does this effectively and does not require an employee's time for anything other than to hand it over to the applicant.

The preliminary interview is short, perhaps no more than twenty minutes. Questions about the company and the job are answered while the company employee determines whether the applicant meets minimum qualifications. If this hurdle is over and the applicant expresses interest, he or she is asked to fill out a formal application form, and an appointment is made for one or more formal interviews.

(ii) ***Formal Application:*** The formal application form serves as a central record for all pertinent information collected during the selection process. A formal application is filled out after a preliminary interview indicates that a candidate has promise as a company salesperson. The application form may be filled out by the applicant personally or by an interviewer who records the applicant's responses. Sometimes, sections are reserved for later recording of the results of such selection steps as reference and credit checks, testing, and physical examination.

(iii) ***The Interview:*** The interview is the most widely used selection step and in some companies it comprises the entire selection system. Some experts criticize the interview as an unreliable tool, but it is an effective way to obtain certain information. No other method is quite so satisfactory in judging an individual as to ability in oral communication, personal appearance and manners, attitude toward selling and the life in general, reaction to obstacles presented face to face, and personal impact upon others.

Good interviewers avoid covering the same ground as other selection devices. The interviewer reviews the completed application form before the interview and refrains from asking questions already answered.

Questions during interviewing: The questions asked to the applicant should reflect the following:

- Attitude
- Motivation
- Initiative
- Stability
- Planning
- Insight
- Social skills

Interview Techniques

There are different interviewing techniques and they are as follows:

- ***Patterned Interview:*** Here a interviewer uses a prepared outline of questions to elicit the basic core of information. The interviewer may directly work from the outline, recording answers as they are given, but this may make the conversation suited and the applicant nervous.
- ***Non-directive Interview:*** In this technique, the applicant is encouraged to talk freely about his or her experience, training, and future plans. The interviewer asks a few direct questions and says only enough to keep the interviewee talking.
- ***Interaction (stress) Interview:*** The interaction interview stimulates and stresses the applicant that would meet in actual selling and provides way to observe the applicant's reaction to them. This interviewing technique has long been used by sales executives who, in interviewing prospective sales personnel, hand the applicant an ashtray or other object and say "Here, sell this to me".
- ***Rating Scale:*** One shortcoming of personal interview is its tendency to lack objectivity, a defect that is reduced through rating scales. These are so constructed that interviewer's ratings are channelled into a limited choice of responses. In evaluating an applicant's general appearance, for e.g., one much used form forces an interviewer to choose one of five descriptive phrases: very neat, nicely dressed, presentable, untidy, slovenly.

(iv) ***References:*** References provide information on the applicants not available from other sources. Some employers deny the value of references saying that references hesitate to criticize personal friends, ex-employees. But the experienced employer reads between the lines, and sees where, for example, the weak candidate is not praised.

Personal contact is best way to obtain information from references, since facial expressions and voice intonations reveal a great deal, and most people are more frank orally than in writing.

- *Credit Check:* Many companies run credit checks on applicants for sales positions. When a heavy burden of personal debt is found, it may indicate financial worries interfering with productivity, motivating factor serving to spur productivity to determine which requires further investigation.

(v) ***Employment Tests:*** The purpose of testing is to determine whether applicants have the traits the company feels leads to selling successfully. In turn, this results in advantages such as lower turnover and increased performance.

Types of Tests: Four types of psychological tests are used in selection system for sales personnel:

- Tests of ability measure how well a person can perform particular tasks with maximum motivation (tests for best performance).
- Tests of habitual characteristics gauge how prospective employees in their daily work normally (tests of typical performance).
- Interest test measures an individual's interest in a particular type of job.
- Achievement tests measure how much individuals have learnt from their experience, training, or education.
- Effective sales executives recognize that psychological testing, although capable of making valuable contribution, is the first step in selection system.

(vi) ***Physical Examination:*** Since good health is important to a salespersons success, most companies do physical examination. Because of the relatively high cost, the physical examination generally is one of the last steps.

Appropriate selection procedures, and their skilful execution, result in greater selling efficiency. A higher grade salesperson is produced, and the advantage of having such employees makes any impressive list—better work quality improved market coverage, superior customer relations, and a lower ratio of selling expense to sales. Thus, good selection fits the right person to the right job, thereby increasing job satisfaction and reducing the cost of personnel turnover.

TRAINING SALES REPRESENTATIVES

Today's customers expect salespeople to have deep product knowledge, offer ideas to improve customer operations, and be efficient and reliable. These demands require companies to make a much higher investment in training their sales reps. Companies use training to help sales reps: (1) know and identify with the company; (2) learn about the company's products; (3) know customers' and competitors' characteristics; (4) make effective sales presentations; and (5) understand sales procedures and responsibilities. Training time varies with the complexity of the selling task and the type of person

recruited into the sales organization. The median training period is 28 weeks in industrial products companies, twelve in service companies, and four in consumer products companies. At IBM, new reps receive extensive initial training and may spend 15 per cent of their time each year in additional training.

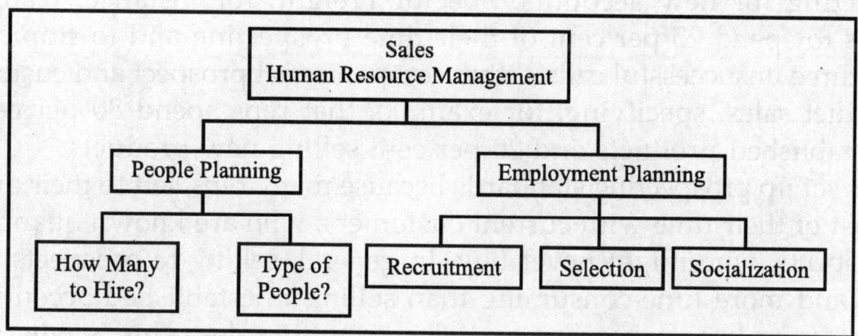

Fig. 3.3. Activities involved in managing a sales force's human resources.

Training often involves a variety of methods, including role playing, audio- and videotapes, CD-ROMs, and Web-based distance learning. For instance, reps at the tandem division of Compaq used to complain that they could not keep up with the printed information and training materials the company sent them. Now field reps carry their own miniature training rooms with them—they simply slip a CD-ROM disk into their laptop computers.

SUPERVISING SALES REPRESENTATIVES

New sales representatives need more than a territory, a compensation package, and training – they also need proper supervision. Reps paid mostly on commission generally receive less supervision, while those who are salaried and must cover definite accounts are likely to receive substantial supervision. In the course of supervising sales reps, successful companies set norms for calls on customers and prospects, and they help reps make the most efficient use of sales time.

Norms for Customer Calls

In the early 1980s, the average salesperson made five calls a day; by 1989, that number had dropped to just 4.2 sales calls a day. Today salespeople make even fewer in-person sales calls because they are using phone, fax, and e-mail to sell. In addition, more firms are using automated ordering systems to reduce reliance on sales calls.

How many calls should a company make on a particular account each year?

Research shows that additional calls generally produce more sales, but companies still need to determine whether the increase in sales justifies the increase in sales costs. Some studies and experience suggest that sales reps may be spending too much time selling to smaller, less profitable accounts when they should be focusing more of their efforts on selling to larger, more profitable accounts.

Therefore, in setting norms, management needs to weigh the cost of a customer sales call against the sales and profit payback for that account.

Norms for Prospect Calls

Knowing the high cost of sales calls, companies often specify how much time reps should spend prospecting for new accounts. Spector Freight, for instance, wants its sales representatives to spend 25 per cent of their time prospecting and to stop calling on a prospect after three unsuccessful calls. Other companies set prospect and customer norms based on product sales, specifying, for example, that reps spend 80 per cent of their time selling established products and 20 per cent selling new products.

Companies set up prospecting standards because many reps, left to their own devices, will spend most of their time with current customers, who are known quantities, rather than with prospects, who might never buy. In general, selling to prospects tends to be more difficult and more time-consuming than selling to established accounts, yet it is the road to customer base expansion and closing more sales. This is why some firms deploy a special missionary sales force to open new accounts.

Using Sales Time Efficiently

Not surprisingly, studies confirm that the best sales reps are those who manage their time effectively. One popular efficiency tool is configurator software to automate the order preparation process. This type of program is offered by Massachusetts-based Concentra Corporation, among others. On a sales call, reps can use configurator software to present product specifications and pricing information, show customization options, and handle scheduling. Integrating all of this information, the configurator software can virtually write up the order in minutes. This software not only saves time; it also builds goodwill by reducing errors and letting both customer and supplier see the same information from the same source. Concentra's customers say this software has helped them increase sales and reduce cancellations.

Another tool is time-and-duty analysis, which helps reps understand how they spend their time and how they might increase their productivity. In general, sales reps spend time in (1) preparation (getting information and planning call strategy); (2) travel (which can be more than 50 per cent of total time); (3) food and breaks (some portion of every workday); (4) waiting (to see buyers); (5) selling (time spent with the buyer); and (6) administration (writing reports, billing, attending sales meetings, and so on). With so many duties, it is no wonder that actual face-to-face selling time can amount to as little as 25 per cent of total working time!

To improve sales force productivity, many companies train their reps in the use of "phone power," simplify record-keeping, and use computerized methods to develop call and routing plans and to supply reps with customer and competitive information.

Seeking to reduce the time demands on their outside sales force, many firms have increased the size and responsibilities of their inside sales force. Inside salespeople are of three types. Technical support people provide technical information and answers to customers' questions. Sales assistants provide clerical backup for the outside reps by confirming appointments, carrying out credit checks, following up on deliveries, and answering customers' questions. Telemarketers use the phone to find new leads, qualify and sell to them, reactivate former accounts, and give more attention to neglected accounts.

The best sales reps spend time getting to know their customers' preferences, needs, and buying patterns so they can plan their calls accordingly. Technology speeds up this process. For example, before telecommunications reps at TimePlex go on a sales call, they use their laptops to dial into the firm's data network and retrieve status reports on that account's previous orders and other background information. When deals are struck, the reps use their laptops to record each order, double-check for errors, and then transmit everything electronically to the firm's New Jersey headquarters.

In addition, Internet technology is helping to make prospecting more efficient. Company's Websites provide an introduction to self-identified potential customers and, for some businesses, may lead to online orders. For more complex transactions, the site provides a way for the buyer to contact the seller, for example, through a link to an e-mail address. The Pall Corporation, which makes fluid filtration and purification technologies, has all e-mail directed to company headquarters, with leads going directly to the appropriate sales rep. The quality and quantity of leads generated by its Website (www.pall.com) has prompted the firm to promote its home page more aggressively.

As another example, Lucent Technologies (www.lucent.com) combines e-mail with Web marketing to generate more qualified sales leads. A typical campaign starts with an e-mail inviting prospects to learn more about a particular offer (and qualify for a free gift) by visiting a customized Web page. Once there, prospects answer a few qualifying questions and can then request information to be sent by mail. Lucent's automated system separates these leads based on product needs, and contacts the best prospects 2 weeks later, offering free, downloadable software for analyzing total product costs. Prospects who choose the download are considered hot leads, so the system sends Lucent's sales force complete contact data on these prospects for immediate follow-up. "We never had to pick up the phone, and we've already established a relationship with them," notes Lucent's senior manager of marketing services.

Special Characteristics of the Sales Job

A salesman is an ambassador of his company to the external world. He leaves a lasting impression on those with whom he interacts and forms an opinion about the company from his behaviour. By no stretch of imagination, we can consider the production staff or, for that matter any other staff of the organization wielding the same influence as the salesman does.

A salesman is out in the field; with no direct or little direct supervision, whereas other employees have to work under close supervision. Field involves hard physical labour, and is never a bed of roses. Besides, selling demands creativity, doggedness and initiative. Thus, a successful salesman should have a combination of brain and brawn. As he is to be self-directed, he needs strong motivation.

A salesman needs human relation skills much more than others. As he interacts with a variety of people in diverse situations he must show diplomatic skills and composure. He should show tact and intelligence while dealing with his customers.

A salesman is authorized to spend company's money for his lodging, boarding, travelling and entertainment. Very few in the company are so authorized to use the company's funds.

A salesman cannot enjoy family life like people in other walks of life do. He has to travel his territory while servicing it. Besides, selling is a high pressure job. All this makes him prone to stress. Thus, a salesman has to brave all kinds of adverse situations, while being away from home. It is, thus, a very tough job.

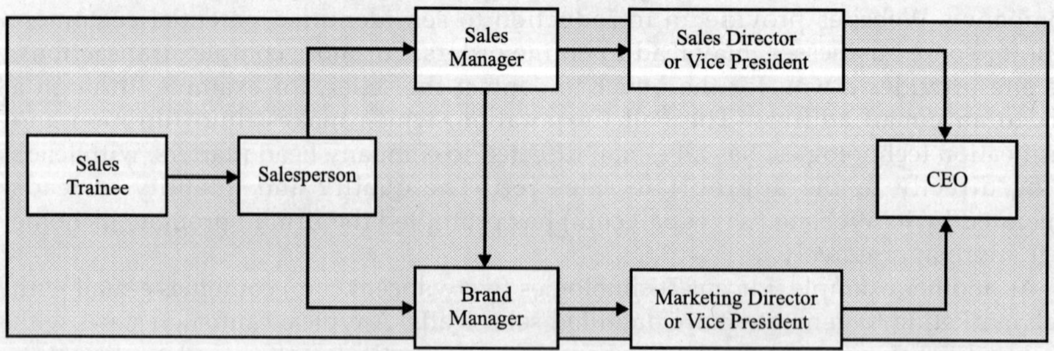

Fig. 3.4. Possible career track in sales job.

BUYER-SELLER DYADS

Salesmanship involves person-to-person communication between the seller and the buyer. This is called a dyad in sociology to describe two-party interaction. There is a dyad in selling as well as in advertising. The desired response of the buyer is a function of the type of interaction they have. Advertising of course, is less interactive than personal selling but they support each other.

Research indicates that if prospects know more about the companies and the salespeople working for it, they are more favourably inclined towards the products. Research also indicates that the matching of prospects and salesperson in terms of physical and demographic characteristics also increases the chances of a sale. This leads to a successful dyadic relationship. In industrial marketing, this type of matching is fairly common. The dyadic relationship is further enhanced by the perception of the buyer about a salesperson's performance and its conformance to his concept of ideal performance.

TYPES OF SELLING JOBS

We can see a wide spectrum of selling jobs–ranging from mere order taking as in the case of a soft-drink salesman to a technological presentation as in the case of a sales engineer selling complex products like industrial machinery, aircraft and computer. Selling jobs can be classified on the basis of the creative input needed to perform them.

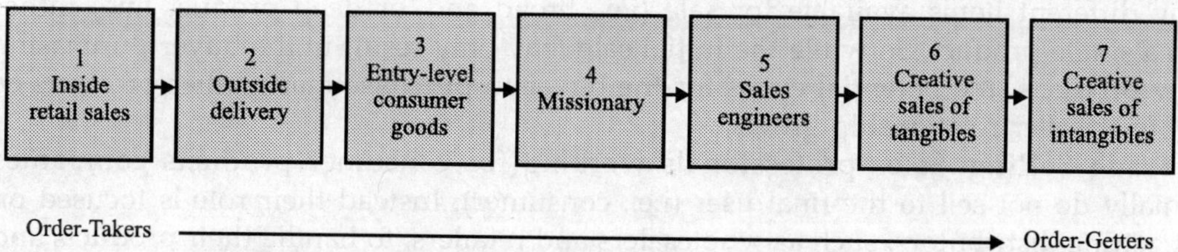

Fig. 3.5. The complexity and difficulty of these seven sales job categories increase as they move from left to right.

Order Getters

The role most synonymous with selling is a position in which the salesperson is actively engaged in using their skills to obtain orders from customers. Such roles can be further divided into:

New Business Development: A highly challenging yet potentially lucrative sales position is one where the main objective is to find new customers. Sales jobs in this category are often in fields that are very competitive, but offer high rewards for those that are successful. The key distinguishing factor of these positions is that once a sale is made new business salespeople pass customers on to others in their organization who handle account maintenance.

Business Equipment Sales: These salespeople are often found in industries where the company's main profits come from the sale of supplies and services that come after an initial equipment purchase. The key objective of business equipment salespeople is to get buyers to purchase the main piece of equipment for which supplies and service are needed for the equipment to function. For instance, in the photocopier industry certain salespeople only seek out new accounts and once a photocopier sale is made they pass along the account to other sales personnel who handle maintenance and supply products.

Telemarketing: This category includes product sales over the phone, whether aimed at business or consumer. While in the US laws restrict unsolicited phone selling, the practice is still widely used in the business market.

Consumer Selling: Certain companies are very aggressive in their use of salespeople to build new consumer business. These include: retailers selling certain high priced consumer products including furniture, electronics and clothing; housing products including real estate, security services, building replacement products (e.g., windows); and in-home product sellers including those selling door-to-door and products sold at "home party" events such as cosmetics, kitchenware and decorative products.

Account Management: Most people engaged in sales are not only involved in gaining the initial order, but also build and maintain relationships with clients that are intended to last a long time. Salespeople involved in accounts management are found across a broad range of industries. Their responsibilities involve all aspects of building customer relationships from initial sale to follow-up account servicing.

Business-to-Business Selling: These salespeople sell products for business use with an emphasis on follow-up sales. In many cases, business-to-business salespeople have many different items available for sale (i.e., broad and/or deep product line) rather than a single product. So while the initial sale may only result in the buyer purchasing a few products, the potential exists for the buyer to purchase many other products as the buyer-seller relationship grows.

Trade Selling: Sales professionals working for consumer products companies normally do not sell to the final user (i.e., consumer). Instead their role is focused on first getting distributors, such as wholesalers and retailers, to handle their products and once this is accomplished, helping distributors sell their product by offering ideas for product advertising, in-store display and sales promotions.

Order Takers

Selling does not always require a salesperson to encourage customers to make a purchase. In fact, the greatest number of people engaged in selling are not order getters, rather they are considered order takers. In this role, salespeople primarily assist customers with a purchase in ways that are much less assertive than order getters. As might be expected, compensation for order takers is generally lower than that of order getters. Among those serving an order taker role are:

Retail Clerks: While some retail salespeople are involved in new business selling, the vast majority of retail employees handle order taking tasks, which range from directing customers to products to handling customer checkout.

Industrial Distributor Clerks: Industrial purchase situations, such as distributors of building products, will also have clerks to handle customer purchases.

Customer Service: Order taking is also handled in non face-to-face ways through customer service personnel. Usually, this occurs via phone conversations, though newer technologies are allowing for these tasks to be handled through electronic means such as online chat.

Order Influencers

Some salespeople are not engaged in direct selling activities at all. That is, they do not sell directly to the person who is the ultimate purchaser for their product. Instead these salespeople concentrate on selling activity that targets those who influence purchases made by the final customer. The primary example of an order influencer is the missionary salesperson:

Missionary: These salespeople are used in industries where customers make purchases based on the advice or requirements of others. Two industries in which missionary selling is commonly found are pharmaceuticals, where salespeople, known as product detailers, discuss products with doctors (influencers) who then write prescriptions for their patients (final customer) and higher education, where salespeople call on college professors (influencers) who make requirements to students (final customer) for specific textbooks.

Sales Support

A final group involved in selling mostly assist with the selling activities of other sales professionals. These include:

Technical Specialists: When dealing with the sale of technical products, particularly in business markets, salespeople may need to draw on the expertise of others to assist with the process. This is particularly the case when the buying party consists of a buying centre. In business selling many people from different functional areas may be involved in the purchase decision. If this buying centre includes technical people, such as scientists and engineers, a salesperson may seek assistance from members of their own technical staff, who can help address specific questions.

Office Support: Salespeople also may receive assistance from their company's office staff in the form of creating promotional materials, setting up sales appointments, finding sales leads, arranging meeting space or organizing trade shows exhibits.

There are other types of selling jobs as mentioned below:

(i) There are manufacturer's salesmen, wholesaler's salesmen and retailer's salesmen.

(ii) Some are counter salesmen while some others are travelling salesmen.

(iii) Some salesmen sell consumer goods like soap, shoe, toothpaste, etc. some sell industrial goods like hand tools, nuts and bolts, motors, machineries, etc. and some others sell agricultural products like fruit , vegetables, grains, seeds, etc.

(iv) Some salesmen sell tangible products like textiles, soaps, cycles, watches, etc. while some others sell intangible goods like insurance policy, securities, advertisement space, etc.

(v) New and competitive goods need expensive selling efforts. Therefore, energetic, hardworking and aggressive salesmen are required for selling new and competitive goods.

(vi) For selling products like medicines, books, magazines, etc. extensive travelling by salesmen is required.

(vii) Some selling jobs require detailed and technical knowledge about the product like machines, electronic equipment, medicine, etc. Some other selling jobs are quite single and therefore do not require thorough and detailed knowledge about the product as in the case of consumer goods and grocery articles.

(viii) Some salesmen are required to sell directly to the ultimate consumers. Another set of salesmen sell to the middlemen like wholesalers and retailers instead to the final consumers.

(ix) Some selling jobs like insurance policies, motor cars, land, etc. require continuous effort on the part of the salesman. Therefore, it takes time to finalize sales in such cases. Some sales may even take months and years to finalize. On the other hand, some sales are finalized immediately and on the spot like pen, food articles, grocery items, etc. since little effort is required to sell these articles.

(x) Costly items like automobiles, video cassette recorders, refrigerators, vacuum cleaners, televisions, air-conditioners, etc. require technical advice and service both before and after the actual sales. Therefore, for selling these articles technically qualified salesmen who possess adequate knowledge about the various aspects of the products are needed.

(xi) There are certain selling jobs which can be best performed by women. Products most ideally suited for saleswomen are ladies garments, cooking utensils, cosmetics, etc. Hence, saleswomen are preferred to sell such articles.

SALESMAN MOTIVATION

Motivation is the process through which hidden needs are aroused. Some salespeople will put forth their best effort without any coaching from the management. For them selling is the most fascinating activity in the world. They are ambitious and self status, but majority of sales representatives require encouragement and special incentives from the management to work at the best level. This is specially true of field selling for the following reasons:

The Nature of the Job

The selling job is one of frequent frustrating, sales representatives usually work alone, their laws are irregular and they are away from home, they confront aggressive, competing sales representatives, they do not have the authority to do what is necessary to in the account they lose large orders that they have worked hard to obtain.

Human Nature

Most people operate below capacity in the absence of special incentives such as financial gain or social recognition.

Personal Problems

Sales representatives are usually preoccupied with personal problems such as sickness in the family, marital discord or debt etc.

MOTIVATION MODEL

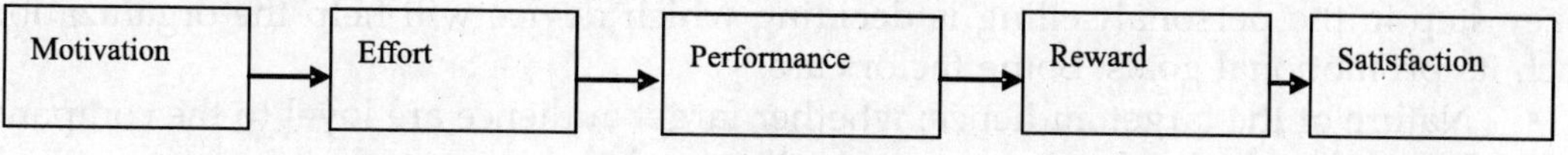

Fig. 3.6. Motivation model.

The above model suggests that higher the salesperson motivation the greater is his or her effort, greater effort will lead to greater performance which will lead to greater rewards and greater rewards will lead to greater satisfaction which will again lead to reinforce motivation.

The model implies the following

- Sales manager must be able to convince the salespeople that they can sell more by working harder or being trained to work smarter. But if sales are largely determined by economic conditions or competitive action this linkage is undermined.
- Sales manager must be able to convince the salespeople that the rewards for better performance are worth the extra effort, but if the rewards are too small or of the wrong kind the linkage is undermined

DISCIPLINED WORK

Whatever the incentive package if the salespersons aren't organized and focused, and if they don't work hard they are not able to meet the ever increasing demand of the customers these days, following points are very important.

1. Set Goals

First of all, sales representatives have to set goals for themselves, what they want to achieve in the future, accordingly they make plans.

2. Make Plans

Planning is very important in the salesperson job, they make schedule for the future great salesperson are very conscious about laying down detailed, organized plans than they follow through in a timely disciplined way, e.g., if they say that they are going to make a follow-up call on a customer in six months, you can insure that they will be on the doorstep in six month.

3. Work Hard

They have to work hard because this job is very demanding and they have to work in irregular hours, travel a lot and most of the times have to work alone and away from home.

4. Selecting the Appropriate Technique

A key step in the personal selling is deciding which device will help the organization reach its promotional goals. Some factors are:

- Nature of the target audience: whether target audience are loyal to the company brand if not higher level of personal selling and convincing techniques are required.
- Nature of the product: Does the product level itself to sampling, demonstration or multiple item purchase.
- Current economic conditions: Sales representatives must also see what the economic conditions of the country are. Premiums and rebates are good in periods of recessions and inflation.

Motivation is goal-directed behaviour, underlying which are certain needs or desires. The term "needs" suggests a lack of something that reaching the goal could satisfy, while the term "desires" suggests positive ardor and strength of feeling. The complex of needs and desires stemming from within individuals leads them to act so as to satisfy these needs and desires.

Specifically, as applied to sales personnel, motivation is the amount of effort the salesperson desires to expend on the activities associated with the sales job, such as calling on potential accounts, planning sales presentations, and filling out reports. Expending effort on each activity making up the sales job leads to some level of achievement on one or more dimensions of job performance: total sales volume, profitability, and sales to new accounts, quota attainment, and the like.

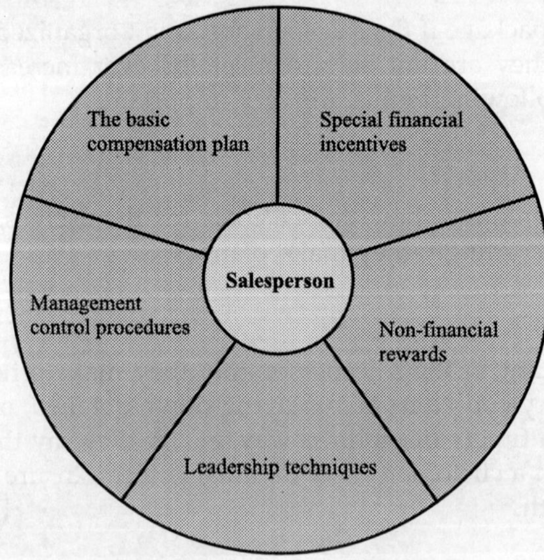

Fig. 3.7. Sales manager's motivation mix.

Motivational "Help" from the Management

Most sales personnel require motivational "help" from the management to reach and maintain acceptable performance levels. They require motivation as individuals and as group members. As individuals, they are targets for personalized motivational efforts by their superiors. As member of the sales force, they are targets for sales management efforts aimed toward welding them into an effective selling team. Four aspects of the salesperson's job affect the quality of its performance. The following discussion focuses on these aspects; each is an important reason why sales personnel require additional motivation.

Inherent Nature of the Sales Job

Although sales jobs vary from one company to the other, sales jobs are alike in certain respects. Every sales job is a succession of ups and downs—a series of experiences resulting in alternating feelings of exhilaration and depression. In the course of day's work, salespersons interact with many pleasant and courteous people, but some are unpleasant and rude and are difficult to deal with. They are frustrated, particularly when aggressive competing sales personnel vie for the same business, and they meet numerous turndowns. Furthermore, sales personnel spend not only working time but considerable afterhours time away from home, causing them to miss many attractive parts of family life. These conditions cause salespersons to become discouraged, to achieve high performance levels, or even to seek non-selling positions. The inherent nature of the sales job, then, is the first reason that requires additional motivation.

Salesperson's Boundary Position and Role Conflicts: The salesperson occupies a "boundary position" in the company and must try to satisfy the expectations of people both within the company (in the sales department and elsewhere) and in customer organizations. There is linkage with four groups: (1) sales management, (2) the company organization that handles order fulfilment, (3) the customers, and (4) other company sales personnel. Each group imposes certain behavioural expectations on the salesperson, and, in playing these different roles, the salesperson faces role conflicts, such as:

1. **Conflict of identification** arises out of multigroup membership. As the salesperson works with the customer, identification is with the customer rather than the company. On returning to the company, the salesperson drops identification with the customer and identifies with the company.
2. **Advocacy conflict** arises when the salesperson identifies with the customer and advocates the customer's position to other groups in the company organization. This may be important and may be encouraged by the sale management group, but the advocator is in a difficult position.
3. **Conflict** is inherent in the salesperson's dual role as an advocate for both the customer and the company. As an entrepreneur paid directly or indirectly on the basis of sales volume, the salesperson has a pecuniary interest in selling as much as possible in the shortest time. However, the salesperson may uncover facts that limit the product's usefulness. If the salesperson tells the customer about these

conditions and that, in all probability, the product will not meet the customer's needs, the salesperson risks losing the sale and the income that goes with it.

Not much can be done to reduce the role conflicts of sale personnel. Some evidence exists that experienced sales personnel perceive significantly less role conflict than do those with less experience. This suggests that a salesperson's perceptions of, and ability to cope with role conflict are influenced not only by experience but by the effectiveness of sales training. It also suggests that those who become experienced sales personnel may cope better with role conflicts (that is, psychologically) than those leaving the sales organization earlier. So improving sales training effectiveness and revising selection criteria are two roads to reducing the impact of role conflict on sales force morale.

Role conflicts traceable to the salespersons linkage with groups that have divergent interests, then, is another reason why additional motivation is required.

Tendency Toward Apathy

Some sales personnel naturally become apathetic, get into a rut. Those who, year after year, cover the same territory and virtually the same customers, lose interest and enthusiasm. Gradually their sales calls degenerate into routine order taking. Because they know the customers so well, they believe that good salesmanship is no longer necessary. Their customer approach typically becomes: "Do you need anything today, Joe?" They fail to recognize that friendship in no way obviates the necessity for creative selling and that most customers do not sell themselves on new products and applications. The customer's response, as often as not, is, "Nothing today, Bill". Later a competing salesperson calls on the same account, uses effective sales techniques, and gets an order. Many salespeople require additional motivation to maintain continuing enthusiasm to generate renewed interest in their work.

Maintaining a Feeling of Group Identify

The salesperson, working alone, finds it difficult to develop and maintain a feeling of group identity with other company's salespeople. Team spirit, if present at all, is weak. Thus, the contagious enthusiasm—conducive to improving the entire group's performance—does not develop.

If sales management, through providing added motivation, succeeds in developing and maintaining team spirit, individual sales personnel strive to meet group performance standards. Few people who consider themselves members of the sales team want to appear as poor performers in the eyes of their colleagues, providing the kind of working atmosphere in which all members of the sales force feel that participating in a cooperative endeavour is not easy. Nevertheless, effective sales management works continuously to achieve and maintain it.

Need Gratification and Motivation

Behavioural research studies show that all human activities including the salesperson's job behaviour is directed towards satisfying certain needs (that is, reaching certain goals).

Patterns of individual behaviour differ because individuals seek to fulfil different sets of needs in different ways. Some salespersons, in other words, are more successful than others because of the differing motivational patterns and amounts and types of efforts they exert in performing their duty.

How particular individuals behave depends upon the nature of their fulfilled and unfulfilled needs modified by their environmental and social backgrounds. The motives lying behind any specific action drive from tensions build up to satisfy particular needs, some beneath the threshold of consciousness. Any action taken is for the purpose of reducing these tensions (fulfilling a need or needs to reach a goal or goals). Needs are either primary or secondary. Primary needs are the inborn or physiological needs for food, water, rest, sleep, air to breathe, sex, and so on, the fulfilment of which are basic to life itself. Until primary needs are satisfied, other needs have little motivational influence. Secondary needs arise from an individual's interaction with the environment, and are not inborn but develop with maturity. Secondary needs include those for safety and security, belongingness and social relations, and self-esteem and self-respect.

MOTIVATION THEORY

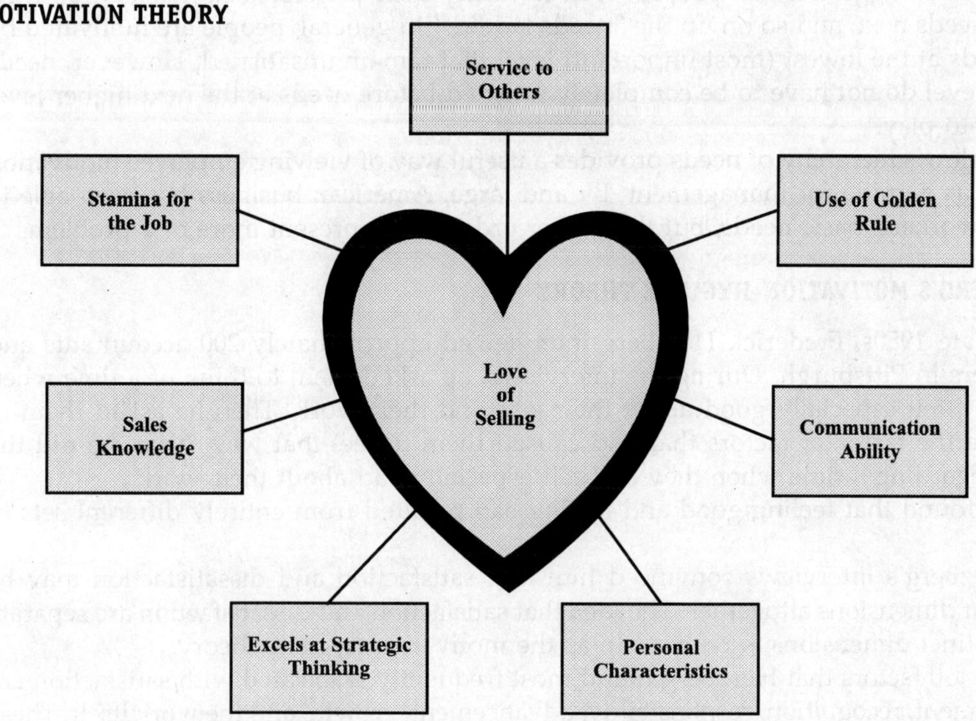

Fig. 3.8. Love of selling is at heart of helping others.

MASLOW'S HIERARCHY OF NEEDS

The concept of a hierarchy of needs was advanced by Abraham Maslow, a psychologist. Maslow assumed that humans are "wanting" beings who seek to fulfil a variety of needs. He assumed that these needs can be arranged according to their importance in a sequence known as Maslow's hierarchy of needs.

At the most basic levels are physiological needs, the things we require to survive. These needs include food and water, clothing, shelter, and sleep. At the next level are safety needs, the things we require for physical and emotional security. They may be satisfied through job security, health insurance, pension plans, and safe working conditions.

Next are the social needs, the human requirements for love, affection, and a sense of belonging. To an extent, these needs can be satisfied through the work environment and the informal organization. But they also include relationships beyond the workplace. Esteem needs include the need for respect and recognition (the esteem of others) as well as a sense of accomplishment and worth (self-esteem). These needs may be satisfied through personal accomplishment, promotion to more responsible jobs, honours and awards, and other forms of recognition.

At the uppermost level are self-actualization needs, the needs to grow and develop as people and to become all that we are capable of being. These are the most difficult needs to satisfy, and the means of satisfying them tend to vary with the individual.

Maslow suggested that people work to satisfy their physiological needs first, their safety needs next, and so on up the "needs ladder." In general, people are motivated by the needs at the lowest (most important) level that remain unsatisfied. However, needs at one level do not have to be completely satisfied before needs at the next higher level come into play.

Maslow's hierarchy of needs provides a useful way of viewing employee motivation as well as a guide for management. By and large, American business has been able to satisfy workers' basic needs, but the higher order needs present more of a problem.

HERZBERG'S MOTIVATION-HYGIENE THEORY

In the late 1950s, Frederick Herzberg interviewed approximately 200 accountants and engineers in Pittsburgh. During the interviews, he asked them to think of a time when they had felt especially good about their jobs and their work. Then he asked them to describe the factor or factors that had caused them to feel that way. Next, he did the same regarding a time when they had felt especially bad about their work.

He found that feeling good and feeling bad resulted from entirely different sets of factors.

Herzberg's interviews convinced him that satisfaction and dissatisfaction may be different dimensions altogether. The idea that satisfaction and dissatisfaction are separate and distinct dimensions is referred to as the motivation-hygiene theory.

The job factors that Herzberg found most frequently associated with satisfaction are achievement, recognition, responsibility, advancement, growth, and the work itself. These factors are generally referred to as motivational factors because their presence increases motivation. However, their absence does not necessarily result in feelings of dissatisfaction.

Job factors cited as causing dissatisfaction are supervision, working conditions, interpersonal relationships, pay, job security, and company policies and administration. These hygiene factors reduce dissatisfaction when they are present to an acceptable degree. However, they do not necessarily result in high levels of motivation.

Using Herzberg's Motivation-Hygiene Theory: Herzberg provides explicit guidelines for using the motivation-hygiene theory of employee motivation. He suggests that the hygiene factors must be present to ensure that a worker can function comfortably. But he warns that a state of no dissatisfaction never exists. Managers should make hygiene as good as possible but should then expect only short-term improvement in motivation.

Managers must work to provide the motivational factors, which will presumably enhance motivation and long-term effort. Employee pay has more effect than is explained by Herzberg's theory.

THEORY X AND THEORY Y

The concepts of Theory X and Theory Y were advanced by Douglas McGregor in his 1960 book, The Human Side of Enterprise. They are, in reality, sets of assumptions that underlie management's attitudes and beliefs regarding worker behaviour.

Theory X is a concept of employee motivation generally consistent with Taylor's scientific management. The basic assumptions of Theory X include the following:

- People dislike work and try to avoid it. Because people dislike work, managers must coerce, control, and frequently threaten employees to achieve organizational goals.
- People generally must be led because they have little ambition and will not seek responsibility. They are concerned mainly with security.

Theory Y is a concept of employee motivation generally consistent with the ideas of the human relation's movement. The basic assumptions of Theory Y include the following:

- People do not naturally dislike work. In fact, work is an important part of their lives.
- People will work toward goals to which they are committed. People become committed to goals when it is clear that accomplishing the goal will bring personal rewards.
- People often seek out and willingly accept responsibility. Employees have the potential to help accomplish organizational goals. Organizations generally do not make full use of their human resources. McGregor argued that most managers behave in accordance with Theory X. But he maintained that Theory Y is more appropriate and effective as a guide for managerial action.

Theory Z: In the 1970s, William Ouchi, a management professor at UCLA, began to study business practices in United States and Japanese firms. In Japan, Ouchi found what he calls Type J firms. They are characterized by:

- Lifetime employment for employees collective (or group) decision-making
- Collective responsibility for the outcomes of decisions
- Slow evaluation and promotion implied control mechanisms
- non-specialized career paths

- A holistic concern for employees as people.

American industry is dominated by what Ouchi calls Type A firms. These firms are characterized by:

- short-term employment
- individual decision making
- individual responsibility for the outcomes of decisions
- rapid evaluation and promotion
- explicit control mechanisms
- specialized career paths
- a segmented concern for employees only as employees

A few very successful American firms represent a blend of the Type J and Type A patterns. These Type Z organizations emphasize:

- long-term employment
- collective decision making
- individual responsibility for the outcomes of decisions
- slow evaluation and promotion
- informal control along with some formalized measures
- moderately specialized career paths
- a holistic concern for employees

Theory Z is the belief that some middle ground between Ouchi's Type A and Type J practices is best for American business.

CONTEMPORARY VIEWS ON MOTIVATION

In recent years, managers have begun to explore four other models that take a more dynamic view of motivation: equity theory, expectancy theory, reinforcement theory, and Theory Z.

Equity Theory

The equity theory of motivation is based on the premise that people are motivated first to achieve and then to maintain a sense of equity. As used here, equity refers to the distribution of rewards in direct proportion to the contribution of each employee to the organization. Everyone need not receive the same rewards, but the rewards should be in accordance with individual contribution.

According to the theory, we tend to implement the idea of equity as follows:

First, we develop an input-to-outcome ratio. Inputs are the things we contribute to the organization. Outcomes are the things we get from the organization. Next, we compare this ratio with what we perceive as the input-to-outcome ratio for some other person, called the "comparison other." If the two ratios are roughly the same, we feel that the organization is treating us equitably and are motivated to leave things as they are. If our ratio is the lower of the two, we feel under-rewarded and are motivated to change things. We may decrease our own inputs by not working so hard.

- Try to increase our total outcomes by asking for a raise in pay.
- Try to get the comparison other to increase some inputs or receive decreased outcomes.
- Leave the work situation.
- Do a new comparison with a different "comparison other".

Equity theory is most relevant to pay as an outcome.

Expectancy Theory

Expectancy theory, developed by Victor Vroom, is a very complex model of motivation that is based on a simple assumption. According to expectancy theory, motivation depends on how much we want something and on how likely we are to get it.

Consider three sales representatives who are candidates for promotion to one sales manager's job. Bill has had a very good sales this year and always gets good performance evaluations. But he isn't sure he wants the job because it requires a great deal of travel, long working hours, and much stress and pressure. Paul wants the job but he doesn't think he has much chance of getting it. He has had a terrible sales this year and gets only mediocre performance evaluations from his present boss.

Susan wants the job as much as Paul, and she thinks she has a good chance of getting it. Her sales have improved significantly this past year, and her evaluations are the best in the company. Expectancy theory would predict that Bill and Paul are not very motivated to seek the promotion. But Susan is highly motivated to seek the promotion, because she wants it and thinks she can get it.

Expectancy theory is complex because each action we take is likely to lead to several different outcomes, some that we may want and others that we may not want. For example, if people work hard and put in a lot of extra hours, several things may happen.

- They may get a pay raise.
- They may be promoted.
- They may gain valuable new job skills.
- They may have less time to spend with their families.
- They may have to cut back on their social life.

Expectancy theory is difficult to apply, but it does provide several useful guidelines for managers. It suggests that managers must recognize the following:

- Employees work for a variety of reasons.
- These reasons, or expected outcomes, may change over time.
- It is necessary to clearly show employees how they can attain the outcomes they desire.

Reinforcement Theory

Reinforcement theory is based on the premise that behaviour that is rewarded is likely to be repeated, whereas behaviour that has been punished is less likely to recur.

Kinds of Reinforcement: Reinforcement is an action that follows directly from a particular behaviour. Reinforcements can take a variety of forms and can be used in a number of different ways.

- A positive reinforcement strengthens desired behaviour by providing a reward.
- A negative reinforcement strengthens desired behaviour by eliminating an undesirable task or situation.
- Punishment is an undesired consequence that follows from undesirable behaviour.
- Managers who rely on extinction hope to eliminate undesirable behaviour by ignoring it.

Using Reinforcement: The effectiveness of reinforcement depends on which type is used and how it is timed. Generally, positive reinforcement is considered the most effective action, and it is recommended when the manager has a choice. Continual, repetitive reinforcement can become tedious for both managers and employees, especially when the same behaviour is being reinforced over and over in the same way.

Goal-Setting Theory

Goal-setting theory suggests that employees are motivated to achieve goals they establish together with managers.

- There are three requirements for the goals that are set.
- They should be specific.
- They should be moderately difficult.
- They should be goals that the employee will commit to achieve.
- Employee rewards should be tied to goal achievement.
- There are several benefits of using goal-setting theory.
- It allows managers to design rewards that fit employee needs.
- It clarifies expectations.
- It maintains equity.
- It provides reinforcement.

Unionization of Sales Personnel

There are several reasons why unions have made little progression organizing sales personnel. First, it is difficult to develop strong group identification in most sales departments because each person works alone and sees other members of the sales force infrequently. Little opportunity exists for mutual exchange of grievances. Second, in contrast to most employee groups, salespersons think of themselves as independent operators rather than as cogs in an industrial machine. Third, sales personnel have some control over their workday and workweek.

If they work excessive hours, it is often to add to their complementation, and there are no time clocks. Fourth, the prospect of higher wages has never served as a strong organizing incentive for sales personnel, as sales personnel have been made to feel that low earnings are the result of personal ineffectiveness, not of the employer's niggardliness.

Only about one in ten salespersons belongs to a union. When unionization has occurred, it usually traces to a failure of sales management. Grievances stem from such failures as too many reports, competition of house accounts, inadequate expense allowances, poor territories, too many people on the sales force (which results in inadequate territories), and too many non-selling duties.

Unionization has made headway in industries where sales personnel are paid straight salaries, where they work together in the same premises (retail selling), and where the selling job is combined with that of delivery, as in the distribution of beer and soft drinks. Unions have made little progress in organizing sales personnel who sell directly to industrial users or those who make calls on middlemen. Sales personnel in these classifications, paid in whole or part according to productivity, frown upon union affiliation. Many sales executives oppose unionization. Their opposition is based chiefly upon the effect that unionization has on the motivation and control of sales personnel and upon the limitations that union contracts place on management. Managerial action is circumscribed by the collective-bargaining agreement, and uses of incentive compensation are restricted.

Commonly, unions object to sales contests and other devices for motivating the sales force; sometimes they insist that all additions to the sales force be recruited through the union, they discourage the use of quotas and other standards of performance, and a strict system of seniority is demanded. Sales executives maintain that the organizational structure of unions does not harmonize with the demands of the selling job. Selling and sales management require more flexibility than does running a plant or an office. They argue that all salespeople are called upon at times for extra effort, this being the price paid for freedom from day-to-day supervision.

Evaluating Sales Force Performance

One of the most important responsibilities of sales managers is to evaluate the performance of the sales personnel. The performance appraisal period can become one of those times that a salesperson dreads, unless the appraisal is effectively conducted. Ineffective performance appraisal tends to become a time-consuming and unpleasant activity for the sales manager as well as the sales personnel.

The factors affecting sales peoples' performance are many. Some of these are beyond the control of the individual, while some can be modified. Aspects like motivation, skill-set, job satisfaction, role perception, personal factors like age, sex, height, etc; the ego drive, and empathy towards the customers are inherent in the individual salesperson. Environmental and organizational factors, along with the different functions of sales management come under external factors. It is difficult for the sales manager to predict the influence of the external factors on the performance of the sales force.

To measure performance, it is necessary for the sales manager to put in place a performance evaluation procedure. A proper evaluation process ensures that the organization is well managed. It also provides the sales personnel with information on their performance and gives recommendations for further improvement. Performance evaluation can also help in improving the relationships between the sales force and superiors by minimizing suspicion and improving interaction. The performance evaluation process generally involves five steps.

The first step is to determine the factors that affect the performance of the sales force. The next step involves the selection of criteria that will be used to evaluate the performance. Step three involves establishing performance standards that can be used as a basis to compare the performance of the sales force. Step four involves monitoring actual performance. The last step is to review and provide feedback to the sales personnel. The purpose of conducting performance evaluation is to crosscheck whether the sales force activities are in alignment with the organizational objectives. It also helps monitor the sales force activities and provide remedial action, if required. Performance evaluation also helps to prepare a future action plan for the sales personnel and fulfil the organizational objectives. It exerts an influence on the mode of compensation, fixing of sales quotas, and decisions on the transfer or removal of the salesperson from the organization. In most organizations, it is the immediate superior or the sales manager who conducts the performance appraisal. Sometimes a team of people including the personnel manager and the department head, along with the sales manager, appraise the sales personnel. The timing of appraisal also varies for different organizations. It depends on the complexity of the sales plan, the costs involved, and the current objectives of the organization.

Periodic performance appraisal is necessary to identify any discrepancies in the overall sales plan and correct them. The sales manager or the concerned person involved in appraising the sales force can take the help of quantitative or qualitative criteria. These are also termed the behaviour and outcome components.

Qualitative criteria include sales skills, territory management skills, personality traits, etc. The quantitative factors include the sales volume, average calls per day, sales orders, etc. Quantitative criteria are those aspects that measure the sales performance in terms of the end results whereas qualitative criteria involve all those activities that the salesperson does to achieve the end results.

The sales manager must ensure that the performance standards are set to compare and evaluate the actual performance of the sales force. The standards vary from industry to industry and are different for different job profiles. Performance standards come under quantitative standards, qualitative standards, time-based standards, or cost-based standards. All the sales force activities can be segregated into one of these four categories and compared with the base standard.

Many methods of performance evaluation have been developed over the years. Yet, there is no single method that can be considered ideal for all organizations. Some of the commonly used methods are essays, rating scales, rankings, management by objectives and behaviourally-anchored rating scales. Several modern methods like critical incident appraisal, work-standards method, family of measures, etc., have been developed to suit variations and other requirements. Finally, regular monitoring and review of the sales force activities is also necessary to ensure that the organizational activities are aligned to the sales plan.

SALESMAN COMPENSATION

Requirements of a Good Compensation Plan

A good sales compensation plan meets seven requirements. First, it provides a living wage, preferably in the form of a secure income. Individuals worried about money matters do not concentrate on doing their jobs well. Second, the plan fits with the rest of the motivational programme—it does not conflict with other motivational factors, such as the intangible feeling of belonging to the sales team. Third, the plan is fair, it does not penalize sales personnel because of factors beyond their control within the limits of seniority and other special circumstances, sales personnel receive equal pay for equal performance. Fourth, it is easy for sales personnel to understand that they are able to calculate their own earning. Fifth, the plan adjusts pay to changes in performance. Sixth, the plan is economical to administer. Seventh, the plan helps in attaining the objectives of the sales organization.

Devising a Sales Compensation Plan

Whether contemplating major or minor changes or drafting a completely new sales compensation plan, the sales executive approaches the project systematically. Good compensation plans are built on solid foundations. A systematic approach assures that no essential step is overlooked.

Define the Sale Job

The first step is to reexamine the nature of the sales job. Up-to-date written job descriptions are the logical place to start. If job descriptions are outdated, if they are not accurate, or incomplete, descriptions of the sales job objectives and work are not given, then a revision is in order. The effective sales executive asks:

Does this description convey a realistic picture of what the salesperson is supposed to accomplish and to do? If there are no written sales job descriptions, they are prepared. Other aspects of company operations are considered in relation to their impact upon the sales job. Sales department objectives are analyzed for their effect on the salesperson's job.

Sales volume objectives, for instance, whether in dollars, units of product, or numbers of dealers and distributors, are translated into what is expected of the sales personnel, as group and individually. The impact of sales-related marketing policies is determined. Distribution policies, credit policies, price policies, and other policies affect the salesperson's job. Current and proposed advertising and sales promotional programmes assist in clarifying the nature of the salesperson's goal, duties, and activities.

Consider the Company's General Compensation

Structure

Most large companies, and also many smaller ones, use job evaluation systems to determine the relative value of individual jobs. Job evaluation procedure is not scientific;

it is an orderly approach based on judgement. It focus on the jobs, without considering the ability or personality of individuals who do the work. Its purpose is to arrive at fair compensation relationships among jobs. There are four job evaluation methods. Two are non-quantitative: simple ranking and classification or grading. The other two are quantitative: the point system and the factor comparison method.

Simple Ranking

In this inexpensive job evaluation method, widely used by small businesses, an executive committee sorts job descriptions in the order of worth. This is done without considering the individuals currently in the jobs or their compensation levels. No attempt is made to determine critical factors inherent in the jobs; only overall appraisals of the relative worth of different jobs are made.

Classification or Grading

This approach utilizes a system of grades and grade descriptions, against which individual jobs are compared. The grades, sometimes called classes, are described in terms of job responsibility, skills required, supervision given and received, exposure to unfavourable and hazardous working conditions, and similar characteristics. Job descriptions are then classified into appropriate grades. This is done by an executive committee or by personnel specialists. The basic process is to compare job descriptions with grade descriptions. All jobs within a grade are treated alike with respect to base compensation.

Point System

The point system is the most widely used job evaluation method. It involves establishing and defining the factors common to most jobs that represent the chief elements of value inherent in all jobs. The specific factors chosen differ from one company to another, but generally include mental and physical skills, responsibility, supervision given and received, personality requirements, and minimum education required.

Each factor is assigned a minimum and maximum number of points, different ranges being associated in line with the relative importance of the factors, Net, appraised factor scores are combined into a total point value. Finally, bands of points are decided upon and become the different compensation classes. Less arbitrary judgment is required than under the classification method; the use of point values makes it possible to determine the gap, or distance, between job classes.

Factor-comparison Method

This method resembles the point system but is more complex. It utilizes a scheme of ranking and cross-comparisons to minimize error from faulty judgement. In a process similar to that used in the point system, the factor-comparison method employs selected factors and evaluation scales. However, the scale values are in dollars and cents, and no upper limit exists to the valuation that can be assigned to any one factor. Number of key jobs, typical of similar jobs throughout the company, is then evaluated, factor by factor. This is done by arranging them in rank order, from highest to lowest for each factor. As a check against this judgemental evaluation, the compensation actually paid for each job are allocated to the factors; the allocation automatically establishes the relationship among jobs for each factor. The judgment ranking and the ranking by allocation compensation are compared and differences are reconciled, or else the jobs are removed from the key list. On the basis of the amounts assigned to the several factors making up key jobs, additional jobs are evaluated and their monetary values for each factor interpolated into the scale. This procedure is repeated until all jobs are evaluated.

Job Evaluation and Sales Positions

Job evaluation occurs whenever decisions are made about the relative worth of jobs, and it is inescapable in organizational life. If, for example, the owner of an automobile dealership decides that the new car sales manager should be paid more than the service manager, the jobs have been evaluated. So informal job evaluation exists in firms not using formal job evaluation.

Traditionally, sales executives have opposed using formal job evaluations to determine the compensation levels of sales personnel. They contend that compensation levels for sales personnel are more closely related to external supply and demand factors than to conditions inside the company. Sales personnel enjoy greater job mobility than most other employees, and are in everyday contact with potential employers.

If a company has a formal job evaluation programme that includes the jobs of sales personnel, there should be sales department representation on the committee that arrives at quantitative evaluations. If the job evaluation programme does not cover sales personnel programme or the company does not use formal job evaluation, it is important for the sales executive to establish the value of sales jobs relative to other company jobs. This helps assure that the monetary attractiveness of sales positions is no less than for comparable jobs elsewhere in the company. If the sales executive keeps informed on the relative differences between sales jobs and other company jobs, he or she is preparing for the day, which is probably inevitable, when sales positions are regarded as appropriate for inclusion in formal job evaluation programmes.

Consider Compensation Patterns in Community and Industry

Because compensation levels for sales personnel are related to external supply and demand factors, it is important to consider prevailing compensation patterns in the community and industry. Management needs answers to four questions:

(1) What compensation systems are being used?
(2) What is the average compensation for similar positions?
(3) How are other companies doing with their plans?
(4) What are the pros and cons of departing from industry or community patterns?

If there is a companywide formal job evaluation programme, it should take into account the current rates for sales positions in the community and industry. A programme for setting compensation of sales personnel is sound only if it considers the relation of external compensation practices to those of the company. Effective sales executives maintain constant vigilance against the possibility that the pay of sales personnel will get out of line with that paid for similar jobs in the community or industry.

Determine Compensation Level

Management must determine the amount of compensation a salesperson should receive on an average. Although the compensation level might be set through individual bargaining, or on an arbitrary judgement basis, neither expedient is recommended. Management should ascertain whether the calibre of the present sales force measures up to what the company would like to have. If it is too low or if the company should have lower-grade people than those currently employed, management should determine the market value of sales personnel of the desired grade. Management weigh the worth of individual persons through estimating the sales and profit that would be lost if a particular salesperson resigned.

Another consideration is the compensation amount the company can afford to pay. The result of examining these and other factors pertinent to the situation is a series of estimates for the total cost of salespeople's compensation. It is an excellent practice to plot each cost estimate on a break-even style chart. When the several plots are compared with the company's cost goals, the sales volume needed to break even at each compensation level is revealed. The compensation levels for individual salespeople under the proposed plan also should be plotted in break-even style.

In some firms, companywide formal job evaluation programmes are used to set compensation levels for sales positions. The procedure recommended earlier serves as a check on the compensation levels prescribed through job evaluations. Any discrepancies should be reconciled. When the job evaluation programme is sound, there should be a few, if any, discrepancies. It is not unusual to find that two companies operate under similar selling conditions but with different sales compensation levels. Sales personnel in one company earn more than those who do essentially the same work in another company.

Relatively speaking, the first group of salespeople is overcompensated. What explains such situations? Sometimes, management does not know the true worth of individual sales personnel, or managerial inertia prevents adjustment of the compensation level to changed selling conditions. In still other cases, sales managers are biased in favour of high compensation for selling jobs.

Provide for the Various Compensation Elements

A sales compensation plan has as many as four basic elements:

(1) a fixed element, either a salary or a drawing account, to provide some stability of income; (2) a variable element (for example, a commission, bonus, or profit-sharing arrangement), to serve as an incentive; (3) an element covering the fringe or "plus factor,"

such as paid vacations, sickness and accident benefits, life insurance, pensions, and the like; and (4) an element providing for reimbursement of expenses or payment of expense allowances. Not every company includes all four elements. Management selects the combination of elements that best fits the selling situation. The proportions that different elements bear to each other vary. However, most companies split the fixed and variable elements on a 60 : 40 to an 80 : 20 basis.

Special Company Needs and Problems

A sales compensation plan is no panacea for marketing ills, but it is often possible to construct a plan that increases marketing effectiveness. If a company's earnings are depressed because sales personnel overemphasize low-margin items and neglect more profitable products, it may be possible, despite the existence of the managerial alternatives, to adjust the compensation plan to stimulate the selling of better balanced orders. Specifically, variable commission rates might be set on different products, with the higher rates applying to neglected products.

Or, as another example, a firm might have a "smaller-order" problem. It is possible to design compensation plans that encourage sales personnel to write larger orders. Commissions rate can be graduated so that higher rates apply to larger orders. However, it is desirable to supplement such a revised compensation plan with a customer classification and call scheduling system, enabling management to vary call frequency with account size.

As still another example, a company may want to obtain more displays or local advertising by retailers. The presence or absence of point-of-purchases displays can spell the difference between marketing success or failure. Securing retail displays is a task that sales personnel may neglect, especially if they are paid commissions based on sales volume. To overcome this tendency, an incentive payment for obtaining retail displays is often incorporated in the compensation plan.

Numerous other possibilities exist for using the compensation plan to help solve special company problems. Plans may assist in securing new customers and new business, improving the quality of salespeople's reports, controlling expenses of handling complaints and adjustments, eliminating price shading by the sales staff, reducing travelling and other expenses, and making collections and gathering credit information.

Management, however, should recognize that other means exist for dealing with these problems, which are generally transitory in nature. Repeated tempering with the sales compensation plan frequently results in complex and difficult-to-administer plans.

Consult the Present Sales Force

Management should consult the present sales personnel, inasmuch as many grievances have roots in the compensation plan. Management should encourage sales personnel to articulate their likes and dislikes about the current plan and to suggest changes in it. Criticism and suggestions are appraised relative to the plan or plans under consideration. But at this point, management compares the calibre of the present sales force with that of the people whom it would like to have. If the present salespeople are not of the grade that the company wishes to attract, their criticisms and suggestions are of limited usefulness. Since, however nearly every sales force has some people of the desired calibre, more weight can be attached to their opinions than to those of others.

Reduce Tentative Plan to Writing and Pretest it

For classification and to eliminate inconsistencies the tentative plan is put in writing. Then it is pretested. The amount of testing required depends upon how much the new plan differs from the one in use. The greater the difference, the more thorough is the testing. Pretests of compensation plans are almost always mathematical and usually computerized. Past payrolls, perhaps for a year or two, are reworked to check operation of the proposed plan against experience under the old system. Analysts compare what happened with what would have happened had the new plan been in effect. If the sales pattern has shown considerable fluctuation, calculations are made for period's representative of average, good, and poor business. Then a look is taken into the future. Utilizing sales forecast data, new and old plans are applied to future periods. The plan is tested for the sales force as a group and for individuals faced with unique selling conditions. Analysis reveals whether the plan permits earning in line with the desired compensation level. If deficiencies show up, the plan may not be at fault; weaknesses can trace to the way territorial assignments have been made or to inaccuracies in sales forecasts budgets, or quotas.

To conduct a pilot test, several territories representative of different sets of selling conditions are selected. The proposed plan is applied in each one long enough to detect how it works under current conditions. Pilot tests are invaluable for spotting possible source of trouble and other deficiencies.

Revise the Plan

The plan is then revised to eliminate trouble spots or deficiencies. If alterations are extensive, the revised plan goes through further pretests and perhaps another pilot test. But if changes have been only minor, further testing is not necessary.

Implement the Plan and Provide for Follow-up

At the time the new plan is implemented, it is explained to sales personnel. Management should convince them of its basic fairness and logic. The sales personnel are made to understand what management hopes to accomplish through the new plan and how this is to be done. Details of changes from the old plan, and their significance require explanation. All sales personnel should receive copies of the new plan, together with written examples of the method used for calculating earnings. If the plan is at all complex, special training sessions are held and aimed at teaching sales personnel how to compute their own earnings. If sales personnel do not understand the plan or certain of its features, such as quotas and variable commission bases, they may think that the company is taking unfair advantage of them. Inadequate understanding of the sales compensation plan is common and often a cause of low morale. No effort is spared to make certain that everyone on the sales force fully comprehends the compensation plan and its workings. Provisions for follow-up are made. From periodic checkups, need for further adjustments are detected. Periodic checks provide evidence of the plan's accomplishments, and they uncover weaknesses needing correction.

COMPENSATION TECHNIQUE

Straight-Salary Plan

The straight salary is the simplest compensation plan. Under it, salesperson receives fixed sums at regular intervals (usually each week or month but sometimes every two weeks), representing total payments for their services. The straight salary was once the most popular sales compensation plan, but it has been declining in importance. A recent study by Executive Compensation Service, Incl. shows that under 17.5 per cent of all selling organizations use straight-salary plans. Such plans are more common among industrial goods companies than among consumer-goods companies. Firms that formerly used the straight salary have tended to combine a basic salary with a variable element—that is, they have switched to combination plans.

In spite of the trend away from its use, sometimes the straight salary plan is appropriate. It is the logical compensation plan when the selling job requires extensive missionary or educational work, when salespeople service the product or give technical and engineering advice to prospects or users, or when salespeople do considerable sales promotion work. If non-selling tasks bulk large in the salesperson's total time expenditure, the straight-salary is worthy of serious consideration.

Straight-salary plans are commonly used for compensating salespeople heavily engaged in trade selling. These jobs, in which selling amounts to mere order taking, abound in the wholesale and manufacturing fields, where consumer necessities are distributed directly to retailers. Frequently, too, the straight-salary method is used for paying driver-salesperson selling liquor and beverages, milk and bread, and similarly distributed products. From management's standpoint, the straight-salary plan has important advantages. It provides strong financial control over sales personnel, and management can direct their activities along the other productive lines. Component tasks making up salespersons' jobs can be recast with minimum opposition from those affected, so there is flexibility in adjusting field sales work to changed selling situations. If sales personnel prepare detailed reports, follow-up leads, or perform other time-consuming tasks, they cooperate more fully if paid straight salaries because of their basic simplicity, and compared with straight-commission plans, accounting costs are lower. The main attraction of the straight-salary plan for sales personnel is that stability of income provides freedom from financial uncertainties inherent in other plans. In addition, sales personnel are relieved of much of the burden of planning their own activities (the practice of providing detailed instruction, for example, on routing and scheduling, generally goes along with the straight-salary plan). And, because of its basic simplicity, sales personnel have no difficulty in understanding straight-salary plans.

The straight-salary plan, however, has weaknesses. Since there are no direct monetary incentives, many salespeople do only an average rather than an outstanding job. They pass up opportunities for increased business, until management becomes aware of them and orders the required actions. Unless the plan is skilfully administered, there is a tendency to under-compensate productive salespeople and to overcompensate poor performers. If pay inequities exist for long, the turnover rate rises; and it is often the most productive people who leave first, resulting in increased costs for recruiting, selecting and training. Other problems are encountered in maintaining morale, as arguments occur on pay adjustments for ability, rising living costs, and length of service.

Because all the selling expense is fixed, it is difficult to adjust to changing conditions—a knotty problem during business downswings, when selling expenses can be reduced only by cutting salaries or releasing personnel. Moreover, during business upturns, there is difficulty in securing the company's share of rising industry volume, because salaried salespeople commonly are not disposed to exceed previous sales records by any large amount. However, many of the straight-salary plan's weaknesses are minimized through good administration.

In administering a straight-salary plan, individual sales personnel are paid, insofar as possible, according to their relative performance. The difficulty is in measuring performance. Management needs to define "performance" and the meaning of good, average, and poor performances. When management has these definitions and develops methods for performance measurements, it can set individual salaries fairly and intelligently. Users of the salary plan define performance as total job performance, not merely success in securing sales volume or in performing some other aspect of the job—and this is theoretically correct, because the payers of salaries assume they can exercise maximum control over to measure performance by relating the salesperson's total selling expense in using the expense-to-sales ratio as the sole criterion of performance overemphasizes the importance of cost control. In the absence of well-defined quantitative performance standards and few companies have them, the sales job description, if up to date and complete, is the place to start in appraising job performances of sales personnel.

All sales personnel need rating not only on their achievement of sales and cost goals but on their performance of each assigned duty. The total evaluation of an individual is a composite of the several ratings, weighted according to relative performance. Persons rated as average are paid average salaries. Each individual's performance is regularly reviewed and upward adjustments made for those showing improvements, and downward adjustments made for those with deteriorating performances.

Straight-Commission Plan

The theory supporting the straight-commission plan is that individual sales personnel should be paid according to productivity. The assumption underlying straight-commission plans is that sales volume is the best productivity measure and can, therefore, be used as the sole measure. This is a questionable assumption. The straight-commission plan, in its purest form is almost as simple as the straight-salary plan, but many commission systems develop into complex arrangements. Some provide for progressive or regressive changes in commission rates as sales volume rises to different levels. Others provide for differential commission rates for sales of different products, to different categories of customers, or during given selling seasons. These refinements make straight commission plans more complex than straight-salary plans. Straight-commission plans fall into one of two broad classifications:

1. Straight-commission with sales personnel paying their own expenses. Advances may or may not be made against earned commission.
2. Straight-commission with the company paying expenses, with or without advances against earned commissions.

There is a general trend away from the straight-commission plan and today no more than 6 or 7 per cent of all companies use such plans. The straight-commission plan is used in situations where non-selling duties are relatively unimportant and management emphasizes order getting. Straight-commission plans are common in the clothing, textile, and shoe industries and in drug and hardware wholesaling. Firms selling intangibles, such as insurance and investment securities, and manufacturers of furniture, office equipment, and business machines also are frequent users of straight-commission plans.

The straight-commission plan has several advantages. The greatest is that it provides maximum direct monetary incentive for the salesperson to strive for high-level volume. The star salesperson is paid more than he or she would be under most salary plans, and low producers are not likely to be overcompensated. When a commission system is first installed, the sales personnel turnover rate accelerates, but usually the exodus is among the low producers.

Those remaining work longer and harder, with more income to show for their efforts. Straight-commission plans, in addition, provide a means for cost control—all direct selling expenses, except for travelling and miscellaneous expenses (which are reimbursable in some plans), fluctuate directly with sales volume changes and sales compensation becomes virtually an all variable expense. The straight-commission plan also is characterized by great flexibility— by revising commission rates applying to different products, for instance, it is possible to stimulate sales personnel to emphasize those with the highest gross margins. However, the straight-commission method has weaknesses. It provides little financial control over salespeople's activities, a weakness further compounded when they pay their own expenses. Salespersons on straight commission often feel that they are discharging their full responsibilities by continuing to send in customers' orders. They are careless about transmitting reports, neglect to follow-up leads, resist reduction in the size of sales territories, consider individual accounts private property, shade prices to make sales, and may use higher-pressure tactics with consequent loss of customer goodwill. Moreover, unless differential commission rates are used, sales personnel push the easiest-to-sell low-margin items and neglect harder-to-sell high margin items; if management seeks to correct this through using differential commission rates; it incurs increased record-keeping expenses. Under any straight-commission plan, in fact, the costs of checking and auditing salespeople's reports and of calculating payrolls are higher than under the straight-salary method. Finally, some salespersons' efficiency may decline because of income uncertainties. If a sales force has many financially worried salespeople, management may have to invest considerable time, effort, and money to buoy up their spirits.

Determining Commission Base

One important aspect of designing a straight-commission system is to select the base on which to pay commission. Company selling policies and problems strongly influence selection of the base. If obtaining volume is the main concern, then total sales is the base. If sales personnel make collections on sales, commissions are based upon shipments, billings, or payments. To control price cutting by sales personnel, some companies base commission on gross margins. Other companies use net profits as the base, seeking simultaneously to control price cutting, selling expense, and net profit.

Drawing Accounts

A modification of the straight-commission plan is the drawing account method, under which the company establishes separate account for each salesperson, to whom commissions are credited and against whom periodic withdrawals are made. Drawing accounts resemble salaries, since customarily individual sales personnel are allowed to overdraw against future earning. If sales personnel become greatly overdrawn, they may lose in incentive to produce, because earned commissions are used to reduce the indebtedness. More important, some sales personnel become discouraged with the prospects of paying back overdrawn accounts and quit the company.

To forestall quitting by overdrawn salespeople, some firms use "guaranteed" drawing account plans. These do not require the paying back of overdraw. Sales executives in these firms are conservative in setting the size of guaranteed drawing accounts, for they are in effect combination salary and commission plans. Commonly, drawing account plans include a provision that covers the possibility of overdrafts. Legally, an overdraft cannot be collected unless the salesperson specially agrees to repay it, or it is really a personal loan, or the salesperson has given a note acknowledging its receipt. Without a formal understanding, most courts hold that the relationship between the salesperson and the company is a partnership in which the company agreed to finance the salesperson and that the resulting loss is a normal risk incurred in doing business. Even if the company has an ironclad agreement with its sales personnel, there is a problem in collecting money that overdrawn sales personnel do not have.

Combination Salary and Incentive Plan

Salary Plus Commission

Most sales compensation plans are combinations of salary and commission plans. Most developed as attempts to capture the advantages and offset the disadvantages of both the salary and commission systems. Where the straight-salary method is used, the sales executive lacks a financial means for stimulating the sales force to greater effort. Where the straight-commission system is used, the executive has weak financial control over non-selling activities. By a judicious blending of the two basic plans, management seeks both control and motivation. Actual results depend upon management's skills in designing and administering the plan. Unless there is skilful adjustment of salary and commission, weaknesses of both basic systems reappear.

Strengths and Weaknesses of Combination Plans

A well-designed and administered combination plan proves significant benefits. Sales personnel have both the security of stable incomes and the stimulus of direct financial incentive. Management has both financial control over sales activities and the apparatus to motivate sales efforts. Selling costs are composed of fixed and variable elements; thus, greater flexibility for adjustment to changing conditions exists than under the commission method. Nevertheless, selling costs fluctuate with the volume of business. There are beneficial effects upon sales force morale. Disagreements on pay increases and territorial changes are less violent than under a straight-commission plan. Further, if salespeople realize that the company shares their financial risks, a cooperative spirit develops between them and the company.

The combination plan, however, has disadvantages. Clerical costs are higher than for either a salary or a commission system. More records are maintained and in greater detail. There are risks that the plan will become complicated and that sales personnel will not understand it. Sometimes a company seeking both to provide adequate salaries and to keep selling costs down uses commission rates so low that the incentive feature is insufficient to elicit needed sales effort. But, if the incentive portion is increased, salespeople may neglect activities for which they are not directly paid. Therefore, the ratio that the base salary and the incentive portion bear to the total compensation is critical. As mentioned earlier, most companies divide the fixed and variable elements on a 60 : 40 to an 80 : 20 basis.

Use of Bonuses

Bonuses are different from commissions—a bonus is an amount paid for accomplishing a specific sales task; a commission varies in amount with sales volume or other commission base. Bonuses are paid for reaching a sales quota, performing promotional activities, obtaining new accounts, follow-up leads, setting up displays, or carrying out other assigned tasks. The bonus, in other words, is an additional financial reward to the salesperson for achieving results beyond a predetermined minimum.

Bonuses are never used alone—they always appear with one of the three main sales compensation methods. If used with the straight-salary, the plan resembles the combination plan. If used with the straight-commission, the result is a commission plan to which an element of managerial control and direction has been added. If used with the combination salary and commission plan, the bonus becomes a portion of the incentive income that is calculated differently from the commission. Certain administrative actions are crucial when a bonus is included in the compensation plan. At the outset, the bonus conditions require thorough explanation, as all sales personnel must understand them. The necessary records must be set up and maintained. Procedures for keeping sales personnel abreast of their current standings relative to the goals are needed. In addition, any bonus misunderstandings or grievances arising should be dealt with fairly and tactfully.

Fringe Benefits

Fringe benefits, which do not bear direct relationships to job performance, range from 25 to 40 per cent of the total sales compensation package. Some are required by federal and state law—for example, payments for social security premiums, unemployment compensation, and worker's compensation. Often the company provides fringe benefits for other reasons; to be competitive with other companies in the industry or community, to furnish reasons for employees to remain in the company's service, and to comply with the employees' expectations.

Fringe benefits, like monetary compensation, are not motivating factors. In the Maslow hierarchy, fringe benefits contribute to fulfilment of safety and security needs, although some (such as payment of country club dues) contribute to fulfilment of esteem and other higher-order needs. Since fringe benefits are given to all in the company's employment and do not vary with job performance, they help to prevent job dissatisfaction but do not add to job satisfaction (in line with Herzberg's motivation-hygiene theory).

Factors Affecting Remuneration Plan

There is hardly any remuneration plan which can be called best and can be adopted to all types of organization. An ideal compensation scheme necessarily maximizes the goals of the firm as well as of the sales force. No doubt, the method of remuneration differs from firm to firm but there are several factors which influence the remuneration plan of any organization directly. These factors determine the nature and amount of remuneration of the sales force. The important factors which need to be considered while developing any method of remuneration for the salesmen are as follows:

(i) **Nature of sales job**
First, a thorough study of the sales job should be made while determining a remuneration plan. A sales job analysis includes all aspects relating to the duties and responsibilities of salesmen. If the job is complex, time-consuming and needs lot of hard work, the remuneration package should be high. On the other hand, if the job is simple and requires little effort, the payment should be a moderate one.

(ii) **Nature of the product**
The remuneration plan of an organization also depends on the nature and number of products. If the product offered for sale is a consumer product, it needs little selling effort on the part of the salesmen. Therefore, they are usually paid less compared to those who sell specialties, luxuries or technical goods which require sustained selling efforts. Similarly, salesmen who sell a variety of goods are expected to earn more than those who handle a single product.

(iii) **Class of salesman**
Some kind of salesmen like travelling salesmen, creative salesmen are highly paid because their job is time-consuming and requires more selling efforts. On

the other hand, counter salesmen, who perform routine type of activities, are comparatively paid less.

(iv) Financial capacity

Firms which have limited financial capacity, plan the remuneration plan in such a manner so that it does not become a burden for them. In other words, the payment of the sales force should be justifiable. They can follow a remuneration plan entirely based on commission basis. On the other hand, financially sound companies are free to adopt any remuneration policy.

(v) Advertising activities

Advertising and sales promotion measures undertaken by the organization generally make the salesman's job comparatively easier. Firms spending heavily on advertising and other sales promotion activities necessarily make the salesman's job comparatively easier. Therefore, the remuneration package of the sales force of such firms can be kept low as their jobs are made easy and simple. On the other hand, salesmen making selling efforts on their own, without any background support made available through advertising and sales promotion activities have to be handsomely paid.

(vi) Channel of distribution

The channel of distribution also plays an important role in remuneration plan and ultimately influences the income of the sales force. The longer the channel, the easier is the job of the salesman since middleman take a lot of burden from the shoulders of the salesmen. In such cases, where little personal salesmanship is required, the salesmen usually get a moderate remuneration. On the other hand, firms using shorter channels of distribution have to undertake a lot of personal selling efforts. Therefore, the salesmen have to make lots of selling efforts and thus need to be paid handsomely.

Controlling the Sales Effort

Sales Budgeting

Estimating future levels of revenue, selling expenses, and profit contributions of the sales function.

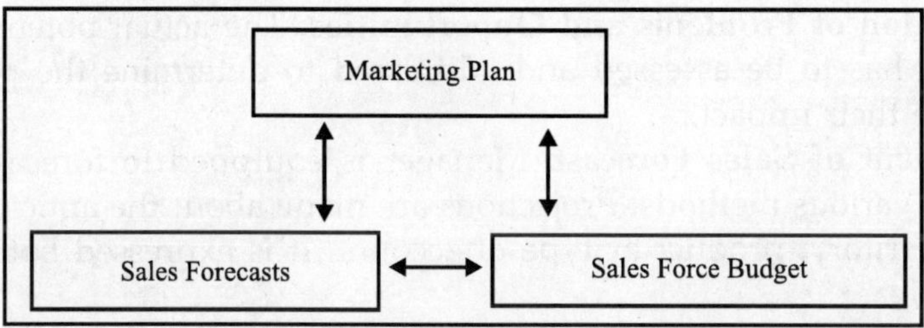

Fig. 3.9. Sales budgeting.

Types of Budget

Financial statement that outlines firms intended actions and the resulting cash flow consequences. Most sales budgets cover a period of one year, but they are often broken down into quarterly or even monthly targets.

- **Sales budget:** Projection of revenue computed from forecast unit sales and average prices.
- **Selling expenses budget:** Approved amount that the department will spend to obtain the revenues projected in the sales budget.
- **Profit budget:** Merged sales budget and the selling expense budget to determine gross profit.

Major Types of Selling Expense Budgets

- **Affordable methods:** Management determines what to spend on selling after accounting for the cost of goods sold and the desired profit level.
- **Percentage of sales method:** The funding level is found by multiplying the sales revenue by a given percentage. Budgeting is based on anticipated rather than historical revenue.
- **Competitive parity method:** Sales budgeting method based on the competitive practices in an industry. They refer to either a specific competitor or the industry average.
- **Objective and task method:** Budget allocation is based on the objective of the firm, tasks necessary to achieve those objectives, and the expenses related to those tasks. It is known as zero-based budgeting.
- **Bidding system:** In this the sales function competes with other functions for limited funds available on the basis of payoffs.
- **Return on investment (ROI):** Some sales managers have begun to use this financial management concept to choose between alternative courses of action. ROI is determined by dividing net income by total assets employed to earn the income.

SALES BUDGETING PROCEDURES

(i) **Situational Analysis:** Sales managers have to look at the magnitude of past differences between budgeted and actual figures and the reasons for these differences.

(ii) **Identification of Problems and Opportunities:** The actual potential threat and challenges has to be assessed and addressed to determine the probabilities of occurrence their impact.

(iii) **Development of Sales Forecast:** Manager is equipped to forecast sales, using one of the various methods. Projections are made about the anticipated levels of sales by territory, product or type of account. It is expressed both in units and rupees.

(iv) **Formulation of Sales Objectives:** Once the forecast has been developed, sales force has to be told what sales target to strive for and what objectives to pursue.

(v) **Determination of Sales Tasks:** Sales manager and sales force have to carry a broad array of sales activities, ranging from recruitment to evaluation, and from prospecting to after-sales service.

(vi) **Specification of Resource Requirement:** The resources that will be required to implement the specified activities and achieve the objectives.

(vii) **Completion of Projections:** Here all the input and requests from various units of the sales function are assembled and tied into a comprehensive package.

(viii) **Presentations and Review:** Present and defend its sales budget proposal to the management.

(ix) **Modification and Revision:** Sales managers have to engage in a series of compromise sessions. Here the sales targets and budgets might be adjusted by the higher management, reflecting both to the needs of the corporation and the true potential of the marketplace.

(x) **Budget Approval:** Final levels are eventually approved and authorized for both the sales and the selling expense budgets. Here onwards budgets are reviewed periodically looking at the ongoing market conditions and other external forces.

SALES QUOTA

Sales quotas are a way of life for the sales force. All activities of the sales force revolve around the fulfilment of sales quotas. Sales quotas are targets assigned to sales personnel. They signify the performance expected from them by the organization. Sales quotas help in directing, evaluating and controlling the sales force. They form an indispensable tool for sales managers to carry out sales management activities. Sales quotas are prepared on the basis of sales forecasts and budgets. Sales quotas serve various purposes in organizations.

They provide targets for sales personnel to achieve; act as standards to measure sales force performance; and help motivate the sales force. Compensation plans are invariably linked to quotas. The commission and bonuses given to salespersons are based on their meeting quotas set for them. The four categories of sales quotas widely used

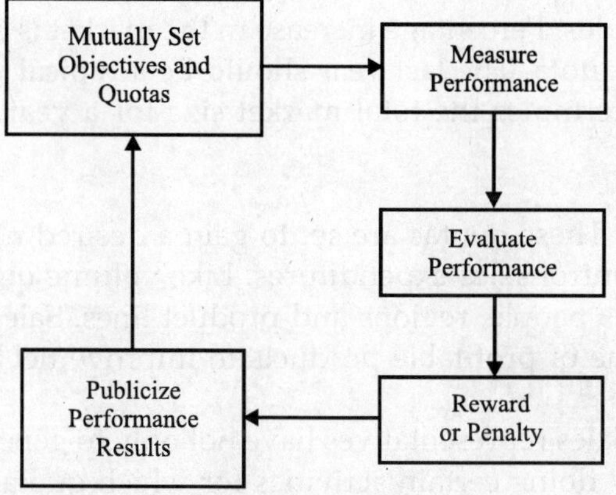

Fig. 3.10. Sales quota.

are: sales volume quotas, expense quotas, activity quotas, and profit quotas. A sales quota should be fair, challenging yet attainable, rewarding, easy to understand, flexible and must satisfy management objectives.

It must also help in the coordination of sales force activities. Setting motivating and easy to understand quotas is essential to obtain the cooperation of the sales force. Various methods are used to set sales quotas, among which, quotas based on sales forecasts and market potential are the most common. Skilful administration by sales managers is required for effective implementation of quotas. Convincing salespeople about the fairness and accuracy of quotas helps the sales management to successfully implement quotas.

Sales quotas have certain limitations such as being time consuming, difficulty in comprehending if complicated statistical calculations have been used and focusing on attaining sales volumes at the cost of ignoring important non-selling activities. Quotas may reduce risk-taking among sales personnel and may influence them to adopt unethical selling practices. With changes in the competitive environment and variations in customer expectations, many companies have started developing compensation plans that are increasingly based on non-traditional aspects, thereby reducing dependency on quotas.

Types of Sales Quota

Quotas are tools for planning and control. There are four types of quotas: (i) Sales volume quota (ii) Financial quota (iii) Activities quota (iv) Combination of the above three.

(i) ***Sales volume quotas:*** They are most widely used and are based on sales volume. Sales volume quota may be (a) units to be sold (b) rupee value of sales (c) combination of (a) and (b).

These are set for a sales representative, or for a product line, or for a geographical area or for a distributor. These management's expectations of the minimum level of performance for a given period of time.

Setting of sales volume quota:

- On basis of past sales: Percentage increase in the market is determined and added to the last year's quota. The last year should be a typical year.
- The company determines the total market size for a year. The volume quota is derived from it.

(ii) ***Financial quotas:*** These quotas are set to gain a desired net profit, control gross margin, and to control sales expenditures. Like volume quotas, these quotas can be applied to sales people, regions and product lines. Sales representatives have to spend their time of profitable products to improve net profit.

(iii) ***Activity quotas:*** Sales representatives have not only to generate sales, but develop the market too by doing certain activities for which quotas are set

- Number of distributors/dealers called on
- Number of new customers contacted

- Number of calls for recoveries of dues
- Number of old customer and institutions called on

These quotas serve as guidelines for younger, inexperienced sales representatives, who may tend to place emphasis on the wrong activities.

(iv) ***Combination quotas:*** These quotas are used when management wants to control the performance of both the selling and non-selling activities of the sales force. These quotas generally use points as common measuring tool to overcome the difficulty of evaluating the different units used by together quotas. Rupee sales volume and activity quotas are combined in large number of pharma companies.

Good quotas are accurate, fair and attainable. Quotas are not useful in short supply situation.

Sales and Cost Analysis

Control is one of the most critical functions performed by a sales manager as it measures the performance of the system and helps the manager take corrective action if the performance of the system is not in agreement with the formulated plans. The present-day dynamic marketplace has forced sales managers to shift their focus in sales control from sales volume alone and to lay equal emphasis on costs incurred in implementing the sales effort.

The objective of sales control is to ensure that the company's sales efforts are in tune with its sales plan by taking necessary measures in case of deviations. The sales control function measures the performance of the sales force and identifies the problems and opportunities that the firm is exposed to. The process of sales control involves setting goals, comparing actual with the targets, and taking up corrective action if necessary. The sales efforts of a company can be studied through a sales analysis that involves gathering, classifying, comparing, and studying the sales data of the company.

A typical sales analysis involves deciding on the purpose of evaluation, comparing the sales figures with some standards and processing the data to generate reports. A sales analysis can be most informative when the sales data is broken down hierarchically. An analysis of volume of sales by categories is very helpful in identifying the root causes of the problems in the sales activities of the firm. Though a sales analysis helps identify the problems associated with the sales activities of the firm, it is also bound by a few limitations like dependency on accounting records, inability to reflect the profitability of sales, etc.

Sales analysis involves analyzing the sales volume or the total sales of the company. It includes the total sales of the company by territory, customer, and product category. A sales audit is periodically taken up by the sales management to examine the entire selling operations of the firm. The audit involves an audit of the sales organization, the sales environment, planning systems, and sales management functions. While a sales analysis measures the sales volume achieved, the marketing cost analysis looks into the costs and expenses incurred to achieve the sales volume and their justification.

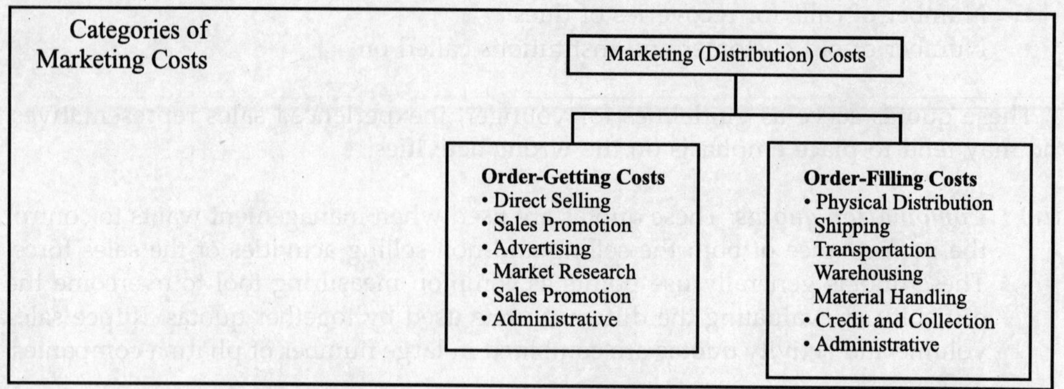

Fig. 3.11. Different types of marketing cost.

Cost analysis involves spreading the natural costs, allocating them to functional units, studying the profitability of the units, and implementing appropriate action depending on the findings of the analysis. Just as a sales audit examines the entire sales operations of a firm, a marketing audit evaluates and enhances the effectiveness of a firm's marketing operations by studying its marketing strategies, policies, and practices.

Sales managers use profitability analysis to relate the sales revenues to marketing costs. This helps sales managers to take necessary measures to ensure higher profitability of the firm's sales transactions. A number of principles such as the iceberg principle, the 80/20 principle and cross-classifications guide sales managers in conducting effective sales and cost analysis. These principles reveal the behaviour of sales data and the actual reasons underlying them. They forewarn sales managers of impending dangers and help them to take measures to counter them.

Time and Territory Management

Effective time management will significantly help a salesperson improve his performance. There has been a fundamental shift in organizations' approach to time management with the advent of better technological options. Advancements in technology have simultaneously led to a significant increase in time pressure on the salesperson. However, technological advancements have also provided several techniques to help salespersons manage their time efficiently.

Efficient time management leads to better customer coverage; helps in reducing selling costs, improving customer service and helps in accurate evaluation of salespeople. A sales territory comprises a number of present and potential customers, located within a given geographical area and assigned to a salesperson, branch, or intermediary. Sales territories should be designed efficiently so that the potential of salespersons can be exploited to the maximum.

Sales territories are designed using the three methods: buildup method, breakdown method and incremental method. The buildup method consists of designing sales territories by assessing the attractiveness of current and prospective customers. In

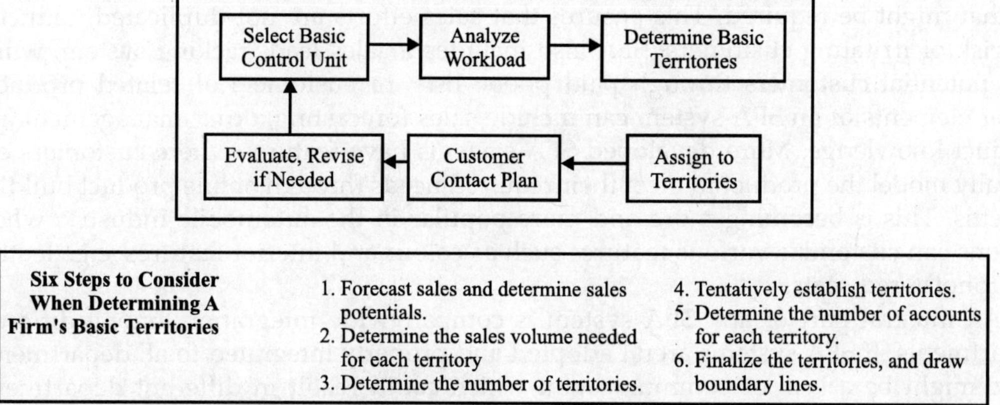

Fig. 3.12. Factors to consider when designing territories.

this method, current and prospective customers are identified and their sales requirements analyzed individually. Subsequently, the salespersons are assigned territories on the basis of the sales volumes and the number of calls they are supposed to make to these accounts.

The breakdown method is the reverse of the buildup method and in this, the market potential for the product is identified and then the market share that the company is targeting assessed. Based on this, sales are forecasted. This is followed by determining the average number of sales that each salesperson is required to make and the territories are then accordingly allocated to individual salespersons. In the incremental method, additional territories are created as long as the revenues generated from them exceed the cost of serving them.

Once the designing of territories is completed, salespersons are allocated to individual territories according to their capabilities. Routing and scheduling are two widely accepted techniques for territory management. Routing refers to the process of deciding the pattern of movement of a salesperson in his territory for making sales calls in a way that minimizes the total distance travelled, the travel expense and the travel time. Scheduling involves allocation of time to the various activities that a salesperson is involved in during a day, week and a month.

SALES FORCE MANAGEMENT SYSTEM

Sales force management systems are information systems used in marketing and management that help automate some sales and sales force management functions. They are frequently combined with a Marketing Information System, in which case they are often called Customer Relationship Management (CRM) systems.

A Sales Force Automation System (SFA), typically a part of a company's customer relationship management system, is a system that automatically records all the stages in a sales process. SFA includes a contact management system which tracks all contact that has been made with a given customer, the purpose of the contact, and any follow-up that might be required. This ensures that sales efforts are not duplicated, reducing the risk of irritating customers. SFA also includes a sales lead tracking system, which lists potential customers through paid phone lists, or customers of related products. Other elements of an SFA system can include sales forecasting, order management and product knowledge. More developed SFA systems have features where customers can actually model the product to meet their required needs through online product building systems. This is becoming more and more popular in the automobile industry, where patrons can customize various features such as colour and interior features, e.g., leather vs. upholstered seats.

An integral part of any SFA system is companywide integration among different departments. If SFA systems aren't adopted and properly integrated to all departments, there might be a lack of communication which could result in different departments contacting the same customer for the same purpose. In order to mitigate this risk, SFA must be fully integrated in all departments that deal with customer service management.

Advantages to the Sales Manager

Sales force automation systems can also affect sales management:

1. The sales manager, rather than gathering all the call sheets from various sales people and tabulating the results, will have the results automatically presented in easy to understand tables, charts, or graphs. This saves time for the manager.
2. Activity reports, information requests, orders booked, and other sales information will be sent to the sales manager more frequently, allowing him/her to respond more directly with advice, product in-stock verifications, and price discount authorizations. This gives management more hands-on control of the sales process if they wish to use it.
3. The sales manager can configure the system so as to automatically analyze the information using sophisticated statistical techniques, and present the results in a user-friendly way. This gives the sales manager information that is more useful in:

- Providing current and useful sales support materials to their sales staff
- Providing marketing research data: demographic, psychographic, behavioural, product acceptance, product problems, detecting trends
- Providing market research data: industry dynamics, new competitors, new products from competitors, new promotional campaigns from competitors, macro-environmental scanning, detecting trends
- Coordinating with other parts of the firm, particularly marketing, production, and finance
- Identifying your most profitable customers, and your problem customers
- Tracking the productivity of their sales force by combining a number of performance measures such as revenue per salesperson, revenue per territory, margin by customer segment, margin by customer, number of calls per day, time spent per contact, revenue per call, cost per call, entertainment cost per call, ratio of orders to calls, revenue as a percentage of sales quota, number of new customers per period, number of lost customers per period, cost of customer acquisition as a percentage of expected lifetime value of customer.

Advantages to the Marketing Manager

- Understanding the economic structure of your industry
- Identifying segments within your market
- Identifying your target market
- Identifying your best customers in place
- Doing marketing research to develop profiles (demographic, psychographic, and behavioural) of your core customers
- Understanding your competitors and their products
- Developing new products
- Establishing environmental scanning mechanisms to detect opportunities and threats
- Understanding your company's strengths and weaknesses
- Auditing your customers' experience of your brand in full
- Developing marketing strategies for each of your products using the marketing mix variables of price, product, distribution, and promotion
- Coordinating the sales function with other parts of the promotional mix (such as advertising, sales promotion, public relations, and publicity)
- Creating a sustainable competitive advantage
- Understanding where you want your brands to be in the future, and providing an empirical basis for writing marketing plans on a regular basis to help you get there
- Providing input into feedback systems to help you monitor and adjust the process

Strategic Advantages

Sales force automation systems can also create competitive advantage:

- As mentioned above, **productivity will increase**. Sales staff will use their time more efficiently and more effectively. The sales manager will also become more efficient and more effective. (see above) This increased productivity can create a competitive advantage in three ways: it can reduce costs, it can increase sales revenue, and it can increase market share.
- **Field sales staff will send their information more frequently**. Typically information will be sent to management after every sales call (rather than once a week). This provides management with current information, information that they will be able to use while it is still valuable. Management response time will be greatly reduced. The company will become more alert and more agile.
- These systems could **increase customer satisfaction** if they are used with wisdom. If the information obtained and analyzed with the system is used to create a product that matches or exceeds customer expectations, and the sales staff use the system to service customers more expertly and diligently, then customers will be satisfied with the company. This will provide a competitive advantage because customer satisfaction leads to increased customer loyalty, reduced customer acquisition costs, reduced price elasticity of demand, and increased profit margins.

Disadvantages

Detractors claim that sales force management systems are:

- difficult to work with

- require additional work inputting data
- dehumanize a process that should be personal
- require continuous maintenance, information updating, and system upgrading
- costly
- difficult to integrate with other management information systems

Encouraging Use

For all the reasons stated above, many organizations have found it difficult to persuade sales people to enter data into the system. For this reason many have questioned the value of the investment. Recent developments have embedded sales process systems that give something back to the seller within the CRM screens. Because these systems help the salesperson plan and structure their selling in the most effective way they give a reason to use the CRM.

Let Us Sum Up

In selecting sales reps, the company can start by asking customers what traits they prefer in salespeople. Most customers want honest, reliable, knowledgeable, and helpful reps. Another approach is to look for traits that are common to successful salespeople. Charles Garfield concluded that super sales performers exhibit risk taking, a powerful sense of mission, a problem-solving bent, care for the customer, and careful planning.

Today's customers expect salespeople to have deep product knowledge, offer ideas to improve customer operations, and be efficient and reliable. These demands have required companies to make a much higher investment in training their sales reps. Companies use training to help sales reps: (1) Know and identify with the company; (2) Learn about the company's products; (3) Know customers' and competitors' characteristics; (4) Make effective sales presentations; and (5) Understand sales procedures and responsibilities.

Motivation is the amount of effort the salesperson desires to expend on the activities associated with the sales job, such as calling on potential accounts, planning sales presentations, and filling out reports. Expending effort on each activity making up the sales job leads to some level of achievement on one or more dimensions of job performance – total sales volume, profitability, and sales to new accounts, quota attainment, and the like.

One of the most important responsibilities of sales managers is to evaluate the performance of the sales personnel. The performance appraisal period can become one of those times that a salesperson dreads, unless the appraisal is effectively conducted. Ineffective performance appraisal tends to become a time-consuming and unpleasant activity for the sales manager as well as the sales personnel.

The factors affecting salespeoples' performance are many. Some of these are beyond the control of the individual, while some can be modified. Aspects like motivation, skill-set, job satisfaction, role perception, personal factors like age, sex, height, etc; the ego drive, and empathy towards the customers are inherent in the individual salesperson. Environmental and organizational factors, along with the different functions of sales management come under external factors. It is difficult for the sales manager to predict the influence of the external factors on the performance of the sales force.

There are different sale force compensation techniques, namely, straight salary plans, straight commission plan, salary plus commission, etc. and along with that many fringe benefits.

Sales budgeting is about estimating future levels of revenue, selling expenses, and profit contributions of the sales function. Sales quotas are targets assigned to sales personnel. Control is one of the most critical functions performed by a sales manager as it measures the performance of the system and helps the manager take corrective action if the performance of the system is not in agreement with the formulated plans. The present-day dynamic marketplace has forced sales managers to shift their focus in sales control from sales volume alone and to lay equal emphasis on costs incurred in implementing the sales effort.

The objective of sales control is to ensure that the company's sales efforts are in tune with its sales plan by taking necessary measures in case of deviations. Effective time management will significantly help a salesperson improve his performance. There has been a fundamental shift in organizations' approach to time management with the advent of better technological options. Advancements in technology have simultaneously led to a significant increase in time pressure on the salesperson. However, technological advancements have also provided several techniques to help salespersons manage their time efficiently.

Question for Discussion

1. Explain the recruitment and selection process of sales representative.
2. What are the traits to be looked into while recruiting a sales representative?
3. Explain the training modules for a newly selected sales representative.
4. What are the different types of selling jobs? Write brief about each type.
5. Write short notes on (i) Order getters (ii) Order takers (iii) Buyer-seller dyads (iv) Order influencers (iv) Sales support.
6. How to motivate the sales force? Explain the various techniques for sales force motivation.
7. Write short notes on (i) Maslow's need hierarchy (ii) Herzberg's hygiene theory (iii) Theory X and Theory Y (iv) Reinforcement theory.
8. What are the contemporary theories in motivation? Explain briefly.
9. How to evaluate sales force performance?
10. Explain different methods of sales force compensation.
11. Write short notes on (i) Straight salary plan (ii) Straight commission plan (iii) Salary plus commission (iv) Fringe benefits to sales rep.
12. Explain briefly various factors affecting sales force remuneration plan.
13. Define sales budget. Explain different types of sales budget.
14. Write short notes on: (i) Sales quota (ii) Control and cost analysis (iii) Time and territory management.
15. Explain briefly about SFA.

4

CHAPTER

Overview of Distribution Management

"Forget logistics, you lose."

—Lt. Gen. Fredrick Franks, USA, 7th Corps Commander, Desert Storm

Basic concepts of distribution systems – consumer marketing channel – industrial marketing channel – different modes of transport in India – functional areas of logistics management – distribution costs – supply chain management.

LEARNING OBJECTIVES

After going through this chapter, students will be able to understand

- Fundamental concepts in distribution
- Different types of distribution channel
- Difference between consumer and industrial marketing channel
- Different modes of transport in India
- Importance of logistic management
- Components of logistic management
- Different types of distribution cost
- Importance of supply chain management

INTRODUCTION

Products must be available to consumers who want to purchase them conveniently, quickly, and with a minimum of effort. The distribution system determines a product's marketing presence and the buyers' accessibility to the product. Distribution (also known as place) provides utility. *Time utility* offer the product when the customers want to purchase it. *Place utility* is offering the product where the customers want to purchase it. *Possession utility* facilitates customer ownership of the product. *Form utility* might be needed if changes have been made to the product in the distribution channel (Coca-Cola concentrate sold to bottlers).

Distribution Management

Distribution management refers to distribution of goods and services in the sales system. An effective distribution management helps in making available goods in the right quantity, at the right time when they are required and giving a reasonable earning to those who are associated with the distribution system like wholesalers, retailers and the like.

Basic Concepts of Distribution System

A distribution channel (also known as a marketing channel) is a set of interdependent organizations or intermediaries involved in the process of making a product available for consumption. A channel directs the flow of products from producers to customers.

According to American Marketing Association: "A channel of distribution, or marketing channel, is the structure of intra-company organization units and extra-company agents and dealers, wholesale and retail through which a commodity, product or service is marketed."

According to William J. Stanton: "A channel of distribution for a product is the route taken by the title to the goods as they move from the producer to the ultimate consumers or industrial user."

According to Cundiff, Still and Govani: "Marketing channels are the distribution networks through which producers' products flow to the market."

Intermediaries are organizations operating in the middle or between the producer and the final buyer. They link producers to other intermediaries or to the ultimate users of the product. Traditionally, intermediaries have been referred to as middlemen.

Distribution without the help of intermediaries:

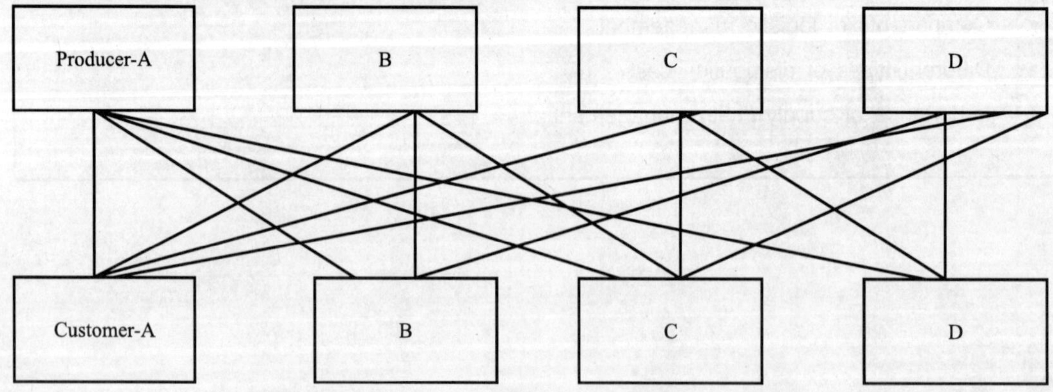

Fig. 4.1. Distribution without the help of intermediaries.

It can be seen from the above diagram, if there is no intermediaries then number of contacts will be more but if there is an intermediary, you can see number of contacts are reduced to very minimum as it can be seen in the following diagram.

Distribution with the help of the intermediaries:

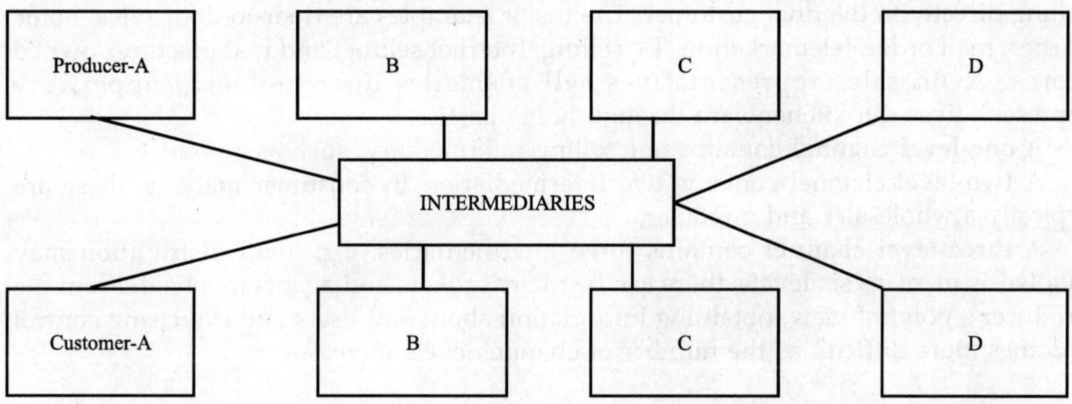

Fig. 4.2. Distribution with the help of the intermediaries.

CONSUMER MARKETING CHANNEL

0-Level
Manufacturer
Consumer

1-level
Manufacturer
Retailer
Consumer

2-level
Manufacturer
Wholesaler
Retailer
Consumer

3-level
Manufacturer
Distributor
Wholesaler
Retailer
Consumer

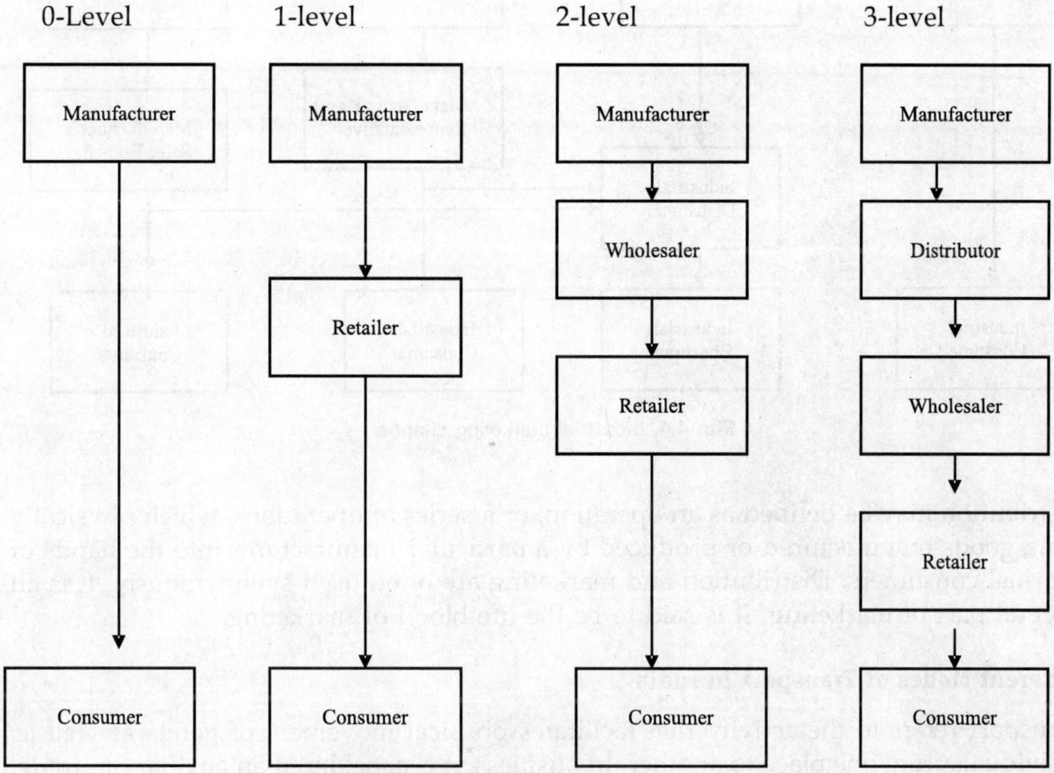

Fig. 4.3. Consumer marketing channel.

The producer and the final customer are part of every channel. We will use the number of intermediary levels to designate the length of a channel. The figure illustrates several consumer goods marketing channels of different lengths.

A **zero-level channel** (also called a *direct-marketing channel)* consists of a manufacturer selling directly to the final customer. The major examples are door-to-door sales, home parties, mail order, telemarketing, TV selling, Internet selling, and manufacturer-owned stores. Avon sales representatives sell cosmetics door-to-door; Tupperware representatives sell kitchenware through home parties.

A **one-level channel** contains one selling intermediary, such as a retailer.

A **two-level** channel contains two intermediaries. In consumer markets, these are typically a wholesaler and a retailer.

A **three-level channel** contains three intermediaries, e.g., food distribution may involve as many as six levels, there can be many brokers and agents involved. From the producer's point of view, obtaining information about end users and exercising control becomes more difficult as the number of channel levels increases.

INDUSTRIAL MARKETING CHANNEL

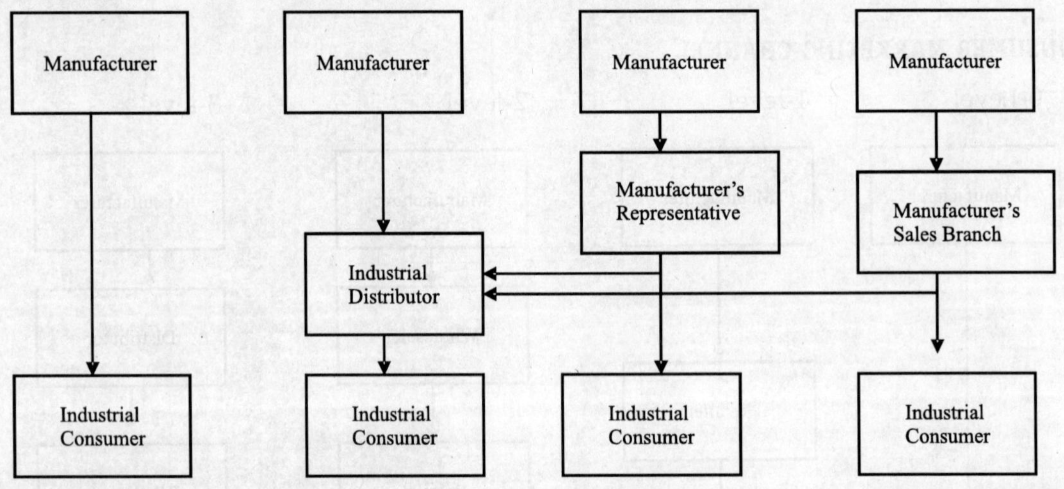

Fig. 4.4. Industrial marketing channel.

Distribution may be defined as an operation, or a series of operations, which physically bring goods manufactured or produced by a particular manufacturer into the hands of the final consumers. Distribution and marketing are often used synonymously. It is an integral part of marketing. It is said to be the life-blood of marketing.

Different Modes of Transport in India

Transport refers to the activity that facilitates physical movement of goods as well as individuals from one place to another. In business, it is considered an auxiliary to trade, that means, it supports trade and industry in carrying raw materials to the place of production and distributing finished products for consumption. Individuals or business firms that engage themselves in such activities are called transporters. Generally, transporters carry raw material, finished products, passengers, etc. from one place to another. So it removes the distance barrier. Nowadays goods produced at one place are readily available at distant places.

People move freely throughout the world because of transport. It is associated with every step of our life. Without transport, we as well as business units cannot move a single step.

Transportation is a barometer of the economic, social and commercial progress of the country. It is the most visible element of the Logistics Management. Transportation is the dynamic part of the supply chain management. A good transportation system is one of the pillars of the growth of trade and economy.

In the olden days modes of transportation were:

- Human beings.
- Camels.
- Horses.
- Bullocks – bullock-carts.
- Ships.
- Elephants to carry wooden logs, etc.

With the passage of time and science and technological development, many innovations happened in the area of transportation system. In modern times, we have wide choice of transportation and these are:

- Rails.
- Water – ships.
- Aircraft.
- Pipelines.
- Ropeways. (rare cases)

Transportation serves two purposes:

1. Material/Product movement from one place to another.
2. In–transit product storage.

The guiding principle for choosing the mode of transportation is: Least cost per unit weight/volume of the product moved over unit distance.

Importance of Transport

- **Makes available raw materials to manufacturers or producers:** Transport makes it possible to carry raw materials from places where they are available, to places where they can be processed and assembled into finished goods.
- **Makes available goods to customers:** Transport makes possible movement of goods from one place to another with great ease and speed. Thus, consumers spread in different parts of the country have the benefit of consuming goods

produced at distant places.

- **Enhances standard of living:** Easy means of transport facilitates large-scale production at low costs. It gives consumers the choice to make use of different quantities of goods at different prices. So it raises the standard of living of the people.
- **Helps during emergencies and natural calamities:** In times of national crisis, due to war or internal disturbance, transport helps in quick movement of troops and the supplies needed in the operation.
- **Helps in creation of employment:** Transport provides employment opportunity to individuals as drivers, conductors, pilots, cabin crew, captain of the ship, etc. who are directly engaged in transport business. It also provides employment to people indirectly in the industries producing various means of transport and other transport equipment.

Factors Influencing Transporting Decision

Transportation plays a prominent role in the distribution of goods. Transportation creates both time and place utilities and also enhances the economic value of the goods. The factors or main considerations about deciding a particular mode of transport are:
(i) Cost (ii) Speed (iii) Handling (iv) Damages (v) Regularity (vi) Flexibility

ROAD TRANSPORTATION

Roads are the means that connect one place to another on the surface of the land. You must have seen roads in your village, in towns and cities. Not all of them look alike. Some of them are made of sand and some may be of chips and cement or coal tar. You find different vehicles plying on roads like bullock-carts, cycles, motorcycles, cars, truck, buses, etc. All of these constitute different means of road transport. The means of road transport may be divided into three types:

- Man driven;
- Animal driven; and
- Motor driven.

You might have seen individuals carrying goods on their head or back or in bicycles moving from one place to other. People also ride a bicycle or use rickshaw to travel short distances. We also find animal-driven vehicles like carts (drawn by bullocks, camels, horses, donkeys, etc.) used in rural areas to carry crops, straw, fodder and sometimes even people. Sometimes even animals are directly used to carry goods from one place to another.

In areas, which are normally covered with snow throughout the year, we find sledges pulled by dogs used to carry both passengers and goods.

Compared with man-driven and animal-driven means of road transport, motor-driven means of transport have become more important over the years. This is due to their speedy movement and larger carrying capacity. Extension of roads to every corner of the country has also enhanced the use of motor-driven transport. The types of motor vehicles used to carry goods and passengers include auto-rickshaws, scooters, vans, buses, tempos and trucks, etc. In Kolkata, tramway also forms part of road transport for carrying passengers.

Advantages of Road Transport

- It is a relatively cheaper mode of transport as compared to other modes.
- Perishable goods can be transported at a faster speed by road carriers over a short distance.
- It is a flexible mode of transport as loading and unloading is possible at any destination. It provides door-to-door service.
- It helps people to travel and carry goods from one place to another, in places which are not connected by other means of transport like hilly areas.

Limitations of Road Transport

It has the following limitations:

- To limited carrying capacity road transport is not economical for long distance transportation of goods.
- Transportation of heavy goods or goods in bulk by road involves high cost.
- It is affected by adverse weather conditions. Floods, rain, landslide, etc., sometimes create obstructions to road transport.

RAILWAYS

This mode of transportation is used to carry material as well as people. It is the cheapest mode of transportation available in our country. 42% of the transportation is occupied by transportation of coal in India. Other contributors are cement, fertilizers, food grains, steel, iron ore, etc.

Transportation of goods and passengers on rail lines through trains is called rail transport. It occupies an important place in land transport system of our country and is the most dependable mode of transport to carry goods and passengers over a long distance. Besides long distance, local transport of passengers is also provided by local trains or metro rail in some metropolitan cities. Rail transport is available throughout the country except some hilly or mountainous regions. In India, two types of trains are found. One is passenger train and other is goods train. While passenger trains carry both human beings and a limited quantity of goods, the goods trains are exclusively used for carrying goods from one place to another. These trains are driven by rail engines and they use team, diesel or electric power to move. Let us now discuss the advantages and limitations of rail transport.

Advantages of Rail Transport

- It is suitable for carrying heavy goods in large quantities over long distances.
- Its operation is less affected by adverse weather conditions like rain, floods, fog, etc.

Limitations of Railway Transport

- It is relatively expensive for carrying goods and passengers over short distances.
- It is not available in remote parts of the country.
- It is a convenient mode of transport for travelling long distances.
- It is relatively faster than road transport.
- It provides service according to fixed time schedule and is not flexible for loading or unloading of goods at any place.
- It involves heavy losses of life as well as goods in case of accident.

WATER TRANSPORT

Water transport refers to movement of goods and passengers on waterways by using various means like boats, steamers, launches, ships, etc. With the help of these means goods and passengers are carried to different places, both within as well as outside the country. Within the country, rivers and canals facilitate the movement of boats, launches, etc. Since the goods and passengers move inside the country, this type of transport is called inland water transport. When the different means of transport are used to carry goods and passengers on the sea route it is termed ocean transport. Let us know further about these two types of water transport.

(i) Inland Water Transport

Inland water transport use boats, launches, barges, steamers, etc. to carry goods and passengers on river and canal routes. These routes are called inland waterways and are used in domestic or home trade to carry bulky goods. Passenger transport through waterways is not so popular in our country. Inland water transport system exists only in few states like West Bengal, Andhra Pradesh, Assam, Tamil Nadu, etc.

(ii) Ocean Transport

Ocean transport refers to movement of goods and passengers with the help of ships through sea or ocean waterways. It plays an important role in the development of international trade. It is also used for transporting goods and passengers in the coastal areas. Ocean transport has its fixed route, which links almost all the countries of the world.

Sea transport may be of the following two types.

Coastal Shipping: In this transport, ships ply between the main ports of a country. This helps in home trade, and also in carrying passengers within the country.

Overseas Shipping: In this transport, ships ply between different countries separated by sea or ocean. It is mainly used for promotion and development of international trade. It is an economical means of transport to carry heavy machines and goods in bulk. Overseas transport is carried out on fixed routes, which connect almost all the countries. In ocean transport, different types of ships are used to carry passengers and goods. These may be classified as under.

Liners: A liner is a passenger or cargo vessel, which belongs to a regular shipping company. These ships ply over a fixed route according to a prescribed schedule or timetable.

Tramps: A tramp is a cargo ship, which does not make regular trips but plies whenever cargo is offered to it. It does not follow a fixed route or a prescribed timetable like that of liners.

Water transport has the following advantages:

- It is a relatively economical mode of transport for bulky and heavy goods.
- It is a safe mode of transport with respect to occurrence of accidents.
- The cost of maintaining and constructing routes is very low as most of them are natural.
- It promotes international trade.

Water transport has the following limitations:

- The depth and navigability of rivers and canals vary and thus, affect operations of different transport vessels.
- It is a slow moving mode of transport and therefore not suitable for transport of perishable goods.
- It is adversely affected by weather conditions.
- Sea transport requires large investment on ships and their maintenance.

AIR

This mode of transportation is costliest of all. It is mainly used for perishable commodities and for the items whose life is short and value is high. Industries use this mode of transportation only in case of **emergency**.

This is the fastest mode of transport. It carries goods and passengers through airways by using different aircraft like passenger aircraft, cargo aircraft, helicopters, etc. Besides passengers it generally carries goods that are less bulky or of high value. In hilly and mountainous areas where other mode of transport is not accessible, air transport is an important as well as convenient mode. It is mostly used for transporting goods and passengers during natural calamities like earthquake and floods, etc. During war, air transport plays an important role in carrying soldiers as well as supplies to the required areas.

Air transport may be classified as domestic and international air transport. While domestic air transport mainly facilitates movement within the country, international air transport is used for carrying goods and passengers between different countries. Air transport is carried out in fixed air routes, which connect almost all the countries.

Advantages of Air Transport

- It is the fastest mode of transport (not an advantage).
- It is very useful in transporting goods and passengers to the area, which are not accessible by any other means.
- It is the most convenient mode of transport during natural calamities.
- It provides vital support to the national security and defence.

Limitations of Air Transport

- It is relatively more expensive mode of transport.
- It is not suitable for transporting heavy and bulky goods.
- It is affected by adverse weather conditions.
- It is not suitable for short distance travel.
- In case of accidents, it results in heavy losses of goods, property and life.

PIPELINES

This mode of transportation was first developed by Mr. Samuel in 1870 to transport petroleum in Pennsylvania. The salient features are:

- Initial investment is very high.
- It works 24 hours.

- It is free of cost once installed (negligible).
- Widely used by corporations for transportation of water, drainage, etc.
- It is eco-friendly.
- At present 27% of the petroleum products are moved through pipelines over a distance of 6350 km.

ROPEWAYS

This is used in hilly areas. In India 16% of the geographical area is covered by hilly regions.

1. They cause least damage to ecology.
2. Inaccessible hilly areas can be reached through the shortest routes.
3. In these zones other modes of transportation are uneconomical.
4. Bulk material can be moved faster over short distances.
5. This is mainly used in Assam, Sikkim, Meghalaya, Mizoram, and Himachal Pradesh.

FREIGHT MANAGEMENT

The selection of mode of transportation depends upon the product characteristics:

- Speed
- Investment
- Freight cost
- Reliability
- Frequency
- Capability

Speed: The speed of the service is important. It is the time elapsed from moving from source to destiny.

- **Reliability:** This means the ability of the carrier to deliver the shipment in good condition, within the stipulated delivery time span to the customer.
- **Frequency**: It is the number of scheduled movements of the carrier between a pair of locations.

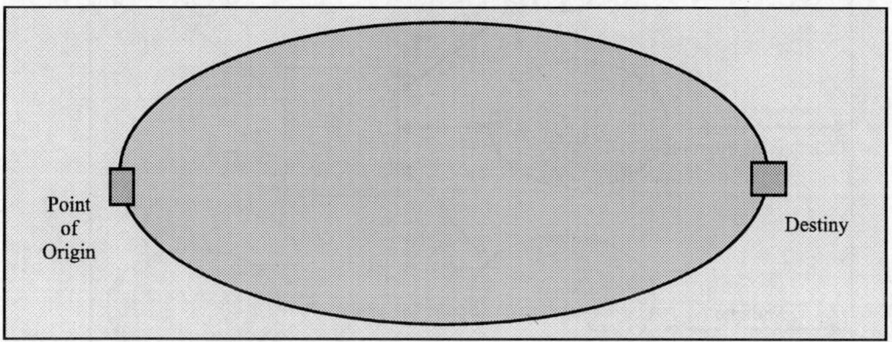

Fig. 4.5. Point-to-point transportation network.

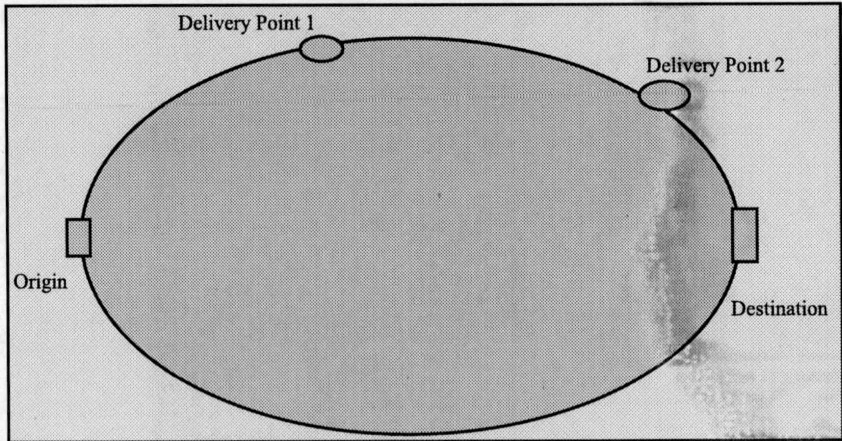

Fig. 4.6. Multiple delivery patterns.

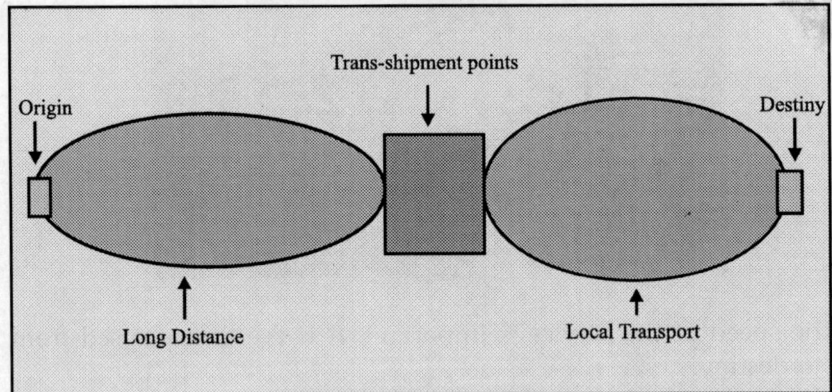

Fig. 4.7. Trans-shipment points.

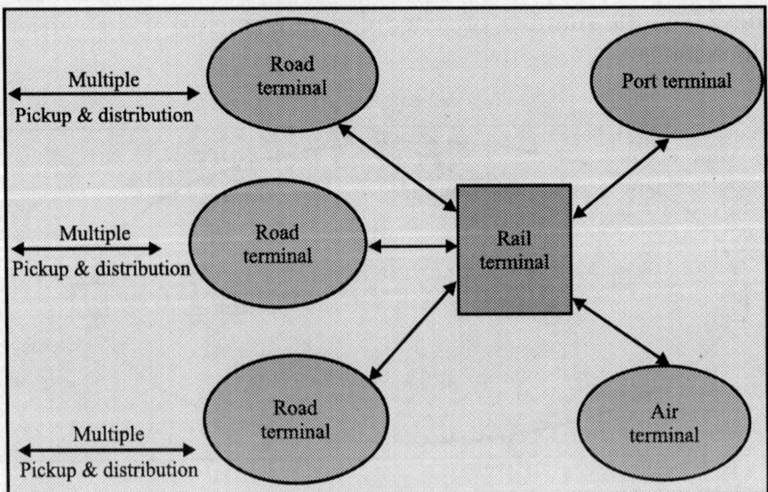

Fig. 4.8. Nodal network.

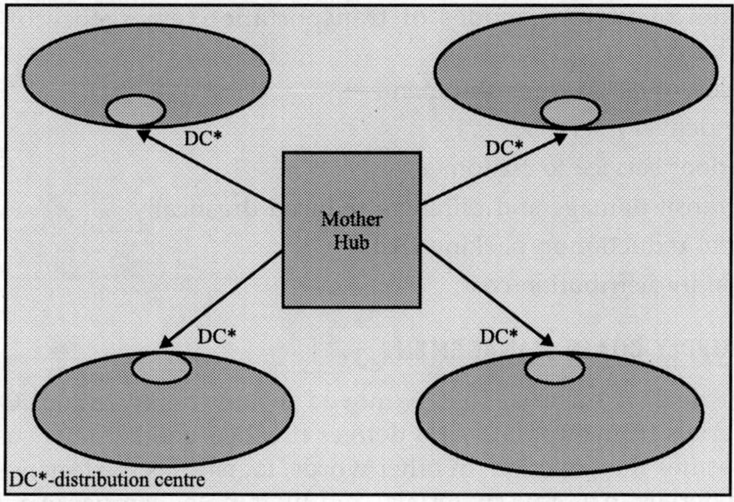

Fig. 4.9. Hub and spoke network.

CONTAINERIZATION

A container can be defined as a transport device to move solid or liquid material. Mr. Malcom McClean introduced the idea in 1956. In shipping business it got introduced in 1960. Now all over the world this concept is accepted and used.

- Integration of various modes of transportation/emergence of inter-modal transportation.
- Elimination of cargo trans-shipment.
- Speedier delivery service.
- Door-to-door service to customer.
- Risk of transit damage and pilferage reduced drastically.
- Substantial reduction in packing cost.
- Reduction in distribution cost.

LOGISTIC AND SUPPLY CHAIN MANAGEMENT

There is a great deal of material that is moved in any organization. Organizations collect raw materials from suppliers and deliver finished goods to the customers. It is logistics that executes this function. In other words, logistics is the function that moves both tangible materials (e.g., raw materials) and intangible material (e.g. information) through the operations to the customers (as a finished product). In continuation to this explanation, we would introduce what a supply chain means. A supply chain consists of a series of activities involving many organizations through which the materials move from initial suppliers to final customers. There may be different supply chains for various products. The chain of activities and organizations is named differently as per the situation. If the emphasis is on operations, then it is called process; if the emphasis is on marketing, then it is called logistics; if the emphasis is on value-addition, then it is called value-chain; if the emphasis is on meeting customer demand, then it is called demand chain; if the emphasis is on movement of material, then we use the most general term, i.e., supply chain. This unit will introduce you with the concept of a supply chain.

A **supply chain** may be considered as a group of organizations, connected by a series of trading relationships. This group covers the logistics and manufacturing activities from raw materials to the final consumer. Each organization in the chain procures and then transforms materials into intermediate/final products, and distributes these to customers.

The supply chain can be defined as the integral management (within the company and through other companies) of the company's various logistical stages such as materials procurement, production, storage, distribution and customer service. The supply chain concept should be seen as a whole, that is, the entire system from the origin of procurement to the final consumption of goods or services.

In supply chain network we must include all the organizations involved in the production of certain goods or services (from the origin of procurement to final consumption), and each of the logistical stages within these organizations. Thus, the supply chain is a network linking and interweaving different supply chains of all the companies involved in a production process. A diagram depicting the typical supply chain is shown below:

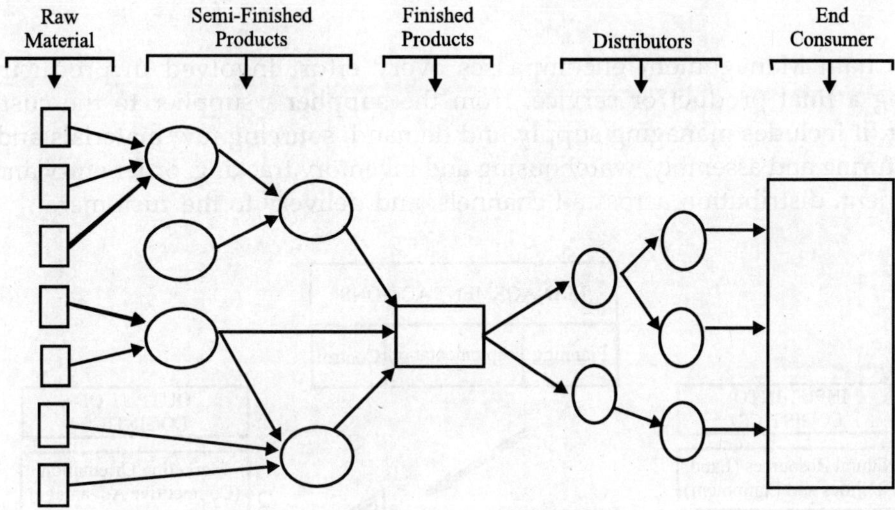

Fig. 4.10. A typical supply chain.

The supply chain activity, therefore, constitutes complex objects, as it involves decision-makers from different companies, who sometimes have no direct relationship and are place in very different geographical locations; yet the decisions they make are mutually dependent upon each other. Hence, there is a need for an information system capable of linking together the different members of the chain so that there is an open communication between them.

The concept of supply chain is not new. Historically we have moved from physical distribution to logistics management and then to supply chain management. The major difference seems to be that supply chain management is the preferred name for the actualization of "integrated logistics", with it acting as an enabler; it is now possible to have an integrated process view about the logistics and all allied processes related to business. Ideally the supply chain should be a "seamless" chain as shown below:

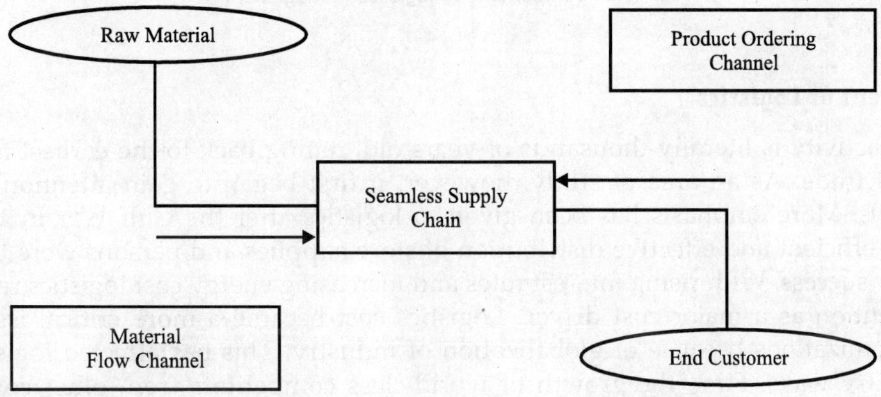

Fig. 4.11. Seamless supply chain.

Concept

Supply Chain Management encompasses every effort involved in producing and delivering a final product or service, from the supplier's supplier to the customer's customer. It includes managing supply and demand, sourcing raw materials and parts, manufacturing and assembly, warehousing and inventory tracking, order entry and order management, distribution across all channels, and delivery to the customer.

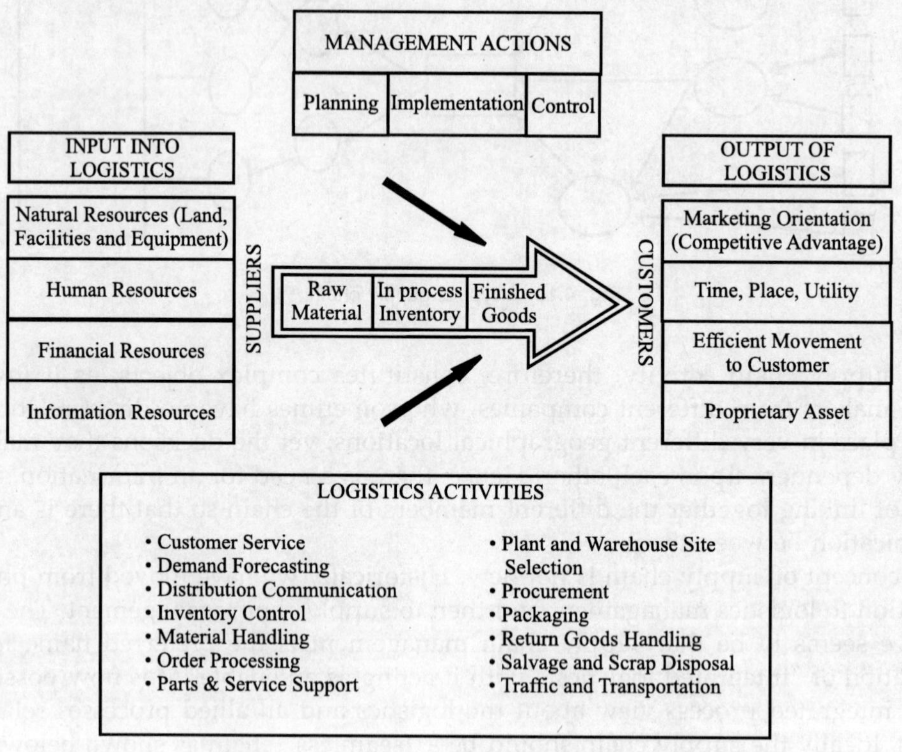

Fig. 4.12. Components of logistics management

Development of Logistics

Logistics activity is literally thousands of years old, dating back to the earliest form of organized trade. As an area of study, however, it first began to gain attention in the early 1990s. More emphasis has been given to logistics after the Gulf War in 1990-91 when the efficient and effective distribution of store supplies and persons were the key factors for success. With rising interest rates and increasing energy cost logistics received more attention as a major cost driver. Logistics cost became a more critical issue for many organizations because of globalization of industry. This has affected logistics in two primary ways. First, the growth of world-class competitors from other countries has caused organization to look for new ways to differentiate their organizations and

Facility Location	Determining location, number and size of facilities needed Allocation demand to facilities
Transportation	Mode and service selection Carrier routing Vehicle scheduling
Inventories	Finished goods stocking policies Record keeping Supply scheduling Short-term sales forecasting
Customer Service	Cooperate with marketing in: determining customer needs and wants for service determining customer response to service
Order Processing and Information Flows	Sales order procedure Information collection storage and manipulation Data analysis
Warehousing and Material Handling	Space determination Stock layout Material handling equipment selection Stock storage and retrieval Equipment replacement policies
Protection Packaging	Design for handling, storage, protection
Product Scheduling	Cooperate with production in: specifying aggregate production quantities sequencing and timing of production

Fig. 4.13. Logistics element.

product offerings. Second, as organizations increasingly buy and sell offshore, the supply chain between the organizations becomes longer, more costly and more complex. Excellent logistics management is needed to fully leverage global opportunities. Information technology input has given a next boom to logistics management. This gave organizations the ability to better monitor transaction intensive activities such as ordering movement and storage of goods and materials.

Combined with the availability of computerized quantitative models, this information increased the ability to manage flows and to optimize inventory levels and movement. Other factors contributing to the growing interest in logistics include advances in information technology, increased emphasis on customer service, growing reorganization of the system approach and total cost concept. The profit leverage from logistics and the realization that logistics can be used as a strategic weapon in competing the marketplace also lead to the growing interest in logistics.

The system approach is a critical concept in logistics. Logistics is in itself a system. It is a network of related activities with the purpose of managing the orderly flow of material and personal within the logistics channel. The system approach simply states that all functions or activities need to be understood in terms of how they effect and are affected by other elements and activities with which they interact. The idea is that if one looks at action in isolation, he or she will not understand the big picture or how such action affects or are affected by other activities. In essence the sum or outcome of a series of activities is greater than its individual parts.

Objectives of Marketing Logistics

The objectives of marketing logistics are:

(i) To improve profitability by reducing operating and administrative costs.

(ii) To improve profitability by carefully assessing the value of company's activities with customers and suppliers.

(iii) To increase revenue growth by providing the level of customer service that keep current customers satisfied while attracting new ones.

(iv) Identify differentiating product and service offerings that will improve customer service as well as revenue operations.

(v) Determining whether or not significant operational improvements are necessary.

The Role of Logistics in Economy

Logistics play a key role in the economy in two significant ways. First, logistics is of the major expenditures for business. Logistics expenditure accounts for around 15-20% of GDP. Thus, by improving the efficiency, logistics make an important contribution to the economy as a whole. Second, logistics support the movement and flow of many economic transactions; it is an important activity in facilitating the sale of virtually all goods and services. To understand this role from a system perspective, consider that if goods do not arrive on time, customer cannot buy them. If goods do not arrive at the proper place or in the proper condition, no sale can be made. Thus, all economic activities throughout the supply chain will suffer.

One of the fundamental ways that logistics add value is by creating utility. From an economic standpoint utility represent the value or usefulness that an item or service has in fulfilling a want or need. There are four types of utilities, namely: form, possession, time and place. Form utility is the process of creating the good or service or putting them in proper form for the customer to use. Possession utility is value added to a product or service because the customer is able to take actual possession like credit arrangement and loans. These two utilities are not directly related to logistics but these are not possible without getting the right item needed for consumption or production to the right place at the right time and in the right condition at the right cost. The time and place utility are directly related to logistics. Time utility is the value added by having an item when it is needed. Place utility is the item or service available where it is needed. The five rights of logistics are the essence of the two utilities provided by logistics time and place utility.

LOGISTICS AND COMPETITIVE PERFORMANCE

Today, logistics department appears on the organization charts of many large organizations. Linking logistics activities directly to organization strategic plan can work effectively to support their organization for achieving competitive advantage. Porter user a tool called the value chain as shown in the below figure to separate buyers, supplier and a firm into the discrete but interrelated activities from which value stems. The value chain concept may be used to identify and understand the specific source of competitive advantage and how they related to buyer value. Value is the amount a customer is willing to pay for the products, services provided by an organization. Value added is the difference between what the customer pays and the cost to the organization in providing that product or service. Porter defines the five categories of primary activity involved in competing in any industry.

Inbound logistics: Activity associated with receiving, storing and disseminating input to the product.

Operation: Activity associated with transforming input into the final product form.

Outbound logistics: Activity associated with collecting, storing and physical distribution of the product to buyers.

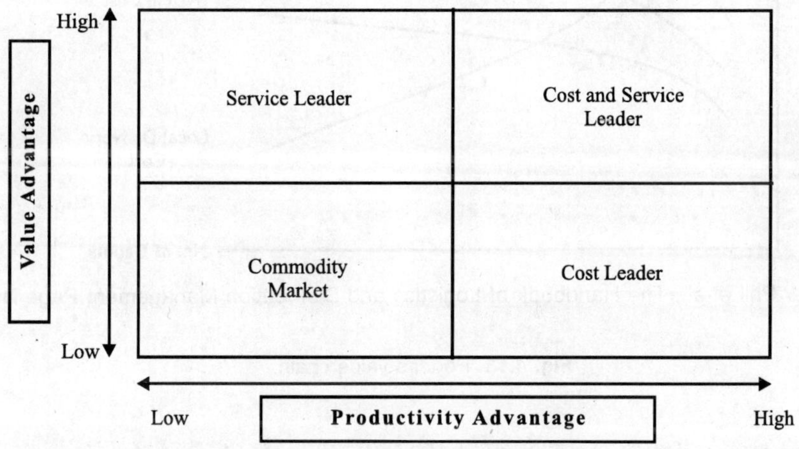

Fig. 4.14. Porter's value chain.

Marketing and Sales: Activities associated with providing a means by which buyers can purchase the product and inducing them to do so such as advertising, promotion, etc.

Service: Activity associated with providing service to enhancer maintains the value of the product such as installation, repair, etc.

The effective logistics management can provide a major source of competitive advantage. The source of competitive advantage is found firstly in the ability of the organization to differentiate itself in the eyes of the customer from its competitor and secondly by operating at a lower cost and hence at greater profit. There are two bases of success in any competitive context. One is the cost advantage and second is the value advantage. Cost advantage is achieved through greater productivity and value advantage is pursued through a different plus over competitive offerings.

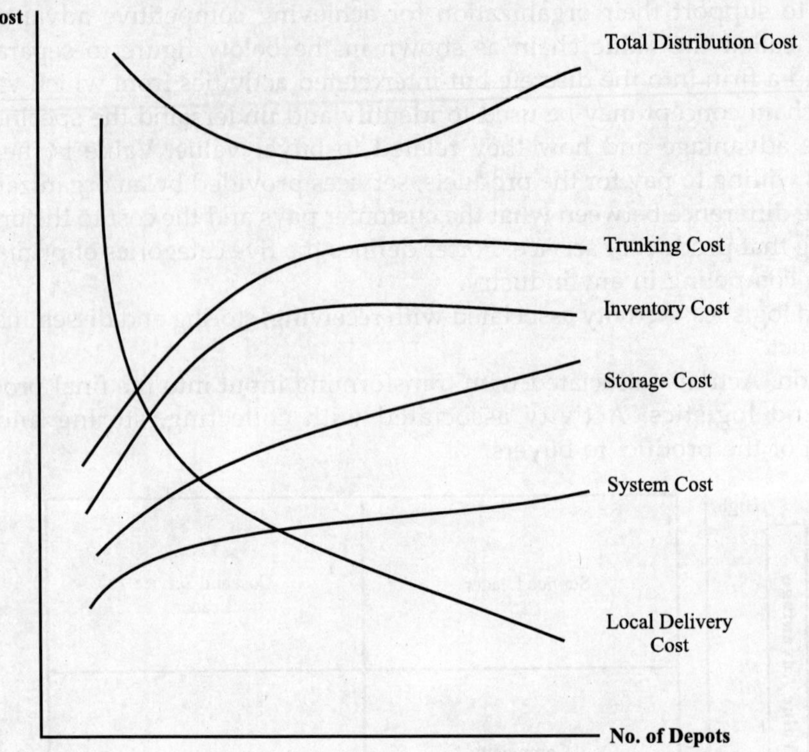

Source: Croucher Phil et al., The Handbook of Logistics and Distribution Management Page No. 123

Fig. 4.15. Porter's value chain.

From the matrix shown in Figure 4.15, it is clear that successful companies will often seek to achieve a position based upon both a productivity advantage and a value advantage. Logistics management can play a critical role to gain both the advantages. In many industries logistics cost represents such a significant proportion of total cost that it is possible to make major cost reduction through fundamentally reengineering logistics process. In terms of value advantage, companies can gain through service differentiation. Today, markets have become more service sensitive. Customers in all industries are seeking greater responsiveness and reliability from suppliers, they are looking for reduced lead time, just-in-time delivery and value-added services that enable them to do better job of serving their customers.

Traditionally, most organizations have viewed themselves as entities that exist independently from others and indeed need to compete with them in order to survive. However, such a philosophy can be self-defeating if it leads to an unwillingness to cooperate in order to compete. Behind this seemingly paradoxical concept is the idea of supply chain integration. Supply chain integration links a firm with its customers, suppliers and other channel members. As such it integrates their relationships, activities, functions, processes and locations. The purpose is to improve the effectiveness and efficiency of SC for ultimate consumers.

PHYSICAL DISTRIBUTION MANAGEMENT

There are many decisions that must be taken, when a company organizes a channel or network of intermediaries, who take responsibility for the management of goods as they move from the producer to the consumer. Each channel member must be carefully selected and the company must decide what type of relationship it seeks with each of its intermediate partners. Having established such a network, the organization must next consider how these goods can be efficiently transferred, in the physical sense, from the place of manufacture to the place of consumption. Physical distribution management (PDM) is concerned with ensuring the product is in the right place at the right time.

It is now recognized that PDM is a critical area of overall supply chain management. Business logistical techniques can be applied to PDM so that costs and customer satisfaction are optimized. There is little point in making large savings in the cost of distribution if in the long run; sales are lost because of customer dissatisfaction.

Similarly, it does not make economic sense to provide a level of service that is not required by the customer but leads to an erosion of profits. This cost/service balance is a basic dilemma that physical distribution managers face. The reason for the growing importance of PDM is the increasingly demanding nature of the business environment. In the past, it was not uncommon for companies to hold large inventories of raw materials and components. Although industries and individual firms differ widely in their stockholding policies, nowadays, stock levels are kept to a minimum wherever possible. Holding stock is wasting working capital for it is not earning money for the company. To think of the logistical process merely in terms of transportation is much too narrow a view. Physical distribution management (PDM) is concerned with the flow of goods from the receipt of an order until the goods are delivered to the customer. In addition to transportation, PDM involves close liaison with production planning, purchasing, order processing, material control and warehousing. All these areas must be managed so that they interact efficiently with each other to provide the level of service that the customer demands and at a cost that the company can afford.

Components of PDM

There are four principal components of PDM, namely: order processing, stock levels or inventory, warehousing and transportation

Order Processing

Order processing is the first of the four stages in the logistical process. The efficiency of order processing has a direct effect on lead times. Orders are received from the sales team through the sales department. Many companies establish regular supply routes that remain relatively stable over a period of time ensuring that the supplier performs satisfactorily. Very often contracts are drawn up and repeat orders (forming part of the initial contract) are made at regular intervals during the contract period. Taken to its logical conclusion this effectively does away with ordering and leads to what is called 'partnership sourcing'. This is an agreement between the buyer and seller to supply a particular product or commodity as and when required without the necessity of negotiating a new contract every time an order is placed.

Order-processing systems should function quickly and accurately. Other departments in the company need to know as quickly as possible that an order has been placed and the customer must have rapid confirmation of the order's receipt and the precise delivery time. Even before products are manufactured and sold, the level of office efficiency is a major contributor to a company's image. Incorrect 'paperwork' and slow reactions by the sales office are often the unrecognized source of ill will between buyers and sellers. When buyers review their suppliers, efficiency of order processing is an important factor in their evaluation. A good computer system for order processing allows stock levels and delivery schedules to be automatically updated so management can rapidly obtain an accurate view of the sales position. Accuracy is an important objective of order processing, as are procedures that are designed to shorten the order processing cycle.

Inventory

Inventory, or stock management, is a critical area of PDM because stock levels have a direct effect on levels of service and customer satisfaction. The optimum stock level is a function of the type of market in which the company operates. Few companies can say that they never run out of stock, but if stock-outs happen regularly then the market share will be lost to more efficient competitors. The key lies in ascertaining the re-order point. Carrying stock at levels below the re-order point might ultimately mean a stock-out, whereas too high stock levels are unnecessary and expensive to maintain. Stocks represent opportunity costs that occur because of constant competition for the company's limited resources. If the company's marketing strategy requires that high stock levels be maintained, this should be justified by a profit contribution that will exceed the extra stock carrying costs.

Warehousing

Many companies function adequately with their own onsite warehouses from where goods are dispatched direct to customers. When a firm markets goods that are ordered regularly, but in small quantities, it becomes more logical to locate warehouses strategically around the country. Transportation can be carried out in bulk from the place of manufacture to respective warehouses where stocks are ready for further distribution to the customers. This system is used by large retail chains, except that the warehouses and transportation are owned and operated for them by logistics experts. Levels of service will of course increase when number of warehouse locations increases, but cost will increase accordingly. Again, an optimum strategy must be established that reflects the desired level of service.

Transportation

Transportation usually represents the bulk of distribution cost. It is usually easy to calculate because it can be related directly to the weight or numbers of units. Costs must be carefully controlled through the mode of transport selected amongst alternatives, and these must be constantly reviewed.

The patterns of retailing that have developed, and the pressure caused by low stock holding and short lead times, have made road transport indispensable. When the volume of goods being transported reaches a certain level some companies purchase their own vehicles, rather than using the services of haulage contractors. However, some large retail chains have now entrusted all their warehousing and transport to specialist logistics companies.

For some types of goods, transport by rail still has advantages. When lead-time is a less critical element of marketing effort, or when lowering transport costs is a major objective, this mode of transport becomes viable. Similarly, when goods are hazardous or bulky in relation to value, and produced in large volumes, then rail transport is advantageous. Rail transport is also suitable for light goods that require speedy delivery (e.g., letter and parcel post). Except where goods are highly perishable or valuable in relation to their weight, air transport is not usually an attractive transport alternative. For long-distance overseas routes air transport is popular. Here, it has the advantage of quick delivery compared to sea transport, and without the cost of bulky and expensive packaging needed for sea transportation, as well as higher insurance costs.

The chosen transportation mode should adequately protect goods from damage in transit (a factor just mentioned makes air freight popular over longer routes as less packaging is needed than for long sea voyages). Not only do damaged goods erode profits, but frequent claims increase insurance premiums and inconvenience to customers, endangering future business.

THE SYSTEMS OR 'TOTAL' APPROACH TO PDM

PDM has been neglected in the past; this function has been late in adopting an integrated approach towards its activities. Managers have now become more conscious of the potential of PDM, and recognize that logistical systems should be designed with the total function in mind. A fragmented or disjointed approach to PDM is the principal cause of failure to provide satisfactory service, and causes excessive costs.

PDM is concerned with ensuring that the individual efforts that go to make up the distributive function are optimized so that a common objective is realized. This is called the 'systems approach' to distribution management and a major feature of PDM is that these functions should be integrated.

To plan an efficient logistics structure it is necessary to be aware of the interaction between the different distribution costs and how they vary with respect to the different depot alternatives (number, size, type and location).

DISTRIBUTION AND LOGISTICS COST

Storage Cost: Storage cost will increase as the number of depots will increase because there will be a need for more stock coverage, more storage space, more management, etc.

Delivery Cost: This will concern with the secondary transportation cost, i.e., cost of delivery from the depot to the consumer. The greater the number of depots, the lesser is the secondary mileage and the delivery cost.

Trunking Cost: This is the primary transport cost in the supply of products in bulk to the depots from the central finished good warehouses or production points. As the number of depots increases, this cost will also increase.

Inventory Cost: The main elements of inventory holding costs are:

Capital Cost: The cost of physical stock. This is the financing charge, which is the current cost of capital to a company.

- Service Cost: That is stock management and insurance cost.
- Risk Cost: It occurs through pilferage, deterioration of stock, damage and stock obsolescence.
- System Cost: These costs represent a variety of information or communication requirements ranging from the order processing to load assembly lists.

CHANNEL INFORMATION SYSTEMS

Information technology has made a big difference to channel operations and management. Information systems have revolutionized the way information is collected, stored and transmitted between channel members. They add value to the distribution function and enable channel members to integrate different channel functions, which was not possible in conventional distribution systems.

Channel information systems have also influenced the structure of distribution channels. Lengthy channels have given way to shorter and highly efficient distribution systems. Channel information systems comprise an information database and the hardware and networks that help in the collection, processing and transmission of information. The hardware, software and networks vary depending on the application requirements of channel members. They vary for business-to-business applications, retailing applications, business to consumer applications and interactive applications for consumers. Transaction-Based Information System (TBIS), Continuous Replenishment Program (CRP), Efficient Consumer Response System (ECR), Point-of-Sale Systems (POS), Quick Response System (QR), Electronic Data Interchange (EDI), etc., are some commonly used information systems. Many companies have developed information systems to suit their needs.

McKesson's ECONOMOST system, United Airlines and American Airlines' Apollo and Sabre systems, Analytic Systems Automatic Purchasing (ASAP) by Baxter Healthcare, Johnson & Johnson's Cooperative Action Plus (COACT) and Abbott's Quick Link information systems are some successful information systems. Precision Code, Data

Designs, Archer's Retail Database Management System (ARDMS) and Product Information Management System by IBM are examples of database systems developed by companies.

Channel Information Systems (CIS) have influenced the way in which different channel functions are performed. It has streamlined operations leading to improved channel flow. CIS has also changed the order in which different functions are performed. CIS has influenced the physical distribution of products or distribution flow. Transaction flow, promotion flow, inventory flow and negotiation flow have improved with the advent of information technology in channel management.

Information systems have a profound impact on channel member relationships. They influence the balance of power, intensity of conflict and the extent of cooperation and coordination among channel members. CIS has changed the dynamics of power among channel members. EDI systems have reduced asset specificity, complexity of product specifications and coordination costs. This has led to a shift in the balance of power among channel members. Many retailers like Wal-Mart have developed efficient information systems that offer them substantial leverage over their suppliers.

Even manufacturers like Philip Morris have conducted extensive programmes to build an exhaustive database about consumer preferences, which allowed them to influence downstream channel members. CIS reduce conflicts that may arise between supplier and retailer due to differences in different channel functions. Some common issues that give rise to conflicts are minimum order size, retail assortment, speed of delivery, retail inventory levels, retail promotion and performance management and the issue of retailers carrying competitors' products. However, the use of channel information systems minimizes the chances of conflicts.

Coordination and cooperation among channel members have greatly improved due to CIS. Channel members have opted for collective goals over individual goals and have started looking for benefits to the channel as a whole. Information is easily available to all channel members, resulting in an increase in trust and commitment. Channels differ based on the type of channel members involved in cooperation and the extent to which members cooperate. Different channel systems include consensus systems, vertical systems, horizontal systems and inter-type systems. Channel cooperation and coordination have led to successful and profitable relationships at different levels in the channel – between manufacturers and suppliers, suppliers and retailers and between manufacturers and retailers.

The basic ideas that one should acquire

- Elements of Channel Information Systems
- Hardware and Networks in an Information System
- Databases for Channel Information Systems
- Impact of Information Systems on Channel Flow
- Transaction flow
- Inventory flow
- Distribution flow
- Promotional flow
- Negotiation flow

- Impact of Information Systems on Channel Relationships
- Power
- Conflict
- Cooperation and Coordination.

Let Us Sum Up

Distribution may be defined as an operation, or a series of operations, which physically bring goods manufactured or produced by a particular manufacturer into the hands of the final consumers. Distribution and marketing may be used synonymously. It is an integral part of marketing. It is said to be the life-blood of marketing.

A distribution channel (also known as a marketing channel) is a set of interdependent organizations or intermediaries involved in the process of making a product available for consumption. A channel directs the flow of products from producers to customers. Transportation is a barometer of the economic, social and commercial progress of the country.

It is the most visible element of the Logistics Management. Transportation is the dynamic part of the supply chain management. A good transportation system is one of the pillars of the growth of trade and economy.

In the olden days modes of transportation were:
- *Human beings.*
- *Camels.*
- *Horses.*
- *Bullocks – bullock-carts.*
- *Ships.*
- *Elephants to carry wooden logs, etc.*

With the passage of time and science and technological development many innovations happened in the area of transportation system. In modern times we have wide choice of transportation and these are:
- *Rails.*
- *Water – ships.*
- *Aircraft.*
- *Pipelines.*
- *Ropeways (Rare cases).*

A supply chain may be considered as a group of organizations, connected by a series of trading relationships. This group covers the logistics and manufacturing activities from raw materials to the final consumer. Each organization in the chain procures and then transforms materials into intermediate/final products, and distributes these to customers.

Logistics play a key role in the economy in two significant ways. First, logistics is of the major expenditures for business. Logistics expenditure accounts for around 15-20% of GDP. Thus, by improving the efficiency, logistics make an important contribution to the economy as a whole. Second, logistics support the movement and flow of many economic transactions; it is an important activity in facilitating the sale of virtually all goods and services. To understand this role from a system perspective, consider that if goods do not arrive on time, customer cannot buy them. If goods do not arrive at the proper place or in the proper condition, no sale can be made. Thus, all economic activities throughout the supply chain will suffer.

Questions for Discussion

1. What do you understand by distribution system? Define distribution channel.
2. Explain the importance of distribution channel.
3. Write short notes on (i) Road transport (ii) Rail transport (iii) Air (iv) Sea (v) Pipelines (vi) Ropeways (vii) Freight management.
4. Explain the importance of logistic and supply chain management.
5. Define logistic. Explain the various functions of logistic.
6. What is PDM? Explain its importance.
7. Explain the components of PDM briefly.
8. Write briefly on distribution cost.
9. Explain different types of transportation which are mostly used for distribution of new products in the market.
10. Explain the factors influencing the transporting and warehousing decisions.
11. How developing an effective logistics help an organization and management? Explain.
12. Explain the various functional areas of logistics.

5

CHAPTER

Managing Marketing Intermediaries

"You know, basically in a commodity business, low cost wins, and this is by far the best company in terms of supply chain management, marketing programmes; [it] understands how to get that low cost to the consumer and to the corporate customer through a variety of areas and now they're looking at getting into the printer market."

—Tobias Levkovich

Role and functions of marketing intermediaries – selection of marketing channel – motivation of marketing intermediaries – distribution analysis – channel management and control – CRM.

LEARNING OBJECTIVES

After going through this chapter, students will be able to understand

- Different types of intermediaries and their roles
- Selection of a particular marketing channel
- Analyzing of distribution channel
- Reasons for channel conflict
- Managing channel conflict
- Customer Relationship Management and its importance.

INTRODUCTION

Intermediaries create suspicions in distribution as it adds extra cost to the final products. In the older days there were no problems as it was barter system. And as long as it is seller's market or having monopoly, then there is no problem because consumers have to come and purchase. It is experienced especially in war-time situation. And earlier in some countries limited the exposure of certain items in certain quantity to the people. So, here also no problems. It became a purely matter of rationing. But in the perfect competitive market where every company wants to reach the every part of the world, it is imperative to have a strong distribution channel.

WHOLESALER

Sometimes said it adds extra price to the product. A wholesaler assists the manufacturer in formulating his policy of manufacture according to the demand. It helps manufacturer in securing the market for his goods. Small retailers cannot afford goods in large quantity. The wholesaler extends credits to the retailers. It is the wholesaler who makes it possible for the retailer to offer to the consumer a large variety of lines on a limited stock basis, which requires a small capital investment by the retailer.

The wholesaler has to assess the public demand and see that marketable goods are manufactured thus protecting the manufacturer from wasteful and indiscriminate production as well as the consumer against goods which are neither satisfactory nor of good value.

INTERMEDIARIES

There are two types of wholesale intermediaries:

- Merchant intermediaries
  - Buy products and resells them.
- Functional intermediaries
  - Do not take title; they expedite exchanges among producers and resellers, compensated by fees and/or commission.

MERCHANT WHOLESALERS

They take title of the product.

- *Full Service Wholesalers* offer widest possible range of functions. Categorized as:
  - General Merchandise: wide mix (unrelated), limited depth.
  - Limited Line: only few products but an extensive assortment.
  - Speciality Line: narrowest range of products.
  - Rack Jobbers: are speciality lines that own and maintain display racks, take back unsold products.
- *Limited Service Merchant Wholesalers* only provide some marketing functions.
- *Cash and carry wholesaler:* Customers pay and furnish their own transportation, no credit.

- *Truck wholesalers:* Operate rolling warehouses and sell a limited line of products directly from their trucks to their customers. Follow regular routes, primarily perishable products.
- *Drop shippers* (desk jobbers): Take title, negotiate sales but do not take possession.
- *Mail-order wholesalers:* Use catalogues instead of sales force to sell.

SOLE DISTRIBUTORSHIP

A manufacturer often appoints certain wholesaler or large retailer as sole distributors or agents for his goods in particular territories. The manufacturer thus encourages the wholesaler or retailer concerned to push the goods of his manufacturer by allowing such a monopoly for a sufficiently lengthy period.

Advantages

- Manufacturer has to watch over a smaller number of accounts.
- Large retailers prefer this method as it reduces competition.
- The manufacturers enjoy the influence and reputation of sole distributor.
- The sole distributor is often willing to advertise at his own expense meaning free advertising for the manufacturer.

Disadvantages

- It limits the outlets for sales, thereby possibly limiting the sales volume of the manufacturer in that locality.

FRANCHISING

It is a system of distribution under a licensing system through which the owner of a product, method or service approaches independent businessmen in selected territories, appoints them as sole franchisee for particular areas and encourages them to make profit for themselves whilst make profit for themselves, the owner retains control over the technique or service is merchandised. Example: Coca-Cola, Pepsi, and McDonalds Pizza.

Advantages

- The speed at which widespread distribution can be achieved.
- The offer of immediate access to professional knowledge.
- The sharing of risks with the franchises.

RETAIL OUTLETS

These are the shops from which the consumers ultimately buy except where the manufacturer sells directly to the consumers. These may be small or giant organizations like the departmental stores and the chain stores organization.

DEPARTMENT STORES

A departmental store is a retrial store handling many different lines of merchandise. The main object of such a store is to make it a centre of attraction. The departmental store is like a large shop with a number of smaller shops within its fold. A visit to such a shop can result in the consumer making a large number of purchases.

The main idea of this type of organization is to have a central shop and attract as many customers as possible to that one location.

CHAIN STORES OR MULTIPLE SHOPS

Here a number of shops are opened in different localities and an attempt is made to approach as near the customer as possible. Many of the multiple shops had their origin in small retailers opening further shops with their success.

SUPERMARKETS

In certain advanced countries, supermarkets have become very popular. The shop is arranged so that the customer walks from one place to another and picks up the articles, which he wants and finally pays at the checkout counters.

Purpose/Objective of Distribution Channel

(i) To ensure availability of products at the point of sale.
(ii) To build channel members' loyalty.
(iii) To stimulate channel members to put greater selling efforts.
(iv) To develop managerial efficiency in channel organization.
(v) To identify your organization at the buyer level.
(vi) To have an efficient and effective distribution system, to make your products and services available.

Characteristics of Channels of Distribution

(i) Route or pathway: Channel of distribution is a route or pathway through which goods and services flow from the manufacturers to consumers.
(ii) Flow: The flow of goods and services is smooth and sequential and usually unidirectional.
(iii) Composition: It is composed of intermediaries such as wholesalers, retailers, agents, distributors, etc. also called middlemen who participate in the flow voluntarily.
(iv) Functions: The intermediaries perform such functions which facilitate transfer of ownership, title and possession of goods and services from manufacturers to consumers.
(v) Remuneration: The intermediaries are paid in the form of commission for the services rendered by them. The same is compensated by the manufacturer in the form of commission allowed by the manufacturer or added in the price of the goods sold.
(vi) Time Utility: As they bring goods to the consumers when needed.
(vii) Convenience value: As they bring goods to the consumers in convenient shape, unit, size, style and package.
(viii) Possession value: As they make it possible for the consumers to obtain goods with ownership title.
(ix) Marketing tools: As they serve as vehicles for viewing the marketing organization in its external aspects and for bridging the physical and non-physical gaps which exist in moving goods from the producers to the consumers; and
(x) Supply-demand linkage: As they bridge the gap between the producers and consumers by resolving spatial and temporal discrepancies in supply and demand.

Channel Functions and Flows

A marketing channel performs the work of moving goods from producers to consumers. It overcomes the time, place, and possession gaps that separate goods and services from those who need or want them. Members of the marketing channel perform a number of key functions as mentioned below:

Information: The collection and dissemination of marketing research information about potential and current customers, competitors, and other actors and forces in the marketing environment.

Promotion: The development and dissemination of persuasive communications signed to attract customers to the offer.

Negotiation: The attempt to reach final agreement on price and other terms so that transfer of ownership or possession can he affected.

Ordering: Marketing-channel members' communication of intentions to buy to the manufacturer.

Financing: The acquisition and allocation of funds required to finance inventories at different levels of the marketing channel.

Risk taking: The assumption of risks connected with carrying out the channel work.

Physical possession: The successive storage and movement of physical products.

Payment: Buyers' payment of their bills to the sellers through banks and other financial institutions.

Title: The actual transfer of ownership from one organization or person to another.

Motivating Channel Members

Intermediaries must be continuously motivated to do their job. The terms that lead them to join the channel provide some motivation, but these must be supplemented by training, supervision, and encouragement. The producer must not only sell through the intermediaries but also to them.

For example, dealer incentive programmes can serve as a powerful motivator. When microbrewer Brewski Brewing Company launched its business, it offered attractive incentives to the large and small distributors who had signed on to sell its products. Once the distributors began selling Brewski, they were rewarded with leather jackets valued at $300 for reaching distribution goals in a series of short-term incentive programmes. In addition, the distributors are empowered to offer their top customers a solid wood, hand-carved, hand-painted tap handle that features the Brewski logo.

Producers vary greatly in how they manage their distributors. They can draw on the following types of power to elicit cooperation.

- **Coercive power** is wielded by a manufacturer that threatens to withdraw a resource or terminate a relationship if intermediaries fail to cooperate. This power is quite effective if the intermediaries are highly dependent upon the manufacturer. But the exercise of coercive power produces resentment and can lead the intermediaries to organize countervailing power.
- **Reward power** occurs when the manufacturer offers intermediaries an extra benefit for performing specific acts or functions. Reward power typically produces better results than coercive power but can be overrated. The intermediaries are conforming to the manufacturer's wishes not out of conviction but because of an external benefit. They may come to expect a reward every time the manufacturer wants a certain behaviour to occur. If the reward is later withdrawn, the intermediaries feel resentment.
- **Legitimate power** is wielded when the manufacturer requests a behaviour that is warranted by the contract. Thus, General Motors may insist that its dealers carry certain inventory levels as part of the franchise agreement. The manufacturer feels it has this right and the intermediaries have this obligation. As long as the

intermediaries view the manufacturer as a legitimate leader, legitimate power works.

- **Expert power** can be applied when the manufacturer has special knowledge that the intermediaries value. For example, a manufacturer may have a sophisticated system for sales-lead generation or for distributor sales training. This is an effective form of power, if intermediaries would perform poorly without this help. Once the expertise is passed on to the intermediaries, however, this basis of power weakens. The manufacturer must continue to develop new expertise so that the intermediaries will want to continue cooperating.
- **Referent power** occurs when the manufacturer is so highly respected that intermediaries are proud to be identified with it. Companies such as IBM, Caterpillar, McDonald's and Hewlett Packard have high referent power. To the extent possible, manufacturers will gain cooperation best if they would resort to referent power, expert power, legitimate power and reward power in that order and generally avoid using coercive power.

Intermediaries can aim for a relationship based on cooperation, partnership, or distribution programming. Most producers see the main challenge as that of gaining intermediaries' *cooperation.* To do so, they often use positive motivators, such as higher margins, special deals, premiums, cooperative advertising allowances, display allowances, and sales contests. At times they will apply negative sanctions, such as threatening to reduce margins, slow down delivery, or terminate the relationship. The weakness of this approach is that the producer applies miscellaneous motivators based on crude stimulus-response thinking. McCammon notes that many manufacturer programmes "consist of hastily improvised trade deals, uninspired dealer contests, and unexamined discount structures."

More sophisticated companies try to forge a long-term partnership with their distributors. The manufacturer develops a clear sense of what it wants from its distributors in the way of market coverage, inventory levels, marketing development, account solicitation, technical advice and services, and marketing information. The manufacturer seeks distributor agreement with these policies and may introduce a functional compensation plan for adhering to the policies. For example, a dental supply company, instead of paying a straight 35% sales commission to its distributors, pays 20% for carrying out its basic sales work, another 5% for carrying a 60-day inventory, another 5% for paying its bills on time, and another 5% for reporting customer purchase information.

The most advanced supply/distributor arrangement is distribution programming, which McCammon defines as building a planned, professionally managed, vertical marketing system that incorporates the needs of both the manufacturer and the distributors. The manufacturer establishes a department within the company called distributor-relations planning, and its job is to identify the distributors' needs and build up merchandising programmes to help each distributor operate as efficiently as possible. This department and the distributors jointly plan the merchandising goals, inventory levels, space and visual merchandising plans, sales-training requirements, and advertising and promotion plans. The aim is to convert the distributors from thinking that they make their money primarily on the buying side (through tough negotiation with the manufacturer) to seeing that they make their money on the selling side (by being part of a sophisticated vertical marketing system).

Too many manufacturers think of their distributors and dealers as their customers rather than their working partners.

Up to now, we have treated manufacturers and distributors as separate organizations. But many manufacturers are distributors of related products made by other manufacturers. Furthermore, some industrial distributors, such as Granger, also own or contract for the manufacturing of in-house brands. Such industrial firms therefore must master both the manufacturing and distribution functions.

Channel Selection

(a) Market Consideration

- The nature of the market is regarded as one of the important factors. Under this factor are considered whether the product is meant for the consumer or industrial buyers. If it is for consumer market, retailers will have to be employed. If it is for both markets, more than one channel will have to be employed.
- If the number of potential customers are large, a number of middlemen's services will be needed. And if it is small, company's sales forces may only be used.
- If customers are concentrated in a few areas, direct selling may be done effectively. Otherwise, a large number of middlemen will have to be used if the customers are widely spread over the entire country.
- If the sales volume is large, direct selling may be economically feasible.

(b) Product Consideration

Unit sales value of a product does influence the amount of finance available for distribution. If the product is of high value, more funds may be derived from the units sold and therefore, shorter and more costly channels may be used. If the product is of low value, larger and cheap channels will be used, e.g., industrial installation type products are sold direct, while small accessory equipment are sold through agents.

- If the product is of a perishable nature, shorter channels will be preferred, while in non-perishable products; wide choice of channels may be made.
- Technical and complex product need shorter channel.

(c) Company Consideration

- Financially sound companies can utilize the services of its sales force and branches in a much better way. They can grant credit for a long period or warehouse their products, whereas weak concerns are obliged to get these services by using middleman.
- Desire for control of channel may lead the producer to establish a short and direct channel even though it may be more costly.
- Experience and competence of management also play a major role.

(d) Consumer Consideration

Consumer consideration with regard to time, form, place utilities play a significant role in choice of distribution channel.

Channel Dynamics

Vertical marketing system (VMS)

Comprise the producer, wholesaler and retailer acting as a unified system. The VMS can be dominated by the producer, the wholesaler or the retailer. One channel member owns the others or franchises them or has so much power that they all cooperate.

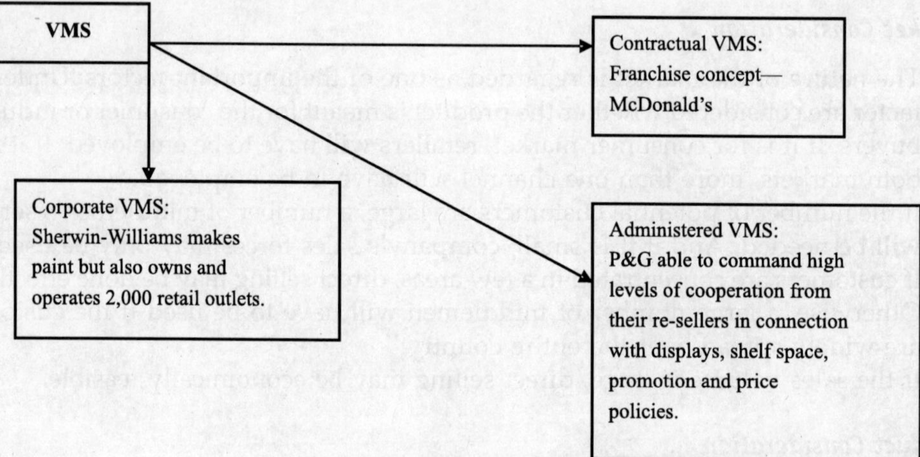

Fig. 5.1. Different types of VMS.

Corporate VMS

More than one stage of the distribution channels under one ownership, IE supermarket chains that own processing plants and large retailers that purchase wholesaling and production facilities.

Examples:

- Sears
- Sherwin Williams
- Giant Foods
- Gallo
- Banana Republic
- Hallmark
- The Gap
- Oil Companies

Administered VMS

Channel members are independent with a high level of inter-organizational management by informal coordination. Agree to adopt uniform accounting policies, etc., and promotional activities. One channel member dominates has a *channel leader*.

Examples:

- Wal-Mart
- Toys R Us
- Kellog
- Pepsi
- Coke
- GE
- P&G
- McKesson Corp
- JC Penney
- Campbell

Channel Leader: Effectiveness of channel hinges on channel leadership. Leader must possess channel power. Power can come in the following forms:

- Reward—provide financial benefits
- Expert—be the expert compared with other members
- Referent—strongly identify with leader
- Coercive—punish members

Contractual VMS

Most popular VMS, inter-organizational relationships formalized through contracts that spell out each member's rights and obligations. McDonald's and KFC.

Wholesaler sponsored, IGA stores-independent retailer's band together under contractual leadership of a wholesaler.

Super value stores, largest food wholesaler in the US, offers a broad package of services to 2800 independent food retailers that voluntarily enter into a buying contract. Retailer sponsored cooperatives, which set up, own and operate their own wholesalers.

Hortizontal marketing system (HMS)

Here, two or more unrelated companies put together resources or programs to exploit an emerging marketing opportunity. Each company lacks the capital, know-how, production or marketing resources to venture alone, or it is afraid of the risk. The companies might work with each other on a temporary or permanent basis or create a separate company.

Multichannel Marketing System

In the past, many companies sold to a single market through a single channel. Today, with the proliferation of customer segments and channel possibilities, more companies have adopted multichannel marketing. Multichannel marketing occurs when a single firm uses two or more marketing channels to reach one or more customer segments.

Causes of Channel Conflict

- **Goal incompatibility:** For example, the manufacturer may want to achieve rapid market growth through a low-price policy. The dealers, in contrast, may prefer to work with high margins and pursue short-run profitability. This is a difficult conflict to resolve.
- **Unclear roles and rights:** IBM sells personal computers to large accounts through its own sales force, and its licensed dealers are also trying to sell to large accounts. Territory boundaries, credit for sales, and so forth are grounds for conflict.
- **Differences in perception:** The manufacturer may be optimistic about the short-term economic outlook and want dealers to carry higher inventory. But the dealers may be pessimistic about the short-term outlook.
- **Great dependence:** The conflict may arise because of the intermediaries' great dependence on the manufacturer. The fortunes of exclusive dealers, such as auto dealers, are initially affected by the manufacturer's product design and pricing decisions. This situation creates a high potential for conflict.

Managing Channel Conflict

- The most important mechanism is the adoption of superordinate goals. The channel members somehow come to an agreement on the fundamental goal they are jointly seeking, whether it is survival, market share, high quality, or customer satisfaction. They, usually do this when the channel faces an outside threat, such as a more efficient competing channel, an adverse piece of legislation, or a shift in consumer desires. Working closely together might help them eliminate or neutralize the threat. There is also chance that the intense cooperation might teach the parties a permanent lesson on the value of working toward the same end.
- A useful conflict management device is the exchange of persons between two or more channel levels. For example, General Motor's executives might agree to work in some dealerships, and some dealership owners might work at General Motors in GM's dealer policy department. Presumably, the participants will grow to appreciate the other's point of view and carry more understanding when retuning to their original position.
- Cooptation is an effort by one organization to win the support of the leaders of another organization by including them in advisory councils, boards of directors and the like. As long as the initiating organization treats the leaders of the other organization seriously and listens to their opinions, cooptation can reduce conflict. But the initiating organization also pays a price in that it may have to compromise its policies and plans in order to win the support of the other side.
- Much can be accomplished by encouraging joint membership in and between trade associations.

- When conflict is chronic or acute, the parties may have to resort to diplomacy, mediation or arbitration diplomacy takes place when each side sends a person or group to other side to resolve the conflict to work more or less continuously with each other to avoid the flaring up of conflicts.

CHANNEL DESIGN

In designing marketing channels, manufacturers have to decide what is ideal, what is feasible, and what is available. A new firm typically starts as a local operation selling in a limited market. Since it has limited capital, it usually uses existing intermediaries. The number of intermediaries in any local market is apt to be limited: a few wholesalers, several established retailers, a few trucking companies and a few warehouses. Deciding on the best channels might not be a problem. The problem might be convincing one or a few available intermediaries to handle the manufacturer's line.

If the new firm is successful, it might branch out to a new market. Again, the manufacturer will tend to work through the available intermediaries, although doing so might mean using different types of marketing channels in different areas. In the smaller markets, the firm might sell directly to retailers; in the larger markets, it might sell through distributors. In rural areas, it might work with general goods merchants; in urban areas, with limited line merchant.

In one part of the country, it might grant franchisees because the merchants normally work this way in another, it might sell through all outlets willing to handle the merchandise. In one country, it might use international sales agents, in another it might partner with a local firm.

Designing a channel system calls for analyzing customer needs, establishing channel objectives and identifying and evaluating the major channel alternatives.

Steps in Channel Designing

(i) ***Analyzing customer needs:*** Understanding what, where, why and how target customers buy is the first step in designing the marketing channel. The market must understand the service output levels desired by the target customers.

(ii) ***Establishing the channel objectives and constraints***: The channel objectives should be stated in terms of targeted service output levels. Channel objectives vary with product characteristics. Perishable products require more direct marketing because of the dangers associated with delays and repeated handling. Bulky products require channels that minimize shipping distance and the number of handlings in the movement from producer to consumer.

(iii) ***Identifying the major channel alternatives:*** A channel alternative is described by three elements: the types of business intermediaries, the number of intermediaries and the terms and responsibilities of each channel participant. The various types of channel alternatives available to a company are company sales force, manufacturer's agency, and industrial distributors. Channel alternatives depend on the kind of product being offered.

(iv) ***Evaluating the channel alternatives:*** Each channel alternative needs to be evaluated against economic control and adaptive criteria.

Each channel alternative will produce a different level of sales and costs. Company sales representatives are better trained to sell the company's products, they are more aggressive and successful because their future depends on company's success.

Legal & Ethical Issues in Channel Relations

For the most part, companies are legally free to develop whatever channel arrangements suit them. In fact, the law seeks to prevent companies from using exclusionary tactics that might keep competitors from using a channel. Here we briefly consider the legality of certain practices, including exclusive dealing, exclusive territories, tying agreements, and dealers' rights.

(i) *Exclusive dealing:* Many producers like to develop exclusive channels for their products. A strategy in which the seller allows only certain outlets to carry its products is called exclusive distribution, and when the seller requires that these dealers not handle competitors' products, this is called exclusive dealing. Both parties benefit from exclusive arrangements. The seller obtains more loyal and dependable outlets, and the dealers obtain a steady source of supply of special products and stronger seller support. Exclusive arrangements are legal as long as they do not substantially lessen competition or tend to create a monopoly, and as long as both parties enter into the agreement voluntarily.

(ii) **Exclusive territories:** Exclusive dealing often includes exclusive territorial agreements. The producer may agree not to sell to other dealers in a given area, or the buyer may agree to sell only in its own territory. The first practice increases dealer enthusiasm and commitment. It is also perfectly legal—a seller has no legal obligation to sell through more outlets than it wishes. The second practice, whereby the producer tries to keep a dealer from selling outside its territory, has become a major legal issue.

(iii) **Tying agreements:** Producers of a strong brand sometimes sell it to dealers only if they will take some or all of the rest of the line. This practice is called full-line forcing. Such tying agreements are not necessarily illegal, but they do violate. Laws if they tend to lessen competition substantially. Producers are free to select their dealers, but their right to terminate dealers is somewhat restricted. In general, sellers can drop dealers "for cause," but they cannot drop dealers if, for example, the dealers refuse to cooperate in a doubtful legal arrangement such as exclusive dealing or tying agreements.

MULTILEVEL MARKETING (MLM)/NETWORK MARKETING

It seems the network marketing, or MLM, industry has been on the verge of an "explosion" for about as long as, well, there has been a network marketing industry. Certainly there have been growth spurts in popularity over the years, but the business just never really exploded, at least for any sustained period of time. Even those occasional

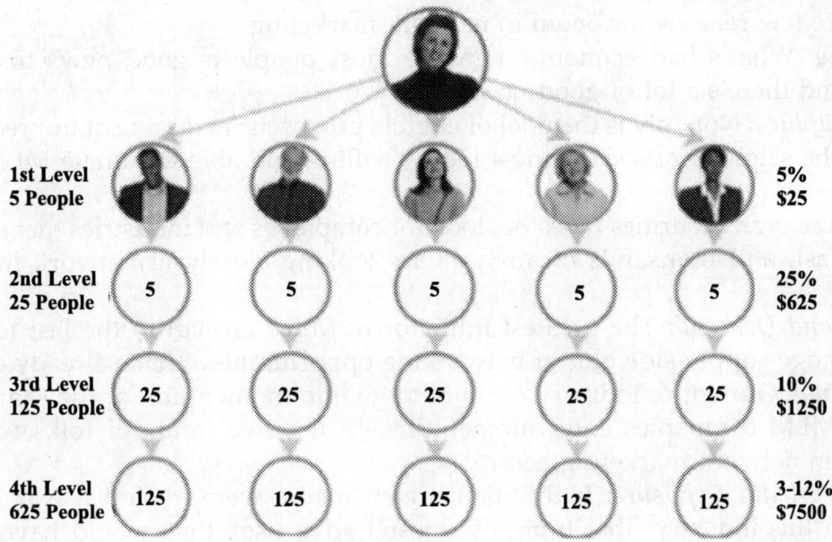

growth pops were always followed by slumps in the MLM economy. Yet, throughout it's history, even in the midst of those slumps, and especially over the last two decades, many of those who would promote it would tell us that, soon, the network marketing industry is going to EXPLODE!

The various promoters of this alleged upcoming MLM boom have always had at least one good reason for believing their claim. It wasn't entirely on hype. Nothing more than the monumental and numerous advantages that network marketing offers to those who want to start a home-based business certainly should have been the reason enough to think that, soon, the masses are going to discover those advantages and flock to MLM en mass. We could surely forgive them for their optimistic delusion.

For the first time in network marketing history, there are solid, logical, verifiable, reasons to believe in an upcoming network marketing boom. In fact, there are eight reasons, any one of which could result in a significant expansion of network marketing in the U.S. over the next few years, and these eight factors will soon by overlaying, one on top of the other, creating the "perfect storm" so to speak, where we have the convergence of several powerful economic, demographic, and psychological factors all hitting at the same time and place in network marketing history. Finally, we can make claim to an upcoming MLM explosion and it won't be just wishful thinking. It absolutely will happen.

For the first time in history there are solid, logical, verifiable, explanations for you to believe in an upcoming network marketing boom. In fact, there are eight reasons, any one of which could result in a significant expansion of network marketing in the U.S. alone over the next few years. And these eight factors will soon be coming together creating a "perfect storm" – the convergence of several powerful economic, demographic and psychological factors all hitting at the exact same time and place. Finally, you and I can honestly make the claim there really is an upcoming MLM explosion. It absolutely will happen, and here's why:

There are few reasons for boom in network marketing:

Economy: What's bad economic news to most people is good news to network marketers and there's a lot of good news.

Demographics: Not only is the pool of eligible prospects increasing at unprecedented levels, but the segment of society most ready, willing and able to pursue MLM is also exploding.

Stock Exchange: Securities investors look for companies and industries that are about to rise up fast, and thousands of analysts are looking closely at network marketing right now.

Supply and Demand: The greatest inhibitor of MLM growth in the last few years has been a huge supply-side glut of networking opportunities. That's already changed.

New Blood: Our entire industry is about to go into momentum for the same reason individual MLM companies enter momentum - a massive influx of folks who have never been in network marketing before.

Positive Media Exposure: If the mainstream media were to find a way to make money from this industry (that typically doesn't advertise), they would have a much greater incentive to promote the positive side of this business.

Last and certainly not the least: The current, positive and powerful growth trends of the network marketing industry itself.

NETWORK MARKETING SUCCESS STORIES IN INDIA

Multilevel marketing is not a very viable concept, even theoretically, nor is it a very profitable means of distribution for all parties involved in multilevel marketing. This non-viability is basically caused by a heightened expectation of easy money.

In fact, the concept of multilevel marketing is no longer new. It is also exempt from the normal rules of the market and the way goods and services are otherwise sold. Many companies have tried the concept of multilevel marketing and most of them have failed.

Some of the multilevel marketing efforts have in fact been miserable failures in spite of the fact that they offer excellent products. After almost 25 years of failed attempts in the area of multilevel marketing, it is time to analyze the reasons for its failures.

Firstly it is important to analyze the driving mechanism of multilevel marketing. The driving mechanisms are intrinsically unstable, and therefore tend to over saturate the market with no one noticing. Multilevel marketing can never equalize into profitability the way companies in the real world can. This is the reason that the organization as a whole cannot be profitable.

It is usually the unfortunate distributor at the bottom who is the loser. Of course money can be made with multilevel marketing. But the money being made is not always legitimate and sometimes made via a sophisticated marketing scheme.

In India, a few companies have introduced multilevel marketing in a very large scale, by quoting and promising very high returns. A large number of the people belonging to the middle class population of India have joined into this dying business of multilevel marketing by paying an entry fee into the business. This only goes to prove the widespread reach of this failing concept in India.

Modicare

MODICARE is a unique business venture established by the Modi Group in 1996 to provide thousands of people, an opportunity to participate as a self-entrepreneur in a business. MODICARE markets products by using a concept called multilevel marketing (MLM). MLM is a method of promoting goods and services through word of mouth advertising, which is a highly successful tool today. Worldwide, MLM accounts for over 18 million people. MODICARE uses this system to market high quality products, developed and manufactured by the company's own highly experienced scientists and technical staff at its R&D centre in Mumbai. These products are backed by a 100% satisfaction guarantee.

MODICARE firmly believes in its commitment to the preservation of the environment. We believe that the efficient management of limited natural resources is the duty of all industries and individuals. Full efforts are being made by MODICARE scientists at its state-of-the-art R&D facility to develop products, which lessen the impact on the environment, while the in-house experts from Holland are developing environment-friendly packaging.

There are no large capital investments required, no employees, no bosses and best of all, no risk. It is your personal business and you decide whom you want to work with, where you want to work and how much you want to earn. MODICARE is here to assist you in aspects of your business.

Swadeshi Marketing

SWADESHI stands for self-reliant nation. Carrying forward the dreams and desires of our freedom fighters on 14th February, 1999, we took a step towards making India self reliant by starting **Swadeshi Marketing & Retail Trading Co. (I) Pvt. Ltd.** in Maharashtra.

The Vision behind SWADESHI is to bring prosperity for every Indian without depending on foreign products or finance. India is one of the biggest democracies in the world with over 100 million populations. If every Indian starts using products made in India and by an Indian, the change in our own economy would be tremendous. In fact, we will export more and import less. Hence, providing every Indian more job opportunities and eliminating poverty. India is what every Indian is...the progress of an Indian is the progress of India.

Today Swadeshi Marketing & Retail Trading Co. (I) Pvt. Ltd has proved that we can achieve success by utilizing our own powers. The ever expanding SWADESHI NETWORK in every state of India has brought over lakhs of members under its single roof. Each member's self-progress through Swadeshi is the evidence of our claim. At Swadeshi there is opportunity for every Indian.

Swadeshi Marketing is led by the dynamic visionary Shri Ramakant Gayakwad as the Managing Director. Also the strong pillars providing support are Shri Sameer Gayakwad as Director Operations. The development of Opportunity Network is handled by Shri Vinaykumar Pandhe as Vice President Development.

Come be a part of a gigantic revolution called SWADESHI and help India be a self-reliant nation.

Customer Relationship Management

There have been a number of studies in the recent times on how customer retention can contribute significantly to profitability. In the times of Internet, it is worthwhile to analyze how this low-cost reach can lead to profitability. Some companies like Siebel, Oracle and Braodvision have created useful CRM products, which can track a number of dimensions of consumer behaviour. There is a basic need on the part of any organization to have a good internal coordination before a CRM package can be used effectively. The impact of consumer behaviour dimensions on CRM is equally important to firms conducting business on the Net. A study indicated that though the acquisition costs of consumers can be high on the Net, they spend more over a period of time if they develop loyalty towards an online store. Even so, McKinsey, study in 1999 proved that among customer attraction, customer conversion and customer retention, the greatest profitability comes from the investments made in customer retention rather than customer attraction or conversion.

Peter Drucker said, "The purpose of a business is to create customers." Implied in his words and his work is the importance of keeping those same customers and of growing the depth of their relationship with you. Initially, new customers cost you money-money spent on advertising and marketing and money spent learning what they want and teaching them how best to do business with you. CRM can be the single strongest weapon you have as a manager to ensure that customers become and remain loyal.

CRM is a comprehensive approach for creating, maintaining and expanding customer relationships.

The relationship marketing approach has great significance from the organizations' point of view due to the following:

- Reduction in customer recruitment cost
- Generation of more and more loyal customers
- Expansion of customer base
- Reduction in advertisement and other sales promotion expenses
- Benefiting customer selectivity approach
- Increase in the number of profitable customers
- Easy introduction of new products
- Easy business expansion possibilities
- Increase in customer partnering.

Building Customer Relationship Management

Step 1: Acquisition: It is a vital stage in building customer relationship. The acquisition process constitutes the following stages.

- Enquiry
- Interaction
- Exchange
- Coordination
- Adoption

Each one of the above stages assumes a significant role in the acquisition process. In the enquiry stage, the prospective buyer undertakes a detailed enquiry with regard to several aspects pertaining to the organization, product, nature of transaction and all other related aspects. Having stored the information he passes on to the interaction stage, where the customer interacts with the organization and obtains additional information, clarifies and ensures already collected information.

Terms of exchange, mode of delivery and other things related to exchange, are settled at the exchange stage. Further coordinated effort on either side would lead the customers moving to adoption of the product or service concerned, and that completes the acquisition process.

Step 2: Customer Interaction Management (CIM): Interaction plays a lead role in building customer relationships. CIM constitutes the customer relationship technologies with additions of technology-based interactive solutions. The interactive channels that are currently available enable very effective customer interactive communications, which leads to CIM, which further leads to relationship building.

In view of technology growth, the interaction management is facilitated by communication in terms of media, message, speed, accuracy, distance, content, reach, repetition, etc. The customer interaction management stands for intensive interaction between customers and the organization, which is supported by technology-enabled mechanisms such as Internet.

CIM can assume the following routes:

- Online routes—e-mails, web communities, chat rooms.
- Offline routes—telephone, fax, mails, interactive television network.
- Outsourcing

Step 3: Customer Retention: The focus of the organizations is more on customer retention than simply on customer acquisition. Customer retention is the process of keeping customers in the customer inventory for an unending period by meeting the needs and exceeding the expectations of those customers. It is the approach of converting a casual customer into a committed loyal customer.

CRM is a complete system with a number of inter-linkages: beginning with what type of consumers should be targeted to finally obtaining efficiency in it. Unless an organization has a holistic view of CRM, it may begin to concentrate on those aspects of CRM may not have critical linkages with the other important dimensions of marketing. Online processing or customer call-centres alone cannot lead to a successful CRM.

A CRM has to start with a good database of consumers and it should have a historical perspective on them. For example, it should be possible for a CRM programme to have specific strategies for prospects, first-time buyers, repeat buyers and advocates. CRM strategies have to take into consideration these differences to qualify consumers for a CRM programme. This is important because a CRM programme has to be beneficial both to the company and its consumers and holds true in the case of both consumer and industrial products.

E-CRM

E-commerce really is not a new game. It's an extension of the game, we have been playing since the dawn of commerce—the game of creating, maintaining, and expanding customer relationships. To play the game of business in this century, it's important to know what e-commerce can do for you and how it's changing customer expectations. Working with the touchstone of your CRM strategy, you will be able to use new rules and the new tools offered by e-commerce to satisfy your customers.

The Internet can enable your CRM strategy in three ways:

Level 1: Getting information out to customer: The Internet can provide an avenue for getting information about your business and your products and services to your current and potential customers. At its most basic level, this means letting them know you are there and how to reach you in the "real world". It can be as simple as a Web-based brochure that describes your products and services and tells customers where you are located and how to reach you by phone.

Level 2: Getting information back from customers: The next level of sophistication means you not only provide information to your customers, but also learn more about them and from them. The Internet allows you to collect all sorts of useful–and sometimes not so useful—data about your customers. Sometimes this means customers respond to questions and provide you useful information. In other cases, you may be able to collect information that's very useful to your business without interfering at all with the customer experience.

Level 3: E-commerce sales: At its highest level, you can use the Internet to deliver products and services to your customers. You can have mutually rewarding relationships with customers you never see, meet, or speak with! Your entire relationship can successfully exist in cyberspace. With the technology available today, you can sell your products over the Internet, respond to customer questions, offer additional products and services based on previous purchases, and evaluate customers' satisfaction with your offerings—all without ever dealing with them in person. Leveraging the Internet can free up resources to deliver higher levels of value to customers in new ways.

Level 4: Getting information out to customers: With half of American households wired to the internet, and the numbers growing throughout the United States and the world, you should expect your customers to search the Web for information about you and your products and services. From a CRM standpoint, it's helpful to think about this level of Internet activity in two ways, passive and active.

CRM and ECRM: The Difference

Being able to take care of your customer via the Internet, or, customers being able to take care of themselves online: that's the difference between CRM and ECRM. It implies a myriad of issues, questions, approaches, technologies, and architecture that are different from client/server-based CRM. Many of them are issues general to the Internet. Others are issues related to certain applications for the Internet. The third group is related directly to ECRM and its actual value to business.

The CRM Process

The final objective of the CRM process is to originate a powerful new tool for customer retention. The focus of any process is to achieve something we have always wanted, but didn't have the proper resources. The CRM implementation and success rate purely depend upon the process, which includes the future, revenue, customer value, customer retention, customer acquisition and profitability.

A Closed-loop CRM Process

Gathering information: Initially, gather information about customers. Customer data comes from sources both internal and external to organization.

Perform data aggregation: It is here that the data is merged and compressed into a complete view of the customer. A large customer data repository is produced.

Create "exploration warehouses": These are extracts of the customer data needed to support specific analyses, such as customer profitability and predictive modelling. Exploration warehouses are the engines for analytical applications that support identification of opportunities and developing strategies.

Execution of strategies: Execute these strategies by developing and launching marketing campaigns across targeted segments of customers. Campaign execution inevitably results in an interaction with customers.

Finally, once a customer interaction takes place and the customer responds, capture that response and "recycle" it to use in the ongoing learning, analysis, and refinement process.

Each time the process loop is completed, more is learnt about the needs and wants of customers. Marketing improves as understanding of customers is enhanced and the ability to anticipate their needs increases.

CRM Implementation

If you attempt to implement a CRM package without knowing how implementation works, it is likely that you will face problems throughout the project and you could be in for a fall, and a big one at that, it could even be a job termination. The statement of work and the change management processes have to be clear prior to starting the installation.

Forget about planning it in the course of customization. Figure it out this way. The industry thumb rule is that the implementation services will cost you at least double to triple the price of the software itself. This definitely needs your attention.

It is definitely necessary to have a formal steering committee that consists of the stakeholders, programme managers, project managers, and so on who would review the project as it moves through the implementation stages.

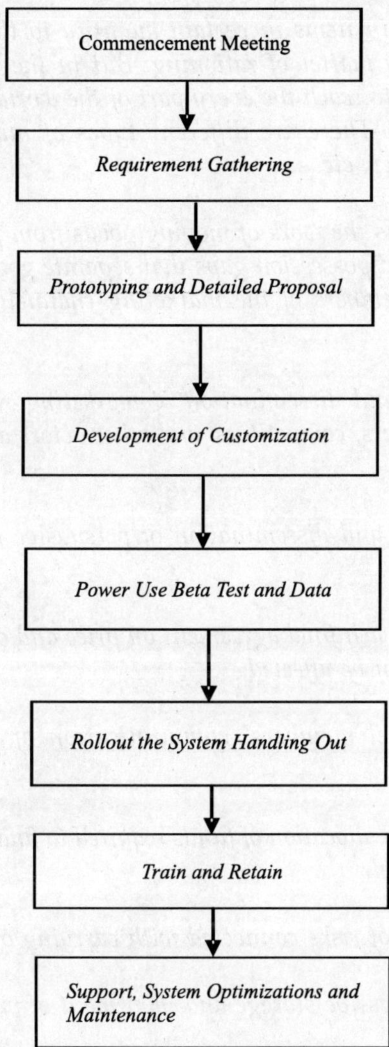

Let Us Sum Up

A distribution channel (also known as a marketing channel) is a set of interdependent organizations or intermediaries involved in the process of making a product available for consumption. A channel directs the flow of products from producers to customers.

Middleman creates suspicion in distribution as it adds extra cost to the final products. In the older days there were no problems as it was barter system. And as long as it is seller's market or having monopoly, then there is no problem because consumers have to come and purchase. It is experienced especially in war-time situation. And earlier in some country limited the exposure of certain items in certain quantity to the people. So, here also no problems. It became a purely matter of rationing. But in the perfect competitive market where every company wants to reach the every part of the world, it is imperative to have a strong distribution channel. There are different types of middlemen like C&F agent, distributor, wholesaler, retailer, etc.

A marketing channel performs the work of moving goods from producers to consumers. It overcomes the time, place, and possession gaps that separate goods and services from those who need or want them. Members of the marketing channel perform a number of key functions.

Information: The collection and dissemination of marketing research information about potential and current customers, competitors, and other actors and forces in the marketing environment.

Promotion: The development and dissemination of persuasive communications signed to attract customers to the offer.

Negotiation: The attempt to reach final agreement on price and other terms so that transfer of ownership or possession can be affected.

Ordering: Marketing-channel members' communication of intentions to buy to the manufacturer.

Financing: The acquisition and allocation of funds required to finance inventories at different levels of the marketing channel.

Risk taking: The assumption of risks connected with carrying out the channel work.

Physical possession: The successive storage and movement of physical products.

Payment: Buyers' payment of their bills to the sellers through banks and other financial institutions.

Title: The actual transfer of ownership from one organization or person to another.

In designing marketing channels, manufacturers have to decide what is ideal, what is feasible, and what is available. A new firm typically starts as a local operation selling in a limited market. Since it has limited capital, it usually uses existing intermediaries. The number of intermediaries in any local market is apt to be limited: a few wholesalers, several established retailers, a few trucking companies and a few warehouses. Deciding on the best channels might not be a problem. The problem might be convincing one or a few available intermediaries to handle the manufacturer's line.

If the new firm is successful, it might branch out to new market. Again, the manufacturer will tend to work through the available intermediaries, although doing so might mean using different types of marketing channels in different areas. In the smaller markets, the firm might sell directly to retailers; in the larger markets, it might sell through, distributors. In rural areas, it might work with general goods merchants; in urban areas, with limited line merchant.

In one part of country, it might grant franchisees because the merchants normally work this way in another, it might sell through all outlets willing to handle the merchandise. In one country it might use international sales agents, in another it might partner with a local firm.

Designing a channel system calls for analyzing customer needs, establishing channel objectives and identifying and evaluating the major channel alternatives.

Questions for Discussion

1. What do you mean by physical distribution system? How is it related to the marketing concept?
2. How physical distributions can contribute the creation of time, form, place and ownership utility?
3. What are the different types of distribution channels are there? Explain.
4. "Physical distribution system should operate at the lowest possible total distribution costs." Explain.
6. What are the reasons for channel conflict? How channel conflict can be managed?
7. What is HMS & VMS? Explain.
8. What are the different functions of channel?
9. Write briefly on "Push vs Pull" strategy.
10. Explain different types of wholesalers.
11. Discuss the purpose/objectives of distribution channel.
12. Explain the characteristics of channels of distribution.
13. How to motivate the channel members? Explain.
14. Discuss the legal and ethical issues in channel designing.
15. List out the emerging trends in network marketing.
16. Write short notes on (i) Network marketing (ii) spatial convenience (iii) utility (iv) Swadeshi marketing (MLM).
17. Write briefly about CRM.

6

CHAPTER

Retail Management

"We are seeing pioneers moving out to the Internet, banks that are taking transactions, retail shopping on the Internet, and although it's going to take most of a decade before most adults are turning to the Internet for a high percentage of their act."

– Bill Gates

Retail management – introduction – key trends in urban India – Indian retail sector – key trends in rural India – hidden challenges – definition – strategies – characteristics of retailing – functions of retailing – extending services – categorizing retailers – retail organization – classification of retail units – retailers classified on the basis of ownership – retailers on the basis of operational structure – retailers on the basis of retail location – trends in retail format – future of retailing – growing importance of retail technology.

LEARNING OBJECTIVES

After going through this chapter, students will be able to understand

- Retail management
- Trends in urban India
- Indian retail sector
- Challenges in retail
- Classification of retailing
- Retail organization
- Trends in retail format
- Future of retailing
- Growing importance of retail technology

INTRODUCTION

The Indian retail scene has witnessed too many players in too short a time, crowding several categories without looking at their core competencies or having a well thought out branding strategy. The growth rate of supermarket sales has been significant in recent years because greater number of higher income Indians prefer to shop at supermarkets due to higher standards of hygiene and attractive ambience. With growth in income levels, Indians have started spending more on health and beauty products. Here also small, single-outlet retailers dominate the market. In recent years, a few retail chains specialized products have come into the market.

Although these retail chains account for only a small share of the total market, their business is expected to grow significantly in the future due to the growing quality consciousness of buyers for these products. Numerous clothing and footwear shops in shopping centres and markets operate all over India. Traditional outlets stock a limited range of cheap and popular items; in contrast, modern clothing and footwear stores have modern products and attractive displays to lure customers. With rapid urbanization, and changing patterns of consumer tastes and preferences, it is unlikely that the traditional outlets will survive the test of time. Despite the large size of this market, very few large and modern retailers have established specialized stores for products.

There seems to be a considerable potential for the entry or expansion of specialized retail chains in the country. The Indian durable goods sector has seen the entry of a large number of foreign companies during the post liberalization period. A greater variety of consumer electronic items and household appliances became available to the Indian customer. Intense competition among companies to sell their brands provided a strong impetus to the growth for retailers doing business in this sector. Increasing household incomes due to better economic opportunities have encouraged consumer expenditure on leisure and personal goods in the country. There are specialized retailers for each category of products (books, music products, etc.) in this sector.

Another prominent feature of this sector is popularity of franchising agreements between established manufacturers and retailers. A strong impetus to the growth of retail industry is witnessed by economic boom and driver of key trends in urban as well as rural India.

KEY TRENDS IN URBAN INDIA

Retailing is still in its infancy in India. In the name of retailing, the unorganized retailing has dominated the Indian landscape so far. According to an estimate the unorganized retail sector has 97% presence whereas the organized accounts for merely 3%. However, the retail industry in India is undergoing a major shake-up as the country is witnessing a retail revolution. The old traditional formats are slowly changing into more complex and bigger formats. Malls and mega malls are coming up in almost all the places be it – metros or the smaller cities, across the length and breadth of the country.

A McKinsey report on India (2004) says organized retailing would increase the efficiency and productivity of entire gamut of economic activities, and would help in achieving higher GDP growth. At 6%, the share of employment of retail in India is low, even when compared to Brazil (14%) and Poland (12%). Govt. of India's plan of changing the FDI guidelines in this sector too speaks of the importance attached to retailing. Recently moves by big corporate houses like Reliance Industries has further fuelled the major investments in retail sector. A strategic alliance, land acquisitions in prime areas give the essence of the mood in this sector.

Both MNCs and Indian firms want to get their share of this burgeoning pie. Notable in Indian firms are Pantaloons Retail & Big Bazaar, Trent's Westside, Shopper's stop, Reliance and Subhiksha, Wills Lifestyle stores, Café Coffee Day, which are present in India in different retail formats. Wal-Mart stores have just started operations in India. Some leading retail coffee chains of the world like Starbucks, Barnies are planning to expand in a major way in India.

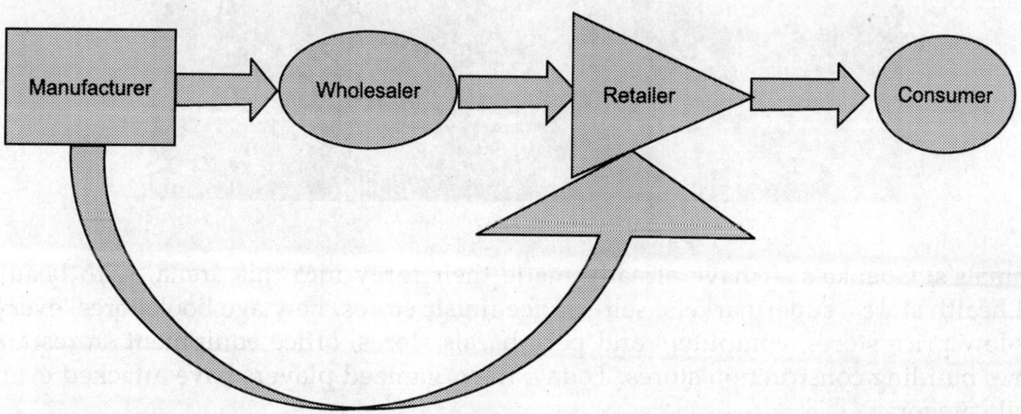

THE INDIAN RETAIL SECTOR

India is the country having the most unorganized retail market. Traditionally, it was a family's livelihood, with their shop in the front and house at the back, while they run the retail business. More than 99% retailer's function in less than 500 square feet of shopping space. Global retail consultants KSA Technopak have estimated that organized retailing in India is expected to touch Rs. 35,000 crore in the year 2005-06. The Indian retail sector is estimated at around Rs. 900,000 crore, of which the organized sector accounts for a mere 2 per cent indicating a huge potential market opportunity that is lying in the waiting for the consumer-savvy organized retailer. Purchasing power of Indian urban consumer is growing and branded merchandise in categories like Apparels, Cosmetics, Shoes, Watches, Beverages, Food and even Jewellery, are slowly becoming lifestyle products that are widely accepted by the urban Indian consumer.

Indian retailers need to advantage of this growth and aiming to grow, diversify and introduce new formats have to pay more attention to the brand building process. The emphasis here is on retail as a brand rather than retailers selling brands. The focus should be on branding the retail business itself. There is no doubt that the Indian retail scene is booming. A number of large corporate houses —Tata's, Raheja's,

Piramals's, Goenka's – have already made their foray into this arena, with beauty and health stores, supermarkets, self-service music stores, new age bookstores, every-day-low-price stores, computers and peripherals stores, office equipment stores and home/building construction stores. Today, the organized players have attacked every retail category.

KEY TRENDS IN RURAL INDIA

- Rural markets emerging as a huge opportunity for retailers reflected in the share of the rural market across most categories of consumption.
- ITC is experimenting with retailing through its e-Choupal and Choupal Sagar – rural hypermarkets.

- Estimated to be US$ 200 billion, of which organized retailing (i.e., modern trade) makes up 3 per cent or US$ 6.4 billion.
- India is rated the fifth most attractive emerging retail market: a potential goldmine.
- Ranked second in a Global Retail Development Index of 30 developing countries drawn up by AT Kearney.
- Food and apparel retailing key drivers of growth.
- Organized retailing in India has been largely an urban phenomenon with affluent classes and growing number of double-income households.

THE HIDDEN CHALLENGES

Modern retailing is all about directly having "first-hand experience" with customers, giving them such a satiable experience that they would like to enjoy again and again. Providing great experience to customers can easily be said than done. Thus, challenges like retail differentiation, merchandising mix, supply chain management and competition from supplier's brands are the talk of the day. In India, as we are moving to the next phase of retail development, each endeavour to offer experiential shopping. One of the key observations by customers is that it is very difficult to find the uniqueness of retail stores. The problem: retail differentiation.

The next problem in setting up organized retail operations is that of supply chain logistics. India lacks a strong supply chain when compared to Europe or the USA. The existing supply chain has too many intermediaries: Typical supply chain looks like:- Manufacturer - National distributor - Regional distributor - Local wholesaler - Retailer - Consumer. This implies that global retail chains will have to build a supply chain network from scratch. This might run foul with the existing supply chain operators. In addition to fragmented supply chain, the trucking and transportation system is antiquated. The concept of container trucks, automated warehousing is yet to take root in India. The result: significant losses/damages during shipping.

Merchandising planning is one of the biggest challenges that any multi store retailer faces. Getting the right mix of product, which is store specific across organization, is a combination of customer insight, allocation and assortment techniques.

The private label will continue to compete with brand leaders. So supplier's brand will take their own way because they have a established brand image from last decades and the reasons can be attributed to better customer experience, value vs. price, aspiration, innovation, accessibility of supplier's brand.

DEFINITION

Retailing includes all of the activities involved in selling goods or services directly to final consumers for personal, non-business use. A retailer or retail store is any business enterprise whose sales volume comes primarily from retailing. Any organization that sells to final consumers—whether a manufacturer (Factory outlet), wholesaler (Cash and carry— Metro, ITC Fresh, Wal-Mart) or retailer—is engaged in retailing.

It does not matter how the goods or services are sold by person. It may be via:

- Mail-publication
- Telephone-telemarketing
- Vending machine-cold drinks, candy or
- Internet-amazon.com, e-bay, India times or where they are sold in a store, on
- The street-newspapers, magazines or in the consumer's home-aquaguard, eureka forbs.

STRATEGIES

Right Positioning: The effectiveness of the mall developer's communication of the offering to the target customers determines how well the mall gets positioned in their minds. At this stage, the communication has to be more of relative nature. This implies that the message conveyed to the target customers must be effective enough in differentiating the mall's offering from that of its competitors without even naming them. The message should also clearly convey to the target audience that the mall offers them exactly what they call the complete shopping-cum-entertainment point that meets all their expectations. The core purpose is to inform the target customers about the offering of the mall, persuade them to visit the mall and remind them about the mall. The mall developer can create awareness about the offering among the target customers in a number of ways. Various communication tools available to the mall developer for this purpose may include advertising, buzz marketing (WoM), celebrity endorsement, use of print media, press releases and viral marketing. Once the message is being conveyed through these channels, the mall developer must add a personal touch to his message by carrying out a door-to-door campaign in order to reinforce the message.

Effective Visual Communication: Retailer has to give more emphasis on display visual merchandising, lighting, signages and specialized props. The visual communication strategy might be planned and also be brand positioned. Theme or lifestyle displays using stylized mannequins and props, which are based on a season or an event, are used to promote collections and have to change to keep touch with the trend. The merchandise presentation ought to be very creative and displays are often on non-standard fixtures and forms to generate interest and add on attitude to the merchandise.

Strong Supply Chain: Critical components of supply chain planning applications can help manufacturers meet retailers' service levels and maintain profit margins. Retailer has to develop innovative solution for managing the supply chain problems. Innovative solutions like performance management, frequent sales operation management, demand planning, inventory planning, production planning, lean systems and staff should help retailers to get advantage over competitors.

Changing the Perception: Retailers benefit only if consumers perceive their store brands to have consistent and comparable quality and availability in relation to branded products. Retailer has to provide more assortments for private level brands to compete with supplier's brand. New product development, aggressive retail mix as well as everyday low pricing strategy can be the strategy to get edge over supplier's brand.

CHARACTERISTICS OF RETAILING

Retailing can be distinguished in various ways from other businesses such as manufacturing. Retailing differs from manufacturing in the following ways:

- There is direct end-user interaction in retailing.
- It is the only point in the value chain to provide a platform for promotions.
- Sales at the retail level are generally in smaller unit sizes.
- Location is a critical factor in retail business.
- In most retail businesses services are as important as core products.
- There are a larger number of retail units compared to other members of the value chain. This occurs primarily to meet the requirements of geographical coverage and population density.

FUNCTIONS OF RETAILING

Retailers play a significant role as a conduit amongst manufacturers, wholesalers, suppliers and consumers. In this context, they perform various functions like sorting, breaking bulk, holding stock, as a channel of communication, storage, advertising and certain additional services.

Sorting: Manufacturers usually make one or a variety of products and would like to sell their entire inventory to a few buyers to reduce costs. Final consumers, in contrast, prefer a large variety of goods and services to choose from and usually buy them in small quantities. Retailers are able to balance the demands of both sides, by collecting an assortment of goods from different sources, buying them in sufficiently large quantities and selling them to consumers in small units.

The above process is referred to as the sorting process. Through this process, retailers undertake activities and perform functions that add to the value of the products and services sold to the consumer. Supermarkets in the US offer, on an average, 15,000 different items from 500 companies. Customers are able to choose from a wide range of designs, sizes and brands from just one location. If each manufacturer had a separate store for its own products, customers would have to visit several stores to complete their shopping. While all retailers offer an assortment, they specialize in types of assortment offered and the market to which the offering is made. Westside provides clothing and accessories, while a chain like Nilgiris specializes in food and bakery items. Shoppers' Stop targets the elite urban class, while Pantaloons is targeted at the middle class.

Breaking Bulk: Breaking bulk is another function performed by retailing. The word retailing is derived from the French word retailer, meaning 'to cut a piece off'. To reduce transportation costs, manufacturers and wholesalers typically ship large cartons of the product, which are then tailored by the retailers into smaller quantities to meet individual consumption needs.

Holding Stock: Retailers also offer the service of holding stock for the manufacturers. Retailers maintain an inventory that allows for instant availability of the product to the consumers. It helps to keep prices stable and enables the manufacturer to regulate production. Consumers can keep a small stock of products at home as they know that this can be replenished by the retailer and can save on inventory carrying costs.

Additional Services: Retailers ease the change in ownership of merchandise by providing services that make it convenient to buy and use products. Providing product guarantees, after-sales service and dealing with consumer complaints are some of the services that add value to the actual product at the retailers' end. Retailers also offer credit and hire-purchase facilities to the customers to enable them to buy a product now and pay for it later.

Retailers fill orders, promptly process, deliver and install products. Salespeople are also employed by retailers to answer queries and provide additional information about the displayed products. The display itself allows the consumer to see and test products before actual purchase. Retail essentially completes transactions with customers.

Channel of Communication: Retailers also act as the channel of communication and information between the wholesalers or suppliers and the consumers. From advertisements, salespeople and display, shoppers learn about the characteristics and features of a product or services offered. Manufacturers, in their turn, learn of sales forecasts, delivery delays, and customer complaints. The manufacturer can then modify defective or unsatisfactory merchandise and services.

Transport and Advertising Functions: Small manufacturers can use retailers to provide assistance with transport, storage, advertising and pre-payment of merchandise. This also works the other way round in case the number of retailers is small. The number of functions performed by a particular retailer has a direct relation to the percentage and volume of sales needed to cover both their costs and profits. As a result of these functions, retailers are required to perform the following activities:

Activities Performed by Retailers: Retailers undertake various business activities and perform functions that add value to the offerings they make to their target segments. Retailers provide convenient location, stock and appropriate mix of merchandise in suitable packages in accordance with the needs of customers. The four major activities carried out by retailers are:

(1) Arrange for assortment of offerings
(2) Breaking quantity
(3) Holding stock
(4) Extending services

Arranging Assortment: An assortment is a retailer's selection of merchandise. It includes both the depth and breadth of products carried. Retailers have to select the combination of assortments from various categories. The assortments must include substitutable items of multiple brands and price points. They should be distinguished on account of physical dimensions and attributes, e.g., colour or flavour. The small retailer takes assortment decision on the basis of his experience; on the other hand, retailers from organized retailing depend on a detailed study of past trends and future projections.

Retailers need to consider certain factors while devising assortment plans for their stores: profitability associated with particular merchandise mix, store image, layout and the level of compatibility between the existing merchandise. For example, FoodWorld, a leading food supermarket positioned as a one-stop shopping centre, deals in multiple product categories along with all possible variants of brands, stock keeping units, and physical attributes in order to meet the expectations of their consumers and survive in the business. Whereas, Subhiksha, a grocery chain in South India has impressive assortments of only the fast moving brands rather than all available variants in the market. Their assortment plan is governed by location, size and store image of their stores.

Breaking Bulk: Breaking bulk means physical repackaging of the products by retailers in small unit sizes according to customer's convenience and stocking requirements. Normally, retailers receive large quantities of sacks and cases of merchandise from suppliers to reduce their transportation costs. In order to meet their customers' requirements retailers have to break or arrange the bulk into convenient units. This entire function of the retailers adds value to the offerings not only for the end customers but also for the suppliers in the value chain. Even in the earlier days of generic and commodity-based trading most of the retailers used to perform this important function in the value chain.

This function receives negligible attention from the retailers now due to the introduction of new product categories, such as FMCG and ready-to-wear apparel.

Holding Stock: To ensure the regular availability of the offerings, retailers maintain appropriate levels of inventory. Consumers normally depend on the retailers directly to replenish their stocks at home. Therefore, retailers, on periodic basis, maintain the required levels of stock to meet the regular or seasonal fluctuations in the demand. Retailers need to maintain equilibrium between the range or variety carried and the sales which it gives rise to. Retailers have to face the negative consequences of holding unwanted levels of stock —for instance, too little stock will hamper the sales volume, whereas, too much stock will increase the retailer's cost of operation. Generally, in small towns of India most retailers have arrangements with the nearby warehouses to stock the goods. Some are so small that they have to stock only on the shop floor. Retailers in the organized sector, to a certain extent, are using effective software packages for maintaining adequate levels of inventory. At the same time, retailers avail of just-in-time deliveries with the help of efficient consumer response systems, which reduces the burden of maintaining high levels of stocks.

Extending Services

Retailing provides multiple services to immediate customers and other members of the value chain. The set of services extended by particular retailers may be part of their core product offerings or it may be 'add on' to their product or service. Retailers offer credit, home delivery, after-sales services and information regarding new products to their customers, thereby making the shopping experience convenient and enjoyable. At the same time, they provide stocking place, reach to the ultimate customers, and information about the concerned target segment to the suppliers. For example, Time Zone, the first organized retail chain of wristwatches in India, started by leading watch manufacturers Titan, set up in all its stores, service centres with proper equipment and trained manpower. This has not only diluted the relevance of service providers in the unorganized sector but has also enhanced the confidence of the customers in the retail services provided by the particular retail chain, as after-sales service is considered to be an integral ingredient of the watch purchase.

CATEGORIZING RETAILERS

Categorizing retailers helps in understanding the competition and the frequent changes that occur in retailing. There is no universally accepted method of classifying a retail outlet, although many categorization schemes have been proposed. Some of these include classifying on the basis of

- Number of outlets
- Margin vs Turnover

- Location
- Size.

The number of outlets operated by a retailer can have a significant impact on the competitiveness of a retail firm. Generally, a greater number of outlets add strength to the firm because it is able to spread fixed costs, such as advertising and managers' salaries, over a greater number of stores in addition to acquiring economies of purchase. While any retailer operating more than one store can be technically classified as a chain owner, for practical purposes a chain store refers to a retail firm which has more than 11 units. In the United States, for example, chain stores account for nearly 95% of general merchandise stores.

Small chains can use economies of scale while tailoring merchandise to local needs. Big chains operating on a national scale can save costs by a centralized system of buying and accounting. A chain store could have either a standard stock list ensuring that the same merchandise is stocked in every retail outlet or an optional stock list giving the outlets the advantage of changing the merchandise according to customer needs in the area. Because of their size, chain stores are often channel captains of the marketing channel—captains can influence other channel partners, such as wholesalers, to carry out activities they might not otherwise engage in, such as extended payment terms and special package sizes.

Big stores focus on large markets where their customers live and work. They use technology to learn more about their customers and target them with point-of-sale machines interactive kiosks, and sophisticated forecasting and inventory systems. They tend to stock a narrow range of inventory that sells well and maintain an extensive inventory of the fast selling products. Branding is important to them. Pricing is often a key area of focus for these retailers. Big stores have many strengths, including regional or national reputation, huge buying power, vast inventory and hassle-free return and exchange policies. Their prime locations, the consistency in their products and services, the fact that they are open when people can and want to shop and the clear consistent image and identity they develop and maintain challenge the abilities and resources of many small retailers. Perhaps their biggest advantage is their knowledge in every aspect of their business, from inventory selection to store layout.

However, large retailers are not perfect. They have competitive weaknesses that small retailers can exploit. Most offer the same standardized assortments of products nationally. Local managers have little say in inventory selection. Often, sales staff has minimal product knowledge. Staff turnover is extremely high. Most large retailers have little connection with the community they serve. They usually do not offer special services.

Larger companies are often slow to recognize and react to changes in their local markets. Independent retailers can coexist and flourish in the shadow of the big chains by developing a niche within the diverse market. The niche should be developed on the basis of new or unusual product offerings, superior service and overall quality. While value is important, price may be less important. Efficient operations, including precise buying practices, are a must. Customer contact within the niche market must be characterized by 'high-touch' service. The key factor is innovation: stores that do not change will perish.

The road to success for the independent retailer lies in doing all the things those big chain stores cannot or will not do. The successful independent retailers embrace the following principles:

- Be prepared for change.
- Move to a narrower niche market and stop competing directly with the big retailers.
- Learn more about customers and include best customers in a database.
- Invest appropriately in advertising and promotion.
- Charge regular prices and avoid discounting (ensure requisite mark-up).
- Buy with precision and search out speciality suppliers.
- Maintain essential inventory.
- Focus on profit instead of volume (be ready to lose an occasional sale).
- Provide extraordinary service.
- Employ the best possible staff.
- Understand the significance of the Internet.

RETAIL ORGANIZATION

The term retail organization refers to the basic format or structure of a retail business designed to cater to the needs of the end customer. Recently, some scholars have started referring to India as a nation of shopkeepers. This epithet has its roots in the huge number of retail enterprises in India, which were over 12 million in 2003. About 78% of these are small family businesses utilizing only household labour.

Retail firms may be independently owned, parts of a retail chain, operated as a franchisee, leased departments, owned by manufacturers or wholesalers, consumers owned or co-operative society.

A retail unit could be owned by:

- Manufacturer (e.g., company owned retail outlets)
- Wholesaler (e.g., Vastra outlet in Rajouri in New Delhi)
- Independent retailer (Chanakya Sweet Shop near Hazratganj in Lucknow)
- Consumer (consumer owned grocery stores in many residential societies)
- Cooperative society (e.g., Mother Dairy milk booths in Delhi)
- Government (e.g., Cottage Emporia)
- Ownership shared among franchiser and franchisee (e.g., Archies Gallery)

Although most Indian retailers fall in the category of small-scale units, there are also some very big retailers. Organized retail stores are generally characterized by large, professionally managed store formats providing goods and services that appeal to customers, in an ambience that is conducive for shopping and provides a memorable experience to customers.

From positioning and operating perspectives, each ownership format serves a marketplace niche and presents certain advantages and disadvantages. Retail executives must not lose sight of this in playing up their strengths and working around their weaknesses.

CLASSIFICATION OF RETAIL UNITS

Conceptual classification of a business unit provides the marketers with strategic guidelines, useful in the design of retailing strategy. Besides, retail businesses are extremely diverse and there are quite a few types of retail units. Therefore, retail units are classified on multiple of ownership, geographical locations, kind of customer interaction, level of services provided, etc.

Retailers Classified on the Basis of Ownership

One of the first decisions that the retailer has to make as a business owner is how the company should be structured. This decision is likely to have long-term implications, so it is important to consult with an accountant and attorney to help one select preferred ownership structure.

There are four basic legal forms of ownership for retailers:

(i) Sole proprietorship: The vast majority of small businesses start out as sole proprietorships. These firms are owned by one person, usually the individual who has the day-to-day responsibility for running the business.

(ii) Partnership: A partnership is a common format in India for carrying out business activities (particularly trading) on a small or medium scale. In a partnership, two or more people share ownership of a single business.

(iii) Joint venture: A joint venture is not well defined in the law. Unless incorporated or established as a firm as evidenced by a deed, joint ventures may be taxed like association of persons, sometimes at maximum marginal rates. It acts like a general partnership, but is clearly for a limited period of time or a single project.

(iv) Limited liability Company (public and private): The Limited Liability Company (LLC) is a relatively new type of hybrid business structure that is now permissible in most states. The owners are members, and the duration of the LLC is usually determined when the organization papers are filed.

Classification of Retailers on the basis of Operational Structure

Retail businesses are classified on the basis of their operational and organizational structure. Operational structure defines the key strategic decision of retail entity, whether to hire employees and manage the distributed sales function internally or to reach customers though franchised outlets owned and operated by local entrepreneurs.

Retail firms can be classified into five heads on the basis of their respective operational structures:

(i) Independent retail unit: The total number of retailers in India is estimated to be over 5 million in 2003. About 78% of these are small family businesses utilizing only household labour. An independent retailer owns one retail unit.

(ii) Retail Chain: A chain retailer operates multiple outlets (store units) under common ownership; it usually engages in some level of centralized (or coordinated) purchasing and decision-making.

(iii) Franchising: Franchising involves a contractual arrangement between a franchiser (which may be a manufacturer, a wholesaler, or a service sponsor) and a retail franchisee, which allows the franchisee to conduct a given form of business under and establishments name and according to a given pattern of business.

(iv) Leased Department or Shop-in-shop: It refers to department in a retail store that are rented to an outside party. Usually, this is done in case of department and speciality stores and also at times, in discount stores.

(v) Cooperative Outlets: Cooperative outlets are generally owned and managed by co-operative societies. In this context, the detailed example of Kendriya Bhandar in India.

Classification of Retailers on the basis of Retail Location

Retailers have also been classified according to their store location. Retailers can locate their stores in an isolated place and attract the customers to the store on their own strength—such as a small grocery store or paan shop in a colony, which attracts the customers staying close by. Classification of retailers on the basis of location is discussed below:

(i) Retailers in a Free-standing Location: Retailers located at a site which is not connected to other retailers depend entirely on their store's drawing power and on the various promotional tools to attract customers. This type of location has several advantages including no competition, low rent, better visibility from the road, easy parking and lower property costs. For example, the Haldiram's outlet on the Delhi-Jaipur highway and the McDonald's outlet on Delhi-Ludhiana highway.

(ii) Retailers in a Business-associated Location: In this case, a retailer locates his store in a place where a group of retail outlets, offering a variety of merchandise, work together to attract customers to their retail area, and also compete against each other for the same customers.

(iii) Retailers in Specialized Markets: Besides the above location-based classification, we also have in India-retailers who prefer specialized markets, particularly traditional independent retailers or chain stores. In India, most of the cities have specialized markets famous for a particular product category. For example, in Chennai, Godown Street is famous for clothes, Bunder Street for stationery products, Usman Street for jewellery, T Nagar for ready-made garments, Govindappan naicleen street for grocery, Poo Kadia for food and vegetables.

(iv) Airport Retailing: For quite some time, duty-free shops and newsstands dominated the small amount of commercial space provided at airports. Lately, serious efforts are being made to design new airport facilities in order to incorporate substantial amounts of retail space.

The key features of airport retailing are:

- Large groups of prospective shoppers
- Captive audience
- Strong sales per square foot of retail space
- Strong sales of gift and travel items
- Difficulty in replenishment
- Longer operating hours
- Duty-free shopping possible.

TRENDS IN RETAIL FORMATS

Retail industry is continuously going through changes on account of liberalization, globalization and consumer preferences. While multinational retail chains are looking for new markets, manufacturers are identifying, redefining, or evolving new retail formats.

The existing retail houses are also gearing up to face the emerging competition from the organized sector and the changing outlook of the consumers. For example, consumer spending is shifting from goods to services. Accordingly the retailers too are fast adjusting to the changing consumer preferences.

Consumers are not only looking for the core products or functional benefits from the retailers but also the non-functional benefits, which need to be compatible with their lifestyles. For example, most of the traditional eating joints in India such as Haldiram, Bikaner and Sagar Ratna have revised their product offerings and atmospherics on the lines of the multinational chains to compete with them and to serve changed expectations of the consumers.

Mom-and-Pop Stores and Traditional Kirana Stores

The retail sector is changing as new store categories have started dominating the marketplace. Mass merchandisers (Wal-Mart, Big Bazaar), discount clubs (Subhiksha), so-called category killers (Home Depot, Vishal chain), and speciality retailers (Time Zone, Tanishq) have all developed a successful retail models. At the same time, the small mom-and-pop stores and the traditional department stores, are finding the competition intense. In 2002, while Wal-Mart and Target saw revenues grow (by 12% and 10%, respectively), department stores such as Saks and Federated experienced declining revenues (down 3% and 1% respectively). Small independent stores, across product categories, is a very common retail formats they are also undertaking large-scale renovations to appeal and attract their target consumer segments.

E-commerce

The amount of retail business being conducted on the Internet is growing every year. Indeed, Forrester Research Agency projects e-commerce revenue to rise to $123 billion in 2004, an increase of some 28% over the previous year and for e-tailing to comprise a bigger slice of the overall retail pie (5.6%, up from 4.5% in 2003). Many major retail organizations and manufacturers have online retail stores. Companies like Amazon.com which helped pioneer the retail e-commerce concept, are now being followed by bricks-and-mortar and catalogue retailers like J. Crew, which are expanding retail e-commerce into new markets.

Department Stores

A few years ago, names like Sears, J.C. Penney, Macy's, and Montgomery Ward dominated malls and downtowns all over America. Over the last decade or so, however, these department stores have suffered badly. In part, this is a result of changing shopping patterns and increased competition from discount stores. It has also come from financial burdens incurred by companies that acquired competing companies and grew too fast. It is unlikely that these players will disappear from the market. However, they should be ready to expect more bumps as the strong get stronger and the weak get absorbed.

Discount Stores

These are giants such as Wal-Mart (the largest retailer in the world, with more than a million employees), Target and Kmart, as well as membership warehouses, such as Costco. These, along with the category killers, have changed the landscape of both the retail industry and America. Where once mom-and-pop and department stores dominated retail, now the discount retailers and category killers are at the top of the heap. And where once shopping malls, anchored by at least one major department store; used to be the dominant retail presence lining the nation's roads, now it is the behemoth Wal-Marts and Home Depots.

Category Killers

These are the giant retailers that dominate one area of merchandise (e.g., Office Depot, Tower Records and The Sports Authority). They are able to buy bathroom tiles, file cabinets, electronic goods or pet food in such huge volumes that they can then sell them at prices even fairly large competitors cannot match. The future of this category is better than that of many of the more general discounters, but the same employment caveats apply. For most job seekers, these companies offer earn-and-learn experiences with vendors and distributors before they move onward and upward.

Speciality Stores

These include Crate & Barrel, the Body Shop, and Victoria's Secret. These stores concentrate on one type of merchandise and offer it in a manner that makes it special. Some are very high-end (Louis Vuitton) while others cater to the price-conscious masses (Old Navy). Many are so successful that department stores have started to emulate their buying, marketing, and merchandise display strategies. Industry experts predict growth in this segment, particularly in home furnishings and home improvement, and it seems to attract many of the best and brightest in retail. Promotion and responsibility come quickly to those willing to work hard, and in many of these stores the hand of bureaucracy is not heavy.

E-tailers

While most retailers have online storefronts, strictly online purveyors with no bricks-and-mortar counterparts are hoping to snare a percentage of the retail profit. Major players, such as Amazon.com, have generated enough business to cause top brick-and mortar competitors to come up with their own Internet sites. Traditional retailers like Wal-Mart and Starbucks, hugely successful in their own right, have also set up online stores so as not to miss out on the revenue opportunities that the Internet offers.

THE FUTURE OF RETAILING

- Retailers operate in a harsh and fast-changing environment, which offers threats as well as opportunities.
- Consumer demographics, lifestyles, and shopping patterns are changing rapidly, as are retailing technologies.
- To be successful, then, retailers will have to choose target segments carefully and position themselves strongly.
- They will have to take the following retailing developments into account as they plan and execute their competitive strategies.
- Although most retailing still takes place the old-fashioned way across countertops in stores, consumers now have an array of alternatives, including mail order, television, phone, and online shopping.

GROWING IMPORTANCE OF RETAIL TECHNOLOGY

- Retail technologies are becoming critically important as competitive tools.
- Progressive retailers are using computers to produce better forecasts, control inventory costs, order electronically from suppliers, send e-mail between stores, and even sell to customers within stores.
- They are adopting checkout scanning systems, online transaction processing, electronic funds transfer, electronic data interchange, in-store television, and improved merchandise-handling systems.
- One innovative scanning system now in use is the shopper scanner, a radar-like system that counts store traffic.
- Perhaps the most startling advances in retailing technology concern the ways in which today's retailers are connecting with customers:

Let Us Sum Up

Indian retailers need to take advantage of this growth and aiming to grow, diversify and introduce new formats have to pay more attention to the brand building process. The emphasis here is on retail as a brand rather than retailers selling brands. The focus should be on branding the retail business itself. There is no doubt that the Indian retail scene is booming. A number of large corporate houses – Tata's, Raheja's, Piramals's, Goenka's – have already made their foray into this arena, with beauty and health stores, supermarkets, self-service music stores, new age book-stores, everyday-low-price stores, computers and peripherals stores, office equipment stores and home/building construction stores. Today, the organized players have attacked every retail category.

Retailing includes all of the activities involved in selling goods or services directly to final consumers for personal, non-business use. A retailer or retail store is any business enterprise whose sales volume comes primarily from retailing. Any organization that sells to final consumers – whether a manufacturer (Factory outlet), wholesaler (Cash and carry–Metro, ITC Fresh, Wal-Mart) or retailer – is engaged in retailing.

It does not matter how the goods or services are sold by person. It may be via:

- *Mail–publication*
- *Telephone–telemarketing*
- *Vending machine–cold drinks, candy or*
- *Internet–amazon.com, e-bay, India times or where they are sold in a store, on the street – newspapers, magazines.*

There are different types of retail outlets like departmental store, speciality store, e-trailers, super-market, discount store, etc.

Question for Discussion

1. Write a short note on trends in retailing in India.
2. Define retailing. Name few retail chains in India.
3. Write about retail trends in rural India.
4. Explain various challenges to retailing in India.
5. Explain various retail strategies.
6. Write short notes on (i) Mom-and-Pop store (ii) departmental store (iii) super-market (iv) speciality store (v) discount store (vi) e-tailers (vii) category killers (viii) E-commerce.
7. What are the characteristics of retailing?
8. How retailers are categorized?
9. Explain classification or retail outlets.
10. Explain various trends in retail format.
11. Discuss the involvement of IT in retail technology.

7
CHAPTER

Logistics Information System and International Logistics

"McDonald's cannot flourish without McDonnell Douglas, the designer of the F-15."

– Thomas Friedman

Logistical information system (LIS) – introduction – importance – primary activities of LIS – functionality – four levels of information functionality – principles of LIS – order management – order processing – distribution operation – transportation and shipping – logistical organization – international logistic – introduction – difference between domestic and international logistic – challenges – developing global logistic strategy : transportation infrastructure, airfreight, export documentation, international inventory issues, international packaging issues, storage facilities, special trade zone, centralized & decentralized logistic management, outsourcing logistic services, supply chain and internet, logistic and security, logistic and environment – supply chain management – introduction – supply chain management problems – evolution of the concept – importance – decision phase in supply chain – effectiveness of supply chain – theories of supply chain – global supply chain concept – technologies in logistic: automatic identification technology, bar-coding, RFI, GPS, E-tracking, automated material handling, AGVS, information directed system, ERP.

LEARNING OBJECTIVES

After going through this chapter, students will be able to understand

- Understanding logistics information system
- Designing logistic information system
- Role of information in logistics
- Logistics organization
- Understanding international logistic
- Basic to supply chain management
- Role of IT in logistics

INTRODUCTION

MIS (Management Information System) is a structure of machines and management technology that enables management to receive, collect, store, transmit and analyze information. Transmission of information involves its movement to and fro processing centre. Order transmitted from customer to the order-processing unit in a firm is an example of transmission activities.

Logistics management is concerned with the functions of storage, handling, moving of materials and information. So MIS performs logistics of information in an organization.

Logistical Information System [LIS] handles information related to Logistics Management. Hence, it is a structure of machines and management technology that enables management to receive, collect, store, transmit and analyze information which has an immensely important role in achieving business goals.

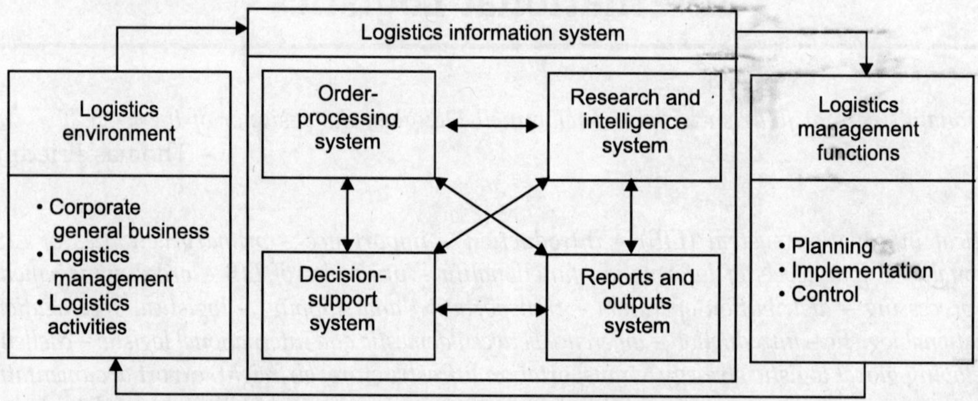

Source: This figure was adapted from the framework for a marketing information system suggested by Philip Kotler[4]

Fig. 7.1. Marketing information system and logistic information system.

Importance of Logistical Information System

There are many advantages of having an efficient LIS. It helps organization

- To develop logistical competence
- Integrates various activities of logistics
- One of the three pipelines managed by logistical management
- Important to customer service
- Underwent revolutionary change due to changes in technology

Primary Activities of LIS

The following are the few salient activities of logistical information system:

- Data flow from external sources
- Processing and storage of information within the firm
- Communication to the decision-maker in the form of reports

- Communication to customers and suppliers and their feedback

LOGISTICAL INFORMATION FUNCTIONALITY

Logistical information functionality is enabling appropriate decision-making at different levels of hierarchy. Information is required in different form and shape at different levels adequate to the requirements of decision-making. Importance of information cannot be overemphasized. Information integrates logistical functions to deliver customer expectations. Logistical information links logistical activities into an integrated process.

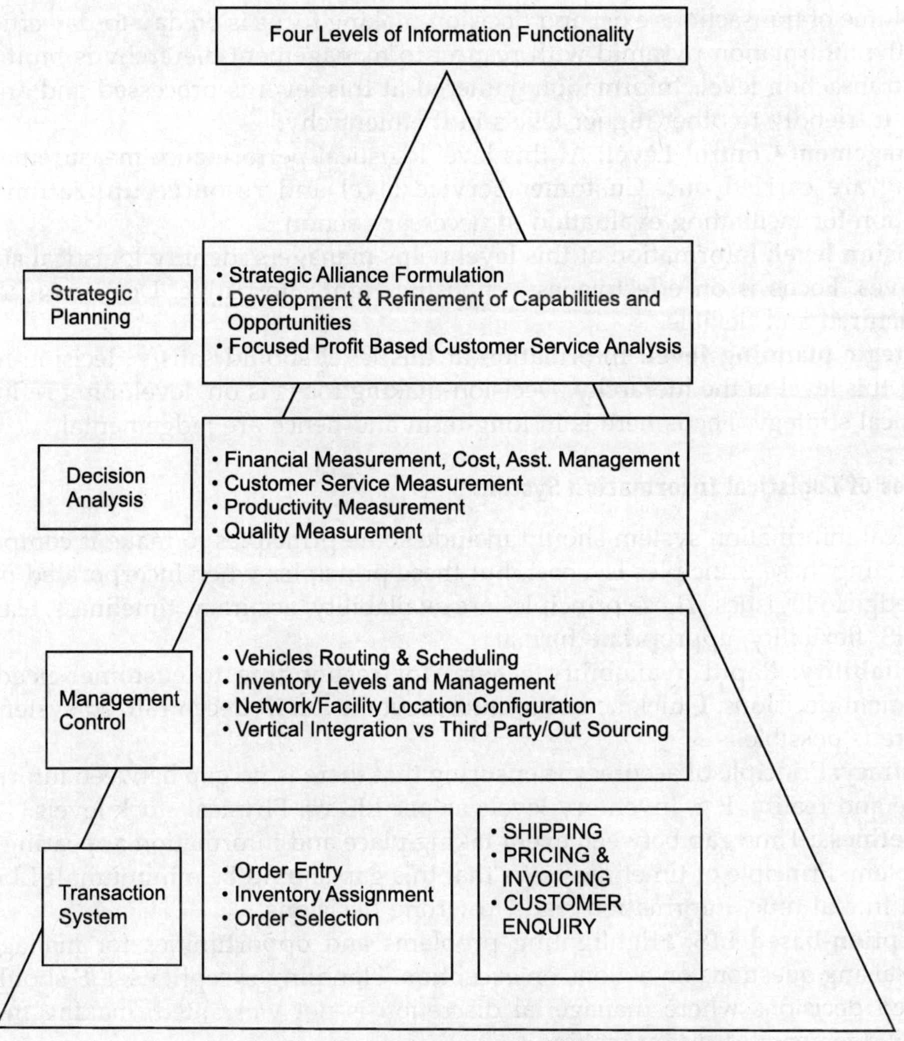

Fig. 7.2. Four levels of information functionality.

Four Levels of Information Functionality

Four levels of information functionality are transaction, management control, decision analysis and strategic planning systems.

Transaction level: The most basic level of information. Customer order triggers a series of transactions from order entry to invoicing. These grass roots level logistical activities are called transactions. Information needed for operational decisions is gathered at this level called transaction level. Information about all these transactions that take place during a customer order performance cycle facilitates decision-making. Information of this level is needed to satisfy some of the customer queries.

Main features of transactions are formalized rules, interfunctional communications, large volume of transactions exist and decision-making focus is on day-to-day efficiency. Rest of the information pyramid with respect to management hierarchy is built on the base of transaction level. Information gathered at this level is processed and analyzed to make it friendly to other higher levels in the hierarchy.

Management Control Level: At this level logistical performance measurement and reporting are carried out. Customer service level and resource utilization is the information for facilitating evaluation of necessary action.

Decision level: Information at this level helps managers identify logistical strategic alternatives. Focus is on effectiveness, choosing right alternative. Decision-making is less structured and flexible.

Strategic planning level: Information at this level should satisfy decision-making needs of this level in the hierarchy. Decision-making focus is on developing refinement to logistical strategy. Focus here is in long-term and hence are judgemental.

Principles of Logistical Information System

A logistical information system should include some principles to make it competitive. Incorporating these principles is a cost. But these principles when incorporated provide cutting edge to logistics. These principles are availability, accuracy, timeliness, exception based LIS, flexibility, appropriate format.

Availability: Rapid availability is vital for responding to customer needs and management decisions. Quick access to information even in decentralized system from anywhere is possible.

Accuracy: Principle of accuracy is ensuring that there is no gap between information available and reality. E.g. Inventory levels as per LIS vs. Physical stock levels.

Timeliness: Time gap between event taking place and information appearing in LIS is a problem. Principle of timeliness says that this gap should be minimum. If LIS is not updated in real time, information leads to wrong decisions.

Exception-based LIS: Highlighting problems and opportunities for management action. Raising questions on actions on exception. Handling exceptions, LIS should take structured decisions where managerial discretion is not warranted, making manager free for judgemental decision-making.

Flexibility: Informational needs are diverse depending on the perspective of the user of the system. A good LIS should be able to provide information as per user's need.

Appropriate format: LIS should structure information in right sequence. Decisions like locating the inventory for order processing or inventory planning is possible when information is structured adequately in right sequence.

Logistical Information System Functionality

Logistical information system integrates the logistical operating system to provide the organization competitive edge. It keeps the necessary information at the fingertips of the manager. LIS functionality areas should be reviewed to identify and eliminate bottlenecks. Logistical information system functionality areas are mentioned below:

Order management

- Entry of the order into the system
- Edit for acceptable orders, find out acceptability of the orders checking against quantity, lead times and quality conformance standard
- Check inventory availability, delivery dates
- Based on the above checks confirmation of customer's requirements is done
- Primary interface between customer service representative and logistical operating system

Order processing

- Allocation of inventory on real time or in batch mode is a policy decision. Order processing is done based on this policy.
- Back-order creation: At this stage backlogging of orders is done keeping the benefits of backlogging and cost of customer dissatisfaction in mind.
- Conflict resolution to match customer requirement by doing necessary modification to the order.
- Order selection (direct distribution function to draw the inventory from which DC).

Distribution operation

- Directing all activities in a distribution centre to meet customer order requirement. This includes receiving, handling, storing, order selecting, etc.

Transportation and shipping: Plan executes and manages all transportation activities like shipment planning, scheduling, shipment consolidation, shipment notification, and document generation and carrier management.

LOGISTICAL ORGANIZATION

The basic function of logistical organization is to give orderly structure to logistical functions. In 1950, the structure was disintegrated or dispersed and various logistical functions were attached to various management functions like finance, manufacturing and marketing.

Logistical Organization Stage I: Late 1950s or early 1960s saw a grouping of logistical activities. Heads of materials management and physical distribution management were created. But these heads remained under the control of traditional management functions of manufacturing and marketing respectively.

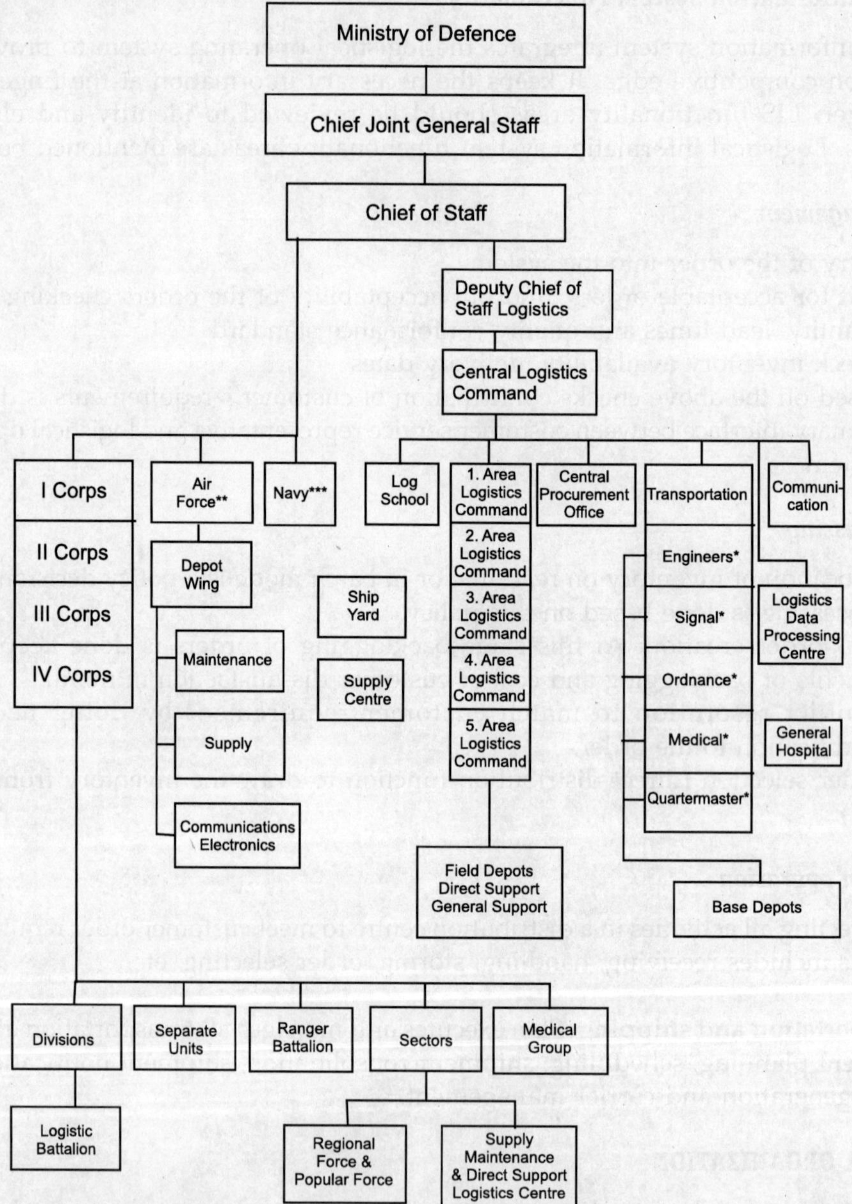

(*Source:* http://www.history.army.mil/books/vietnam/logistic/images/ch18.jpg

Fig. 7.3. Logistic organization of army.

Logistical Organization Stage II: Late 1960s or early 1970s saw emergence of physical distribution management. As an independent function internally integrating all outbound logistical functions. Materials remained attached to manufacturing.

Logistical Organization Stage III: Decade of 1980 saw emergence of a new organization. Organized activities of inbound and outbound logistics were brought under one control. New organization of logistical activities as logistical operations, logistical support and logistical planning emerge.

INTERNATIONAL LOGISTICS

According to The Council of Logistics Management, "International logistics is the process of planning, implementing and controlling the flow and storage of goods, services and related information from a point of origin to a point of consumption located in a different country."

International Logistics is design and management of a system that controls the flow of materials into, through, and out of the international corporation.

By taking a systems approach, the firm explicitly recognizes the linkages among the traditionally separate logistics components within and outside the corporation. Global logistics plans, controls, and manages the movement and storage of goods, services, and related information as it moves across international boundaries from raw material provider to consumer also considering the handling of return goods and containers.

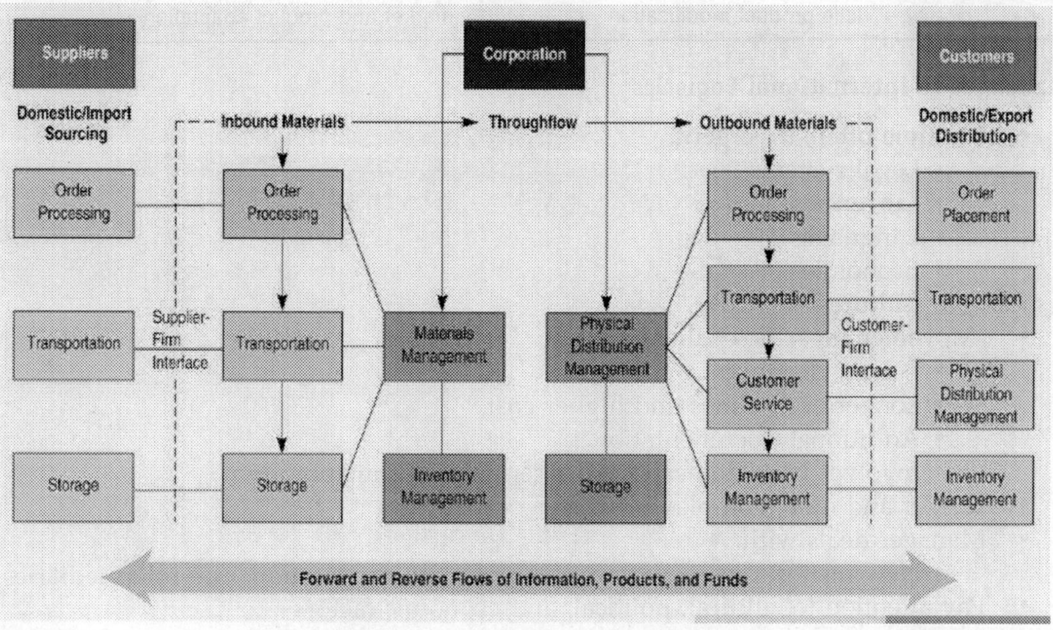

Fig. 7.4. The International supply chain.

Difference between International and Domestic Logistic

Basis	Domestic	International
Cost	About 10% of U.S. GDP today	Estimated at 16% of world GDP today
Transport mode	Mainly truck and rail	Mainly ocean and air, with significant intermodal activity
Inventories	Lower levels, reflecting short-order, lead-time requirements and improved transport capabilities	Higher levels, reflecting longer lead-times and greater demand and transit uncertainty
Agents	Modest usage, mostly in rail	Heavy reliance on forwarders, consolidators, and customs brokers
Financial risk	Low	High, owing to differences in currencies, inflation, levels and little recourse for default
Cargo risk	Low	High, owing to longer and more difficult transit, frequent cargo handling, and varying levels of infrastructure development
Government agencies	Primarily for hazardous materials, weight, safety laws, and some tariff requirements	Many agencies involved (e.g., customs, commerce, agriculture, transportation)
Administration	Minimal documentation involved (e.g., purchase order, bill of lading, invoice)	Significant paperwork; the U.S. Department of Commerce estimates that paperwork cost for an average shipment is $250
Communication	Voice, paper-based system adequate, with growing usage of electronic data interchange and Internet	Voice and paper costly and often ineffective; movement toward electronic interchange but variations in standards hinder widespread usage
Cultural differences	Relative homogeneity requires little product modification	Cultural differences require significant market and product adaptation

Challenges in International Logistics

- Multiple often, divergent:
  - Legal systems
  - Currencies
  - Languages
  - Economies
  - Cultures
- Movement-specific challenges
  - Longer distances
  - Longer cycle times and higher cost
  - Additional documentation
  - Involves both domestic and international transportation
- Riskier and more complex
- Manager deals with:
  - New institutions, new terms, complex documentation, and intermediaries
- Pay attention to cultural, political, and economic factors
- Interpersonal management task more difficult:
  - Multiple players

- Home office
- International business partners
- Officials in central and local government
- Workers in the venture

Guidelines for Developing a Global Logistic Strategy

Logistics planning should be integrated into the company's strategy. Logistics departments need to be guided by a clear vision and must measure output regularly. Import/export management should try to ensure integrated management of all elements of the logistics supply chain, from origin to destination. Opportunities to integrate domestic and international operations should be pursued to leverage total company volumes with globally oriented carriers.

TRANSPORTATION INFRASTRUCTURE

A firm's logistics platform is determined by a location's ease and convenience of market reach under favourable cost circumstances. The public sector's investment priorities, safety regulations, tax incentives, and transport policies can have major effects on the logistics decisions of firms. The logistics manager must learn about existing and planned infrastructures abroad and at home and factor them into the firm's strategy.

Airfreight

Airfreight is available to and from most countries, including the developing world. International airfreight is expected to grow to 190 billion tons in 2005, compared to only 70 billion tons in 1995. Forty per cent of the world's manufactured travel by air. Items that are high-value or high in density tend to travel by air.

Export Documentation

(i) A **bill of lading** is a contract between the exporter and the carrier indicating that the carrier has accepted responsibility for the goods and will provide transportation in return for payment.

(ii) A **commercial invoice** is a bill for the goods stating basic information about the transaction, including a description of the merchandise, total cost of the goods sold, addresses of the shipper and seller, and delivery and payment terms.

(iii) A **freight forwarder** specializes in handling export documentation.

International Inventory Issues

Inventories tie up a major portion of corporate funds, therefore, proper inventory policies should be a major concern to the international logistician. Just-in-time inventory policies minimize the volume of inventory by making it available only when needed.

The purpose of establishing inventory systems is:

- to maintain product movement in the delivery pipeline
- to have a cushion to absorb demand fluctuations

International Packaging Issues

Packaging is instrumental in getting the merchandise to the destination in a safe, presentable condition. Because of the added stress of international shipping, packaging that is adequate for domestic shipping may be inadequate for international shipping. Packaging considerations that should be taken into account are environmental conditions and weight. One solution to the packaging problem has been the development of intermodal containers. Cost attention must be paid to international packaging.

Storage Facilities

A stationary period is involved when merchandise becomes inventory stored in warehouses. The **location decision** addresses how many distribution centres to have and where to locate them. Storage facilities abroad can differ in availability and quality. The logistician should analyze international product sales and then rank order products according to warehousing needs.

Special Trade Zones

Foreign trade zones are areas where foreign goods may be held or processed and then re-exported without incurring duties. Trade zones can be useful as trans-shipment points to reduce logistics cost and redesign marketing approaches. Governments and firms benefit from foreign trade zones.

Export Processing Zones and Economic Zones

In **export processing zones**, special rules apply that are different in other regions of the country. These zones usually provide tax-free and duty-free treatment for production facilities whose output is destined abroad. The **maquiladoras** of Mexico are one example of a programme that permits firms to take advantage of sharp differentials in labour costs. Through the creation of **special economic zones**, the Chinese government has attracted many foreign investors bringing in millions of dollars.

Centralized Logistics Management

In international logistics, the existence of a headquarters staff that retains decision-making power over logistics is important. To avoid internal problems, both headquarters staff and local management should report to one person. This individual can contribute an objective view when inevitable conflicts arise in international logistics coordination.

Decentralized Logistics Management

When a firm serves many diverse international markets, total centralization might leave the firm unresponsive to local adaptation needs. If each subsidiary is made a profit centre in itself, each one carries the full responsibility for its performance. Once products are within a specific market, increased input from local logistics operations should be expected and encouraged.

Outsourcing Logistics Services

The systematic outsourcing of logistics capabilities is a third option. By collaborating with transportation firms, private warehouses, or other specialists, corporate resources can be concentrated on the firm's core product. One-stop logistics allows shippers to buy all the transportation modes and functional services from a single carrier.

The Supply Chain and the Internet

Because of the Internet, firms are able to conduct many more global comparisons among suppliers and select from a wider variety of choices. When customers have the ability to access a company through the Internet, the company must be prepared for 24-hour order-taking and customer service. For all countries, but particularly in developing nations, the issue of universal access to the Internet is crucial.

Logistics and Security

After the terrorist attacks of 2001, companies have to deal with the fact that the pace of international transactions has slowed down and that formerly routine steps will now take longer. Logistics systems and modern transportation systems are often the targets of attacks. The need to institute new safeguards for international shipments will affect the ability of firms to efficiently plan their international shipments.

Logistics and the Environment

Since environmental laws and regulations differ across the globe, the firm's efforts need to be responsive to a wide variety of requirements. Reverse distribution systems are instrumental in ensuring that the firm not only delivers the product to the market, but also can retrieve it from the market for subsequent use, recycling, or disposal. Companies need to learn how to simultaneously achieve environmental and economic goals.

SUPPLY CHAIN MANAGEMENT

Supply chain management (SCM) is the management of a network of interconnected businesses involved in the ultimate provision of product and service packages required by end customers (Harland, 1996). Supply chain management spans all movement and storage of raw materials, work-in-process inventory, and finished goods from point of origin to point of consumption (supply chain).

Another definition is provided by the APICS dictionary when it defines SCM as the "design, planning, execution, control, and monitoring of supply chain activities with the objective of creating net value, building a competitive infrastructure, leveraging worldwide logistics, synchronizing supply with demand, and measuring performance globally."

More common and accepted definitions of Supply Chain Management are:

Supply Chain Management is the systemic, strategic coordination of the traditional business functions and the tactics across these business functions within a particular company and across businesses within the supply chain, for the purposes of improving the long-term performance of the individual companies and the supply chain as a whole (Mentzer et al., 2001).

Global Supply Chain Forum–Supply Chain Management is the integration of key business processes across the supply chain for the purpose of creating value for customers and stakeholders (Lambert, 2008).

According to the Council of Supply Chain Management Professionals (CSCMP), supply chain management encompasses the planning and management of all activities involved in sourcing, procurement, conversion, and logistics management. It also includes the crucial components of coordination and collaboration with channel partners, which can be suppliers, intermediaries, third-party service providers, and customers. In essence, supply chain management integrates supply and demand management within and across companies. More recently, the loosely coupled, self-organizing network of businesses that cooperate to provide product and service offerings has been called the Extended Enterprise.

A supply chain, as opposed to supply chain management, is a set of organizations directly linked by one or more of the upstream and downstream flows of products, services, finances, and information from a source to a customer. Managing a supply chain is 'supply chain management' (Mentzer et al., 2001). Supply chain management software includes tools or modules used to execute supply chain transactions, manage supplier relationships and control associated business processes.

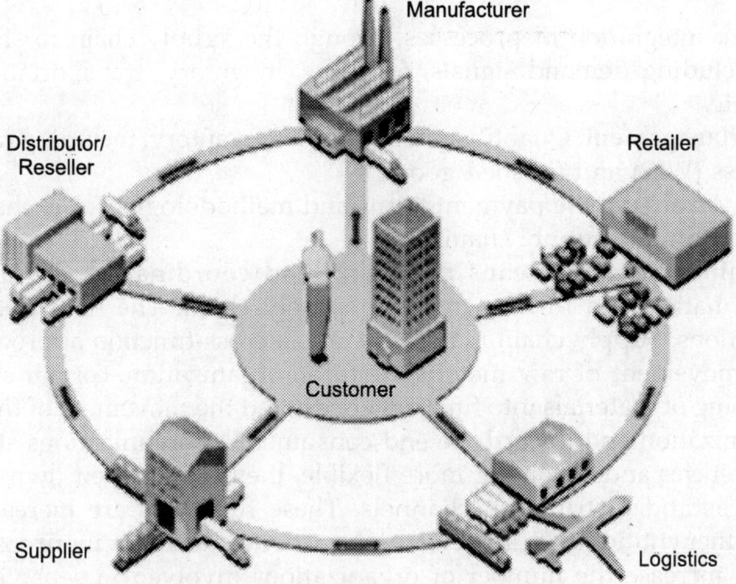

Fig. 7.5. A typical supply chain.

Supply chain event management (abbreviated as SCEM) is a consideration of all possible events and factors that can disrupt a supply chain. With SCEM possible scenarios can be created and solutions devised.

Supply Chain Management Problems

Supply chain management must address the following problems:

Distribution Network Configuration: Number, location and network missions of suppliers, production facilities, distribution centres, warehouses, cross-docks and customers.

Distribution Strategy: Questions of operating control (centralized, decentralized or shared); delivery scheme, e.g., direct shipment, pool point shipping, cross-docking, DSD (direct store delivery), closed loop shipping; mode of transportation, e.g., motor carrier, including truckload, LTL, parcel; railroad; intermodal transport, including TOFC (trailer on flatcar) and COFC (container on flatcar); ocean freight; airfreight; replenishment strategy (e.g., pull, push or hybrid); and transportation control (e.g., owner-operated, private carrier, common carrier, contract carrier, or 3PL).

Trade-offs in Logistical Activities: The above activities must be well coordinated in order to achieve the lowest total logistics cost. Trade-offs may increase the total cost if only one of the activities is optimized. For example, full truckload (FTL) rates are more economical on a cost per pallet basis than less than truckload (LTL) shipments. If, however, a full truckload of a product is ordered to reduce transportation costs, there will be an increase in inventory holding costs which may increase total logistics costs. It is therefore imperative to take a systems approach when planning logistical activities. These trade-offs are key to developing the most efficient and effective logistics and SCM strategy.

Information: Integration of processes through the supply chain to share valuable information, including demand signals, forecasts, inventory, transportation, potential collaboration, etc.

Inventory Management: Quantity and location of inventory, including raw materials, work-in-progress (WIP) and finished goods.

Cash-Flow: Arranging the payment terms and methodologies for exchanging funds across entities within the supply chain.

Supply chain execution means managing and coordinating the movement of materials, information and funds across the supply chain. The flow is bidirectional. Activities/functions: Supply chain management is a cross-function approach including managing the movement of raw materials into an organization, certain aspects of the internal processing of materials into finished goods, and the movement of finished goods out of the organization and toward the end-consumer. As organizations strive to focus on core competencies and becoming more flexible, they reduce their ownership of raw materials sources and distribution channels. These functions are increasingly being outsourced to other entities that can perform the activities better or more cost-effectively. The effect is to increase the number of organizations involved in satisfying customer demand, while reducing management control of daily logistics operations. Less control and more supply chain partners led to the creation of supply chain management concepts. The purpose of supply chain management is to improve trust and collaboration among supply chain partners, thus improving inventory visibility and the velocity of inventory movement.

Several models have been proposed for understanding the activities required to manage material movements across organizational and functional boundaries. SCOR is a supply chain management model promoted by the Supply Chain Council. Another model is the SCM Model proposed by the Global Supply Chain Forum (GSCF). Supply chain activities can be grouped into strategic, tactical, and operational levels. The CSCMP has adopted The American Productivity & Quality Centre (APQC) Process Classification Framework SM a high-level, industry-neutral enterprise process model that allows organizations to see their business processes from a cross-industry viewpoint.

Organizations increasingly find that they must rely on effective supply chains, or networks, to compete in the global market and networked economy. In Peter Drucker's (1998) new management paradigms, this concept of business relationships extends beyond traditional enterprise boundaries and seeks to organize entire business processes throughout a value chain of multiple companies.

During the past decades, globalization, outsourcing and information technology have enabled many organizations, such as Dell and Hewlett Packard, to successfully operate solid collaborative supply networks in which each specialized business partner focuses on only a few key strategic activities (Scott, 1993). This inter-organizational supply network can be acknowledged as a new form of organization. However, with the complicated interactions among the players, the network structure fits neither "market" nor "hierarchy" categories (Powell, 1990). It is not clear what kind of performance impacts different supply network structures could have on firms, and little is known about the coordination conditions and trade-offs that may exist among the players. From a systems perspective, a complex network structure can be decomposed into individual component firms (Zhang and Dilts, 2004). Traditionally, companies in a supply network concentrate on the inputs and outputs of the processes, with little concern for the internal management working of other individual players. Therefore, the choice of an internal management control structure is known to impact local firm performance (Mintzberg, 1979).

In the 21st century, changes in the business environment have contributed to the development of supply chain networks. First, as an outcome of globalization and the proliferation of multinational companies, joint ventures, strategic alliances and business partnerships, significant success factors were identified, complementing the earlier "Just-in-Time", "Lean Manufacturing" and "Agile Manufacturing" practices. Second, technological changes, particularly the dramatic fall in information communication costs, which are a significant component of transaction costs, have led to changes in coordination among the members of the supply chain network (Coase, 1998).

Many researchers have recognized these kinds of supply network structures as a new organization form, using terms such as "Keiretsu", "Extended Enterprise", "Virtual Corporation", "Global Production Network", and "Next Generation Manufacturing System". In general, such a structure can be defined as "a group of semi-independent organizations, each with their capabilities, which collaborate in ever-changing constellations to serve one or more markets in order to achieve some business goal specific to that collaboration" (Akkermans, 2001).

The security management system for supply chains is described in ISO/IEC 28000 and ISO/IEC 28001 and related standards published jointly by ISO and IEC. Developments in Supply Chain Management: Six major movements can be observed in the evolution of supply chain management studies: Creation, Integration, and Globalization (Lavassani et al., 2008a), Specialization.

Evolution of Supply Chain

Creation Era: The term supply chain management was first coined by a U.S. industry consultant in the early 1980s. However, the concept of a supply chain in management was of great importance long before, in the early 20th century, especially with the creation of the assembly line. The characteristics of this era of supply chain management include the need for large-scale changes, re-engineering, downsizing driven by cost reduction programs, and widespread attention to the Japanese practice of management.

Integration Era: This era of supply chain management studies was highlighted with the development of Electronic Data Interchange (EDI) systems in the 1960s and developed through the 1990s by the introduction of Enterprise Resource Planning (ERP) systems. This era has continued to develop into the 21st century with the expansion of Internet-based collaborative systems. This era of supply chain evolution is characterized by both increasing value-adding and cost reductions through integration.

Globalization Era: The third movement of supply chain management development, the globalization era, can be characterized by the attention given to global systems of supplier relationships and the expansion of supply chains over national boundaries and into other continents. Although the use of global sources in the supply chain of organizations can be traced back several decades (e.g., in the oil industry), it was not until the late 1980s that a considerable number of organizations started to integrate global sources into their core business. This era is characterized by the globalization of supply chain management in organizations with the goal of increasing their competitive advantage, value-adding, and reducing costs through global sourcing.

Specialization Era—Phase One: Outsourced Manufacturing and Distribution in the 1990s industries began to focus on "core competencies" and adopted a specialization model. Companies abandoned vertical integration, sold off non-core operations, and outsourced those functions to other companies. This changed management requirements by extending the supply chain well beyond company walls and distributing management across specialized supply chain partnerships.

This transition also re-focused the fundamental perspectives of each respective organization. OEMs became brand owners that needed deep visibility into their supply base. They had to control the entire supply chain from above instead of from within. Contract manufacturers had to manage bills of material with different part numbering schemes from multiple OEMs and support customer requests for work-in-process visibility and vendor-managed inventory (VMI).

The specialization model creates manufacturing and distribution networks composed of multiple, individual supply chains specific to products, suppliers, and customers who work together to design, manufacture, distribute, market, sell, and service a product. The set of partners may change according to a given market, region, or channel, resulting in a proliferation of trading partner environments, each with its own unique characteristics and demands.

Specialization Era—Phase Two: Supply Chain Management as a service specialization within the supply chain began in the 1980s with the inception of transportation brokerages, warehouse management, and non-asset-based carriers and has matured beyond transportation and logistics into aspects of supply planning, collaboration, execution and performance management.

At any given moment, market forces could demand changes from suppliers, logistics providers, locations and customers, and from any number of these specialized participants as components of supply chain networks. This variability has significant effects on the supply chain infrastructure, from the foundation layers of establishing and managing the electronic communication between the trading partners to more complex requirements including the configuration of the processes and workflows that are essential to the management of the network itself.

Supply chain specialization enables companies to improve their overall competencies in the same way that outsourced manufacturing and distribution has done; it allows them to focus on their core competencies and assemble networks of specific, best-in-class partners to contribute to the overall value chain itself, thereby increasing overall performance and efficiency. The ability to quickly obtain and deploy this domain-specific supply chain expertise without developing and maintaining an entirely unique and complex competency in house is the leading reason why supply chain specialization is gaining popularity.

Outsourced technology hosting for supply chain solutions debuted in the late 1990s and has taken root primarily in transportation and collaboration categories. This has progressed from the Application Service Provider (ASP) model from approximately 1998 through 2003 to the On-Demand model from approximately 2003-2006 to the Software as a Service (SaaS) model currently in focus today.

Importance of Supply Chain

Supply chain is about creating value for customers and suppliers of the firm, and value for the firm's stakeholders. Value in supply chain is primarily in terms of time and place. Productions and services have no value unless they are supplied to customers when (time) and where (place) they wish to consume them. Good supply chain management views each activity in the supply chain as contributing to the process of adding value. To many firms throughout world, supply chain has become an increasingly important value-adding process for a number of reasons. They are discussed below.

Costs are Significant: Statistics show that average about 12% of world's GDP accounts supply chain costs. About 7-9% sales accounts physical distribution costs. Supply chain cost, substantial for most firms, rank second only to the cost of goods sold. Value is added by minimizing these costs and by passing the benefits on to customers and to the firm's shareholders.

Increased expectations of the customers: Awareness of customers has gone up. Customers expect rapid processing of their requests, quick delivery and also expect a high degree of product availability. Supply chain assures less error rates, lower order processing costs, reduced inventory, minimum cycle time and lowest transportation costs. To meet the increased exceptions of the present-day customer, it is essential that every firm should implement supply chain management.

Supply and distributions lines are lengthening with greater complexity: Today's trend is towards an integrated world economy. Firms are seeking, or have developed, global strategies by designing their products for a world market and producing them wherever the low-cost raw materials, components, and labour can be found, or they simply produce locally and sell internationally. In either case, supply and distribution lines are stretched, as compared with the producer who wishes to manufacture and sell only locally. As this happens, supply chain takes on increased importance within the firm and can considerably reduce the other costs.

Supply chain is important to strategy: Firms spend a great deal of time finding ways to differentiate their product offerings from those of their competitors. When management recognizes that supply chain affects a significant portion of a firm's costs and that the result of decisions made about the supply chain processes yields different levels of customer service, it is in a position to use this effectively to penetrate new markets, to increase market share, and to increase profits. That is, good supply chain management can generate sales, not just reduce costs.

Supply Chain adds Significant Customer Value: Customers become unsatisfied, if the product/service is not delivered to him/her at the time and place he/she wishes to consume it. When a firm incurs the cost of moving the product toward the customer or making inventory available in a timely manner, customer value has been created. It is value as surely as that created through the production of a quality product or through a low price. Supply chain controls two (time and place) out of four values creating variables.

Customers increasingly want QUICK customized response: Today's customers expect that products and services be delivered at very short time. In addition, improved internet service, quick information systems, and flexible manufacturing systems have led the marketplace toward customization. Rather than consumers having to accept the 'One size fits all' philosophy in their purchase, suppliers are increasingly offering products that meet individual customer needs.

Supply Chain in Service Industry: Service sector of industrialized countries is large and growing. The size of this sector alone forces us to use the supply chain concepts to tap the potentials so far not tapped.

Decision Phase in a Supply Chain

Successful management of supply chain requires many important decisions, such as strategy, planning and operations. They are very important because they affect the flow of information, product and funds in the supply chain. Let us discuss these decisions.

Strategy or Design: Strategy is a grand plan. Supply chain strategy involving decisions how to structure the supply chain over next several years. It decides what the chains configuration will be, how resources will be allocated, and what processes each stage will perform. Strategic decisions made by companies include the location and capacities of production and warehouse facilities, the products to be manufactured or stored at various locations, the modes of transportation to be made available along different shipping legs, and the type of information system to be utilized. A firm must ensure that the supply chain configuration supports its strategic objectives during this decision phase. Supply chain design decisions are made for the long term and are very expensive to alter on short notice.

Consequently, when companies make these decisions, they must take into account uncertainty in anticipated market conditions over the next few years.

(i) **Planning:** The supply chains configuration determined in design phase is fixed for making planning decisions. Companies start the planning phase with a forecast for the coming year of demand in different markets. Planning includes decisions regarding which markets will be supplied from which locations, the sub-contracting of manufacturing, the inventory policies to be followed, and the timing and size of marking promotions. Planning establishes parameters within which a supply chain will function over a specified period of time. In the planning phase, companies must include uncertainty in demand, exchange rates, and competition over this time horizon in their decisions.

    Given a shorter time horizon and better forecast than the design phase, companies in the planning phase try to incorporate any flexibility built into optimize performance. As a result of the planning phase, companies define a set of operating polices that govern short-term operations.

(ii) **Operation:** During operation phase (weekly or daily) companies make decisions regarding individual customer orders. At the operational level, supply chain configuration is considered fixed and planning policies are already defined. The goal of supply chain operations is to handle incoming customer orders in the best possible manner. During this phase, firms allocate inventory or production to individual orders, set a date that an order is to be filled, generate pick lists at a warehouse, allocate an order to a particular shipping mode and shipment, set delivery schedules of trunks and place replenishment orders. Because operational decisions are being made in the short term, there is less uncertainty about demand information. Given the constraints established by the operation phase is to exploit the reduction of uncertainty and optimize performance.

Effectiveness of Supply Chain

The performance of supply chain depends on successful managing of following functional areas:

(a) **Customer service management process:** Customer Relationship Management concerns the relationship between the organizations and its customers. Customer service is the source of customer information. It also provides the customer with real-time information on scheduling and product availability through interfaces with the company's production and distribution operations. Successful organizations use the following steps to build customer relationships:

- determine mutually satisfying goals for organization and customers
- establish and maintain customer rapport
- produce positive feelings in the organization and the customers

(b) **Procurement process:** Strategic plans are drawn up with suppliers to support the manufacturing flow management process and the development of new products. In firms where operations extend globally, sourcing should be managed on a global basis. The desired outcome is a win-win relationship where both parties benefit, and a reduction in time required for the design cycle and product development. Also, the purchasing function develops rapid communication systems, such as electronic data interchange (EDI) and Internet linkage to convey possible requirements more rapidly. Activities related to obtaining products and materials from outside suppliers involve resource planning, supply sourcing, negotiation, order placement, inbound transportation, storage, handling and quality assurance, many of which include the responsibility to coordinate with suppliers on matters of scheduling, supply continuity, hedging, and research into new sources or programmes.

(c) **Product development and commercialization:** Here, customers and suppliers must be integrated into the product development process in order to reduce time to market. As product life cycles shorten, the appropriate products must be developed and successfully launched with ever shorter time-schedules to remain competitive. According to Lambert and Cooper (2000), managers of the product development and commercialization process must:

- Coordinate with customer relationship management to identify customer-articulated needs;
- Select materials and suppliers in conjunction with procurement, and
- Develop production technology in manufacturing flow to manufacture and integrate into the best supply chain flow for the product/market combination.

(d) **Manufacturing flow management process:** The manufacturing process produces and supplies products to the distribution channels based on past forecasts. Manufacturing processes must be flexible to respond to market changes and must accommodate mass customization. Orders are processes operating on a just-in-time (JIT) basis in minimum lot sizes. Also, changes in the manufacturing flow process lead to shorter cycle times, meaning improved responsiveness and efficiency in meeting customer demand. Activities related to planning, scheduling and supporting manufacturing operations, such as work-in-process storage, handling, transportation, and time phasing of components, inventory at manufacturing sites and maximum flexibility in the coordination of geographic and final assemblies postponement of physical distribution operations.

(e) **Physical distribution:** This concerns movement of a finished product/service to customers. In physical distribution, the customer is the final destination of a marketing channel, and the availability of the product/service is a vital part of each channel participant's marketing effort. It is also through the physical distribution process that the time and space of customer service become an integral part of marketing, thus it links a marketing channel with its customers (e.g., links manufacturers, wholesalers, retailers).

(f) **Outsourcing/partnerships:** This is not just outsourcing the procurement of materials and components, but also outsourcing of services that traditionally have been provided in-house. The logic of this trend is that the company will increasingly focus on those activities in the value chain where it has a distinctive advantage, and outsource everything else. This movement has been particularly evident in logistics where the provision of transport, warehousing and inventory control is increasingly subcontracted to specialists or logistics partners. Also, managing and controlling this network of partners and suppliers requires a blend of both central and local involvement. Hence, strategic decisions need to be taken centrally, with the monitoring and control of supplier performance and day-to-day liaison with logistics partners being best managed at a local level.

(g) **Performance measurement:** Experts found a strong relationship from the largest arcs of supplier and customer integration to market share and profitability. Taking advantage of supplier capabilities and emphasizing a long-term supply chain perspective in customer relationships can both be correlated with firm performance. As logistics competency becomes a more critical factor in creating and maintaining competitive advantage, logistics measurement becomes increasingly important because the difference between profitable and unprofitable operations becomes narrower. A.T. Kearney Consultants (1985) noted that firms engaging in comprehensive performance measurement realized improvements in overall productivity. According to experts, internal measures are generally collected and analyzed by the firm including

- Cost
- Customer service
- Productivity measures
- Asset measurement, and
- Quality.

External performance measurement is examined through customer perception measures and "best practice" benchmarking, and includes (i) customer perception measurement, and (ii) best practice benchmarking.

Theories of Supply Chain Management

Currently there is a gap in the literature available on supply chain management studies: there is no theoretical support for explaining the existence and the boundaries of supply chain management. A few authors such as Halldorsson, et al. (2003), Ketchen and Hult (2006) and Lavassani, et al. (2008b) have tried to provide theoretical foundations for different areas related to supply chain by employing organizational theories. These theories include:

- Resource-Based View (RBV)
- Transaction Cost Analysis (TCA).
- Knowledge-Based View (KBV)
- Strategic Choice Theory (SCT)
- Agency Theory (AT)
- Institutional Theory (InT)
- Systems Theory (ST)
- Network Perspective (NP)

Tax Efficient Supply Chain Management

Tax Efficient Supply Chain Management is a business model which considers the effect of tax in design and implementation of supply chain management. As the consequence of globalization, business which is cross-nation should pay different tax rates in different countries. Due to the differences, global players have the opportunity to calculate and optimize supply chain based on tax efficiency legally. It is used as a method of gaining more profit for company which owns global supply chain.

Supply Chain Sustainability

Supply chain sustainability is a business issue affecting an organization's supply chain or logistics network and is frequently quantified by comparison with SECH ratings. SECH ratings are defined as social, ethical, cultural and health footprints. Consumers have become more aware of the environmental impact of their purchases and companies' SECH ratings and, along with non-governmental organizations (NGOs), are setting the agenda for transitions to organically-grown foods, anti-sweatshop labour codes and locally-produced goods that support independent and small businesses. Because supply chains frequently account for over 75% of a company's carbon footprint many organizations are exploring how they can reduce this and thus improve their SECH rating.

For example, in July 2009 the U.S. based Wal-Mart corporation announced its intentions to create a global sustainability index that would rate products according to the environmental and social impact made while the products were manufactured and distributed. The sustainability rating index is intended to create environmental accountability in Wal-Mart's supply chain, and provide the motivation and infrastructure for other retail industry companies to do the same.

Components of Supply Chain Management Integration

The SCM components are the third element of the four-square circulation framework. The level of integration and management of a business process link is a function of the number and level, ranging from low to high, of components added to the link (Ellram and Cooper, 1990; Houlihan, 1985). Consequently, adding more management components or increasing the level of each component can increase the level of integration of the business process link. The literature on business process re-engineering, buyer-supplier relationships and SCM suggests various possible components that must receive managerial attention when managing supply relationships. Lambert and Cooper (2000) identified the following components:

- Planning and control
- Work structure
- Organization structure
- Product flow facility structure
- Information flow facility structure
- Management methods
- Power and leadership structure
- Risk and reward structure
- Culture and attitude

However, a more careful examination of the existing literature leads to a more comprehensive understanding of what should be the key critical supply chain components, the "branches" of the previous identified supply chain business processes, that is, what kind of relationship the components may have that are related to suppliers and customers. Bowersox and Closs states that the emphasis on cooperation represents the synergism leading to the highest level of joint achievement (Bowersox and Closs, 1996). A primary level channel participant is a business that is willing to participate in the inventory ownership responsibility or assume other aspects of financial risk, thus including primary level components (Bowersox and Closs, 1996). A secondary level participant (specialized) is a business that participates in channel relationships by performing essential services for primary participants, including secondary level components, which support primary participants. Third level channel participants and components that support the primary level channel participants and are the fundamental branches of the secondary level components may also be included.

Consequently, Lambert and Cooper's framework of supply chain components does not lead to any conclusion about what are the primary or secondary (specialized) level supply chain components (see Bowersox and Closs, 1996, p. 93). That is, what supply chain components should be viewed as primary or secondary, how should these components be structured in order to have a more comprehensive supply chain structure, and how to examine the supply chain as an integrative one.

Reverse Supply Chain Reverse logistics is the process of managing the return of goods. Reverse logistics is also referred to as "Aftermarket Customer Services". In other words, any time money is taken from a company's warranty reserve or service logistics budget one can speak of a reverse logistics operation.

GLOBAL SUPPLY CHAIN MANAGEMENT

Global supply chains pose challenges regarding both quantity and value. Supply and Value chain trends:

- Globalization
- Increased cross border sourcing
- Collaboration for parts of value chain with low-cost providers

- Shared service centres for logistical and administrative functions
- Increasingly global operations, which require increasingly global coordination and planning to achieve global optimums
- Complex problems involve also midsized companies to an increasing degree

These trends have many benefits for manufacturers because they make possible larger lot sizes, lower taxes, and better environments (culture, infrastructure, special tax zones, sophisticated OEM) for their products. Meanwhile, on top of the problems recognized in supply chain management, there will be many more challenges when the scope of supply chains is global. This is because with a supply chain of a larger scope, the lead time is much longer. Furthermore, there are more issues involved such as multi-currencies, different policies and different laws. The consequent problems include:

- Different currencies and valuations in different countries;
- Different tax laws (Tax Efficient Supply Chain Management);
- Different trading protocols;
- Lack of transparency of cost and profit.

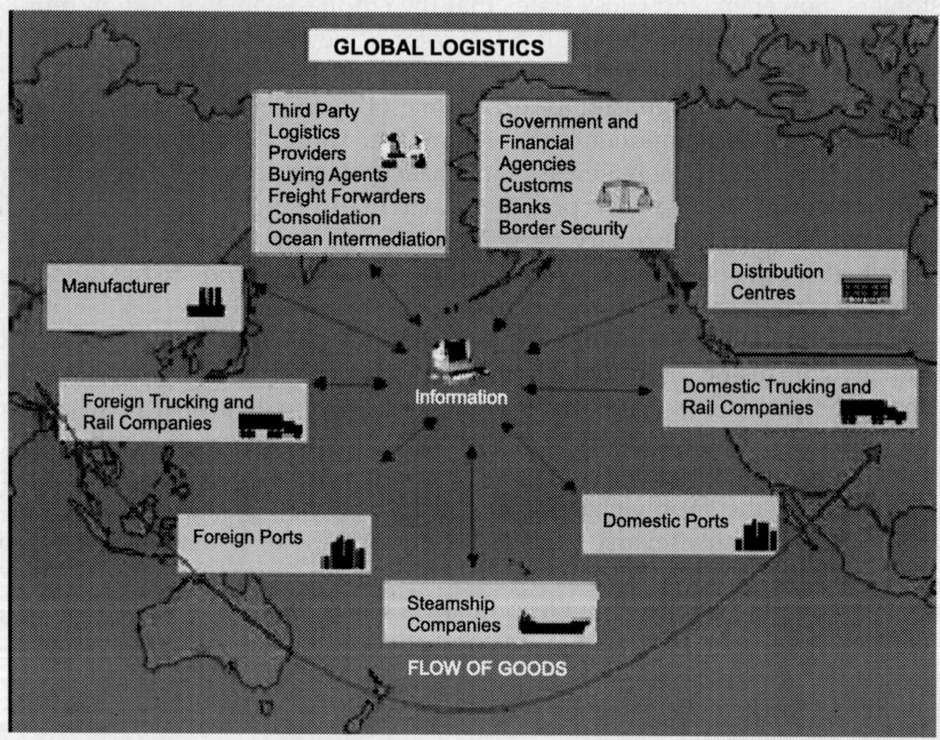

LATEST TECHNOLOGIES IN THE LOGISTICS

Latest technologies in the logistics are in the areas of:

- Automatic identification
- Communication

- Material handling
- Information technology

(i) Automatic Identification Technology

- Direct entry of data or information into computer without operating a keyboard.
- Includes bar coding, RFID, data-communication, magnetic strip and voice recognition.
- It can be used for tracking rail cars, a carton moving on a conveyor belt, etc.

(ii) Bar Coding

- Used for identification, handling, retrieval and storage of goods.
- Individual inventory items, cartons, etc. are affixed with bar codes.
- They are a sequence of parallel lines of different thickness and with spaces in between.
- These bar codes can be read by a bar code scanner attached to an online computer.
- Bar code helps it showing an inventory's identity during storage, retrieval and dispatch.
- They are also used by accounts departments for preparation of bills.
- These bars have information in a codified form which can be decodified with the help of a scanner.

Advantages of bar coding

- Facilitates easy identification of items during storage, packing, dispatch and transit.
- Reduce paper work and time consumed for process.
- Increase the productivity of warehouse.
- Facilitate system automation.

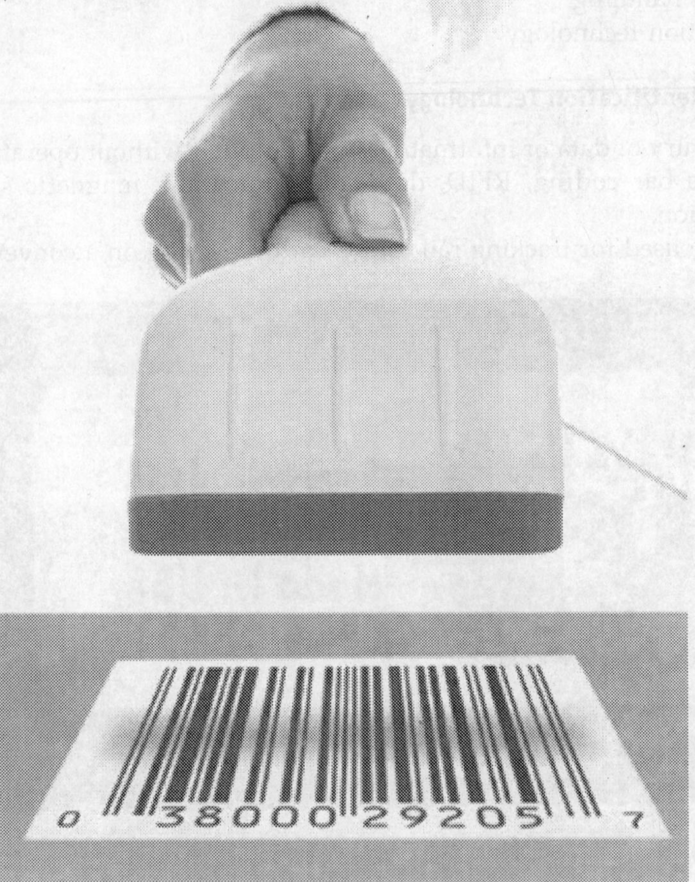

(iii) Radio Frequency Identification

- It is automated identification and data capture technology.
- It is one of the most preferred forms these days.
- It helps in communication between objects and systems.
- It consists of two main elements–a tag and a reader that communicate through radio transmission.
- The tag contains a small chip and an antenna and can be placed on any object.
- Information stored on the tag can be transmitted to an RAD reader over a distance of few metres.
- Information stored may be product type, product item, manufacturer, date expiry, etc.
- RFID is been used in passports.
- The first RFID passport was used in Malaysia in 1998.

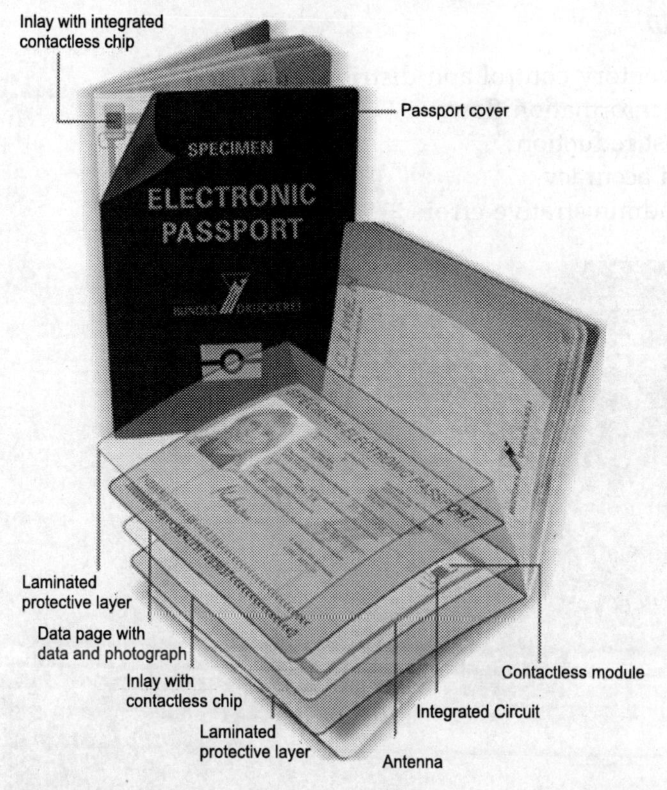

Inlay with integrated contactless chip
Passport cover
SPECIMEN
ELECTRONIC PASSPORT
Laminated protective layer
Data page with data and photograph
Inlay with contactless chip
Laminated protective layer
Antenna
Integrated Circuit
Contactless module

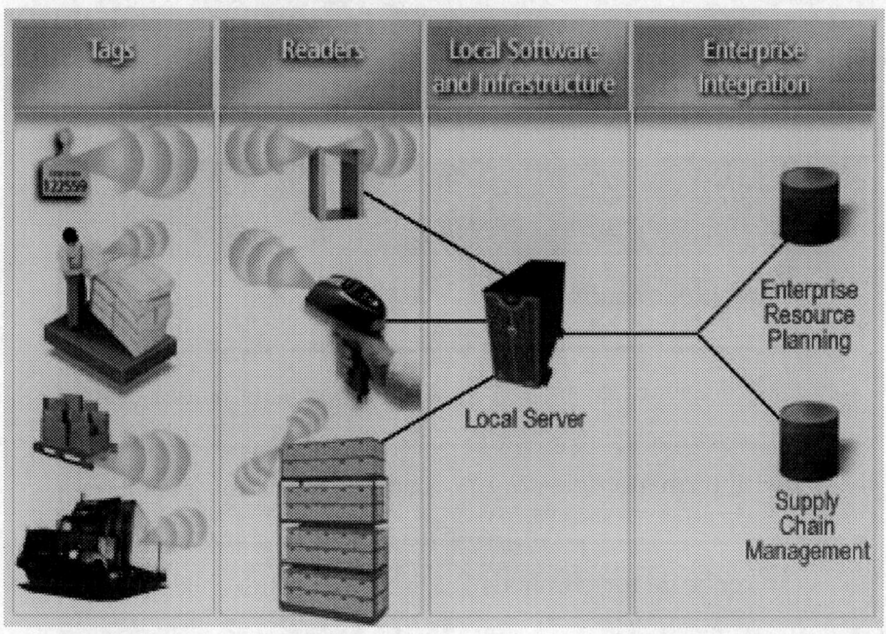

Tags
Readers
Local Software and Infrastructure
Enterprise Integration
Enterprise Resource Planning
Local Server
Supply Chain Management

Advantages of RFID

- Proper inventory control and distribution.
- Improved information flow.
- Labour cost reduction.
- Speed and accuracy.
- Reduced administrative errors.

(iv) Bar Coding vs RFID

Bar coding	**RFID**
Individual reading	Simultaneous reading
High Labour costs	Automated: low labour costs
Limited information memory	Large information memory
Easy to replicate for criminals	Difficult to replicate

(v) Communication Technology

- Communication has a very crucial role in business success.
- Latest technology in communication has ensured that there is speed and accuracy in customer service.
- These technologies have enabled superior customer service leading to competitiveness.

(vi) Global Positioning System

- It is a space-based global navigation system that provides reliable location of objects.
- In logistics, GPS can be used for tracking the locations of trucks carrying goods.
- Once the position of vehicle is known, it can be transmitted through other centres.
- Transmission network will be a mobile phone or Internet.

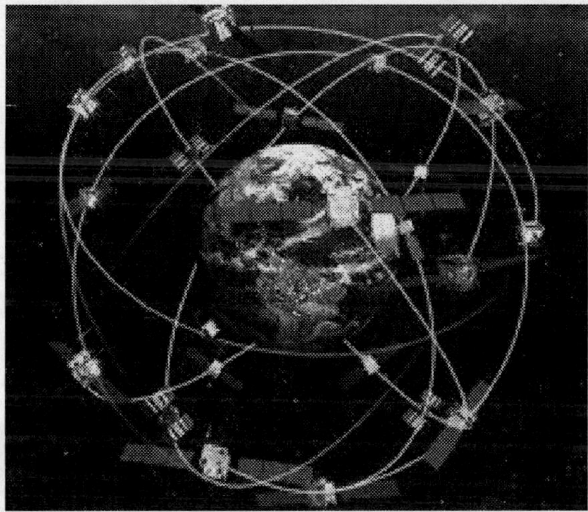

- GPS system has a voice-over facility for driver to speak and hear instructions.
- A GPS receiver needs to be mounted on the truck.
- It also has LCD supported by a keyboard to transmit and receive text massages.
- GPS is mostly used in developed countries.
- In India, its used at very limited place.
- This system costs about Rs. 25,000 per truck.
- GPS is also used for tracking the direction of vehicles, duration of halt, to check overspeeding, etc.
- In India, BMTC uses GPS technology.
- BMTC could recover their lost bus stolen by thieves the very next day using GPS technology.
- Information collected from the GPS would be in latitudes and longitudes.

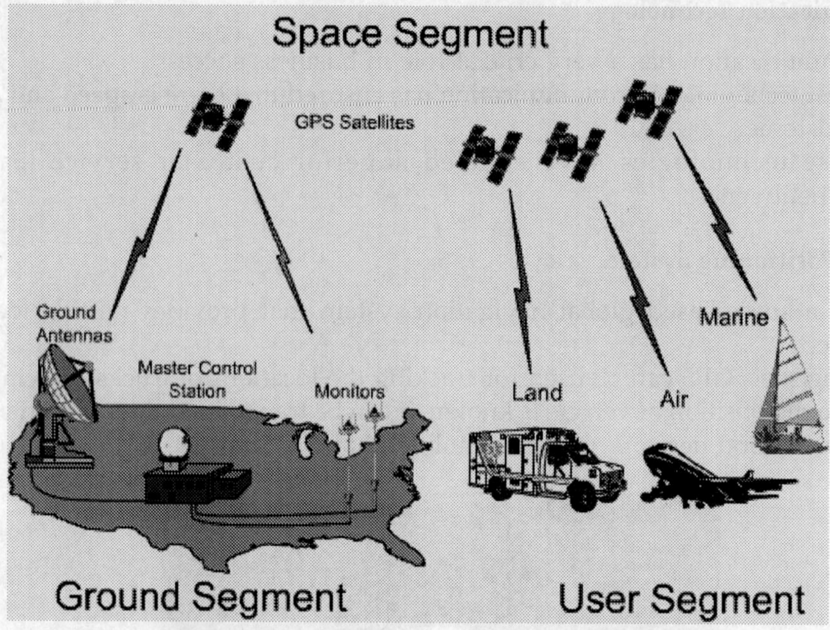

Advantages of GPS

- Greater saving of time.
- Greater security.
- Increased productivity.
- Reduction in cost.

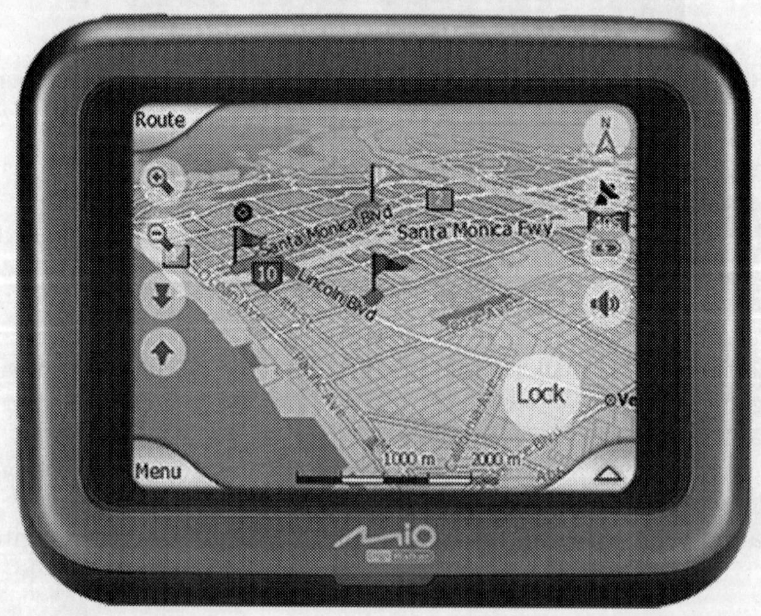

(vii) E-Tracking

- It involves truck drivers calling their offices at regular intervals in a day to notify his position.
- This becomes costly if information is to be conveyed to both consigner and consignee.
- It costs about Rs. 7,000 per vehicle per month.
- For PDS tracking, collector of Tiruchirapalli gifted mobile phones to employees on 14th August 2010.

(viii) Automated Material Handling

- Automation for loading, unloading, storing of goods in warehouses.
- It will reduce the intensity of labour in these activities.
- Automation will be more useful where handling of hazardous material takes place.

(ix) AGVS

- It stands for Automated Guided Vehicle System.
- This system makes use of magnetic or optical guidance system.
- It is a mobile robot that follows markers or wires in the floor.
- These robots can be programmed by built-in microprocessors for performing various tasks in warehouses.
- AGVS can perform its functions without any human involvement.
- In multi-storey warehouses, the ASRS are in use because of greater importance to automated unit load handling.

(x) Information Directed System

- This system keeps all equipment in the warehouse under the control of a centralized computer.
- The required movements are fed into a computer for analysis.
- The computer assigns the jobs to individual equipment.
- The communication is through radio frequency.
- These systems can do a variety of complex material-handling jobs by same equipment.
- This system ensures flexibility in handling a variety of jobs.
- This is recently developed, so it is still in the testing stage.

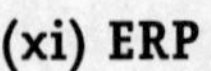

(xi) ERP

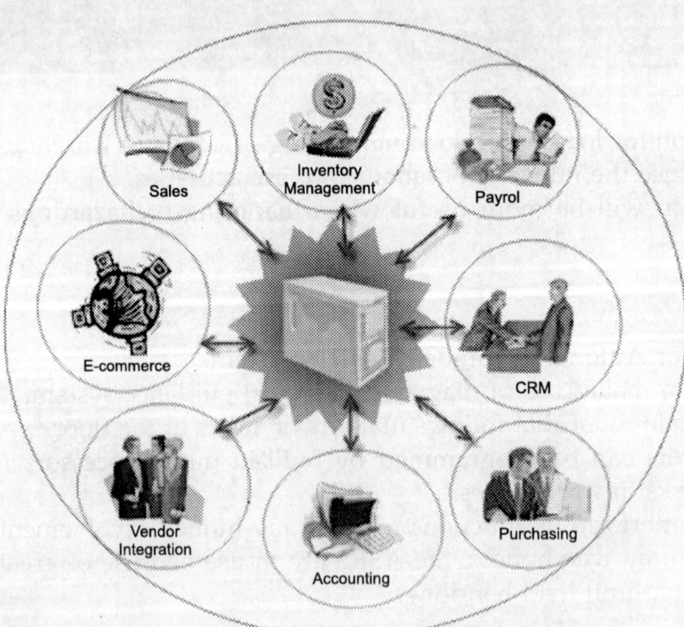

- It stands for Enterprise Resource Planning.
- It is a way to integrate the data and processes of an organization into one single system.
- Its purpose is to facilitate flow of information between all business functions inside the boundaries of the organization.
- ERP is very expensive, large and complex.
- ERP finds its use in SCM as SCM focuses on optimizing movement of goods through the logistic system of the enterprise.
- Indian companies Ramco Systems have developed ERP to suit the Indian business environment.

Advantages of ERP

- Quicker response to customer requirement.
- Reduction in inventory costs.
- Improvement in service levels.
- Reduction in logistical cost.

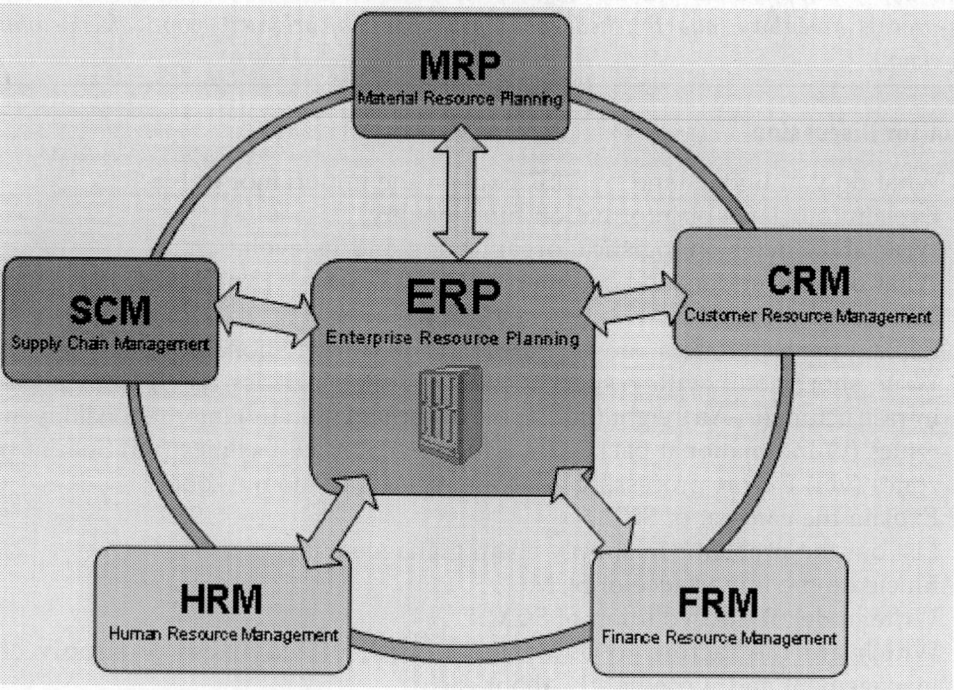

Let Us Sum Up

Logistical Information System (LIS) handles information related to Logistics Management. Hence, it is a structure of machines and management technology that enables management to receive, collect, store, transmit and analyze information which has an immensely important role in achieving business goals.

Logistical organization is to give orderly structure to logistical functions. In 1950, the structure was disintegrated or dispersed and various logistical functions were attached to various management functions like finance, manufacturing and marketing.

International logistics is design and management of a system that controls the flow of materials into, through, and out of the international corporation.

By taking a systems approach, the firm explicitly recognizes the linkages among the traditionally separate logistics components within and outside the corporation. Global logistics plans, controls, and manages the movement and storage of goods, services, and related information as it moves across international boundaries from raw material provider to consumer also considering the handling of return goods and containers.

Supply chain management (SCM) is the management of a network of interconnected businesses involved in the ultimate provision of product and service packages required by end customers (Harland, 1996). Supply Chain Management spans all movement and storage of raw materials, work-in-process inventory, and finished goods from point of origin to point of consumption (supply chain).

Question for Discussion

1. What do you understand by LIS? Explain the importance of LIS.
2. Explain four level of information functionality.
3. Write short notes on logistical organization and its evolution.
4. What do you understand by International Logistics? Explain few challenges in International Logistics.
5. Explain the differences between domestic and international logistics.
6. Write short notes with respect to international logistics on (i) Transportation infrastructure (ii) Airfreight (iii) Export documentation (iv) International inventory issues (v) International packaging issues (vi) Storage facilities (vii) Special trade zones (viii) Export processing zone and special economic zone.
7. Explain the concept of SCM.
8. List out the problems in supply chain management.
9. Elucidate the importance of SCM.
10. Write in detail the evolution of SCM.
11. Which are the factors to be considered for effectiveness of supply chain management and write briefly about each?
12. Name the various theories of supply chain management.
13. Write briefly about global supply chain management.
14. Write short notes on (i) Automatic identification technology (ii) Bar coding (iii) RFI (iv) GPS (v) E-tracking (vi) Automated material handling (vii) AGVS (viii) Information directed system (ix) ERP.

8

CHAPTER

Warehouse Management

"Amateurs talk about tactics, but professionals study logistics."

—Gen. Robert H. Barrow, USMC (Commandant of the Marine Corps) noted in 1980

Warehouse management – introduction – need for warehousing – types of warehouses – characteristics of ideal warehouse – functions – advantages – warehouse location – factors to look before warehouse selection – ideal warehouse location – warehouse cost – storage management – different types of storage system – warehouse design – storage plan – service benefits of warehousing – stacking and storage system – pilferage – product deterioration – shrinkage – pest control – warehouse – inventory management – needs – inventory control – factors affecting – inventory cost – EOQ – ABC analysis – VED classification – FSN analysis – modern warehouse management – automated system.

LEARNING OBJECTIVES

After going through this chapter, students will be able to understand

- Understanding meaning of warehouse management
- Different types of warehouse
- Merchandise handling
- Stacking, pilferage, spoilage, shrinkage
- Pest and insect control
- Receiving and issuing inventory
- Overhead costs
- Inventory cost
- Control systems

INTRODUCTION

A warehouse is a commercial building for storage of goods. Warehouses are used by manufacturers, importers, exporters, wholesalers, transport businesses, customs, etc. They are usually large plain buildings in industrial parts of towns. They come equipped with loading docks to load and unload trucks; or sometimes are loaded directly from railways, airports, or seaports. They also often have cranes and forklifts for moving goods, which are usually placed on ISO standard pallets.

A warehouse is the centre of any retail distribution organization. The fast and accurate tracking of shipments and organization of those shipments is a vital component to any distribution firm. In order to streamline the warehouse tasks, many companies are turning to upgrade current infrastructures to increase efficiency and speed of various warehousing tasks.

Need for Warehousing

Warehousing is necessary due to the following reasons:

(i) **Seasonal Production:** Agricultural commodities are harvested during certain seasons, but their consumption or use takes place throughout the year. Therefore, there is a need for proper storage or warehousing for these commodities, from where they can be supplied as and when required.

(ii) **Seasonal Demand:** There are certain goods, which are demanded seasonally, like woollen garments in winters or umbrellas in the rainy season. The production of these goods takes place throughout the year to meet the seasonal demand. So there is a need to store these goods in a warehouse to make them available at the time of need.

(iii) **Large-scale Production:** In case of manufactured goods, nowadays production takes place to meet the existing as well as future demand of the products. Manufacturers also produce goods in huge quantity to enjoy the benefits of large-scale production, which is more economical. So the finished products, which are produced on a large scale, need to be stored properly till they are cleared by sales.

(iv) **Quick Supply:** Both industrial as well as agricultural goods are produced at some specific places but consumed throughout the country. Therefore, it is essential to stock these goods near the place of consumption, so that without making any delay these goods are made available to the consumers at the time of their need.

(v) **Continuous Production:** Continuous production of goods in factories requires adequate supply of raw materials. So there is a need to keep sufficient quantity of stock of raw material in the warehouse to ensure continuous production.

(vi) **Price Stabilization:** To maintain a reasonable level of the price of the goods in the market there is a need to keep sufficient stock in the warehouses. Scarcity in supply of goods may increase their price in the market. Again, excess production and supply may also lead to fall in prices of the product. By maintaining a balance of supply of goods, warehousing leads to price stabilization.

TYPES OF WAREHOUSES

After getting an idea about the need for warehousing, let us identify the different types of warehouses.

Warehousing caters to the storage needs of different types of commodities. In order to meet their requirement, various types of warehouses came into existence, which may be classified as follows.

- Private Warehouses
- Public Warehouses
- Government Warehouses
- Bonded Warehouses
- Cooperative Warehouses

(i) **Private Warehouses:** The warehouses which are owned and managed by the manufacturers or traders to store, exclusively, their own stock of goods are known as private warehouses. Generally, these warehouses are constructed by the farmers near their fields, by wholesalers and retailers near their business centres and by manufacturers near their factories. The design and the facilities provided therein are according to the nature of products to be stored.

(ii) **Public Warehouses:** The warehouses which are run to store goods of the general public are known as public warehouses. Anyone can store his goods in these warehouses on payment of rent. An individual, a partnership firm or a company may own these warehouses. To start such warehouses, a licence from the government is required. The government also regulates the functions and operations of these warehouses. Mostly these warehouses are used by manufacturers, wholesalers, exporters, importers, government agencies, etc.

(iii) **Government Warehouses:** These warehouses are owned, managed and controlled by central or state governments or public corporations or local authorities. Both government and private enterprises may use these warehouses to store their goods. Central Warehousing Corporation of India, State Warehousing Corporation and Food Corporation of India are examples of agencies maintaining government warehouses.

(iv) **Bonded Warehouses:** These warehouses are owned, managed and controlled by government as well as private agencies. Private bonded warehouses have to obtain licence from the government. Bonded warehouses are used to store imported goods for which import duty is yet to be paid. In case of imported goods the importers are not allowed to take away the goods from the ports till such duty is paid. These warehouses are generally owned by dock authorities and found near the ports.

(v) **Cooperative Warehouses:** These warehouses are owned, managed and controlled by cooperative societies. They provide warehousing facilities at the most economical rates to the members of their society.

Characteristics of Ideal Warehouses

In the above section, you have learnt about different types of warehouses. In each of these warehouses, adequate arrangements are made to keep the goods in proper conditions. However, any warehouse is said be an ideal warehouse if it possesses certain characteristics, which are given below:

- Warehouse should be located at a convenient place near highways, railway stations, airports and seaports where goods can be loaded and unloaded easily.
- Mechanical appliances should be there to loading and unloading the goods. This reduces the wastages in handling and also minimizes handling costs.
- Adequate space should be available inside the building to keep the goods in proper order.
- Warehouses meant for preservation of perishable items like fruits, vegetables, eggs and butter, etc. should have cold storage facilities.
- Proper arrangement should be there to protect the goods from sunlight, rain, wind, dust, moisture and pests.
- Sufficient parking space should be there inside the premises to facilitate easy and quick loading and unloading of goods.
- Round-the-clock security arrangement should be there to avoid theft of goods.
- The building should be fitted with latest firefighting equipment to avoid loss of goods due to fire.

Functions of Warehouses

Warehouses preserve goods on a large scale in a systematic and orderly manner. They provide protection to goods against heat, wind, storm, moisture, etc. and also cut down losses due to spoilage, wastage, etc. This is the basic function of every warehouse. In addition to this, warehouses nowadays also perform a variety of other functions. In this section, let us learn about the various functions of warehouses.

Warehouses perform the following functions:

- Storage of goods
- Protection of goods
- Risk bearing
- Financing
- Processing
- Grading and branding
- Transportation

We shall now discuss each of these functions.

(i) **Storage of goods:** The basic function of warehouses is to store large stock of goods. These goods are stored from the time of their production or purchase till their consumption or use.

(ii) **Protection of goods:** A warehouse provides protection to goods from loss or damage due to heat, dust, wind and moisture, etc. It makes special arrangements for different products according to their nature. It cuts down losses due to spoilage and wastage during storage.

(iii) **Risk bearing:** Warehouses take over the risks incidental to storage of goods. Once goods are handed over to the warehousekeeper for storage, the responsibility of these goods passes on to the warehousekeeper. Thus, the risk of loss or damage to goods in storage is borne by the warehousekeeper. Since it is bound to return the goods in good condition, the warehouse becomes responsible for any loss, theft or damage, etc. Thus, it takes all precautions to prevent any mishap.

(iv) **Financing:** When goods are deposited in any warehouse, the depositor gets a receipt, which acts as a proof about the deposit of goods. The warehouses can also issue a document in favour of the owner of the goods, which is called warehousekeeper's warrant. This warrant is a document of title and can be transferred by simple endorsement and delivery. So while the goods are in custody of the warehousekeeper, the businessmen can obtain loans from banks and other financial institutions keeping this warrant as security. In some cases, warehouses also give advances of money to the depositors for a short period keeping their goods as security.

(v) **Processing:** Certain commodities are not consumed in the form they are produced. Processing is required to make them consumable. For example, paddy is polished, timber is seasoned, and fruits are ripened, etc. Sometimes warehouses also undertake these activities on behalf of the owners.

(vi) **Grading and branding:** On request warehouses also perform the functions of grading and branding of goods on behalf of the manufacturer, wholesaler or the importer of goods. It also provides facilities for mixing, blending and packaging of goods for the convenience of handling and sale.

(vii) **Transportation:** In some cases warehouses provide transport arrangement to the bulk depositors. It collects goods from the place of production and also sends goods to the place of delivery on request of the depositors.

Advantages of Warehousing

Warehousing offers many advantages to the business community. Whether it is industry or trade, it provides a number of benefits which are listed below.

(i) **Protection and preservation of goods:** Warehouse provides necessary facilities to the businessmen for storing their goods when they are not required for sale. It provides protection to the stocks ensures their safety and prevents wastage. It minimizes losses.

(ii) **Regular flow of goods:** Many commodities like rice, wheat, etc. are produced during a particular season but are consumed throughout the year. Warehousing ensures regular supply of such seasonal commodities throughout the year.

(iii) **Continuity in production:** Warehouse enables the manufacturers to carry on production continuously without bothering about the storage of raw materials. It helps to provide seasonal raw material without any break, for production of finished goods.

(iv) **Convenient location:** Warehouses are generally located at convenient places near road, rail or waterways to facilitate movement of goods. Convenient location reduces the cost of transportation.

(v) **Easy handling:** Modern warehouses are generally fitted with mechanical appliances to handle the goods. Heavy and bulky goods can be loaded and unloaded by using modern machines, which reduces cost of handling such goods. Mechanical handling also minimizes wastage during loading and unloading.

(vi) **Useful for small businessmen:** Construction of own warehouse requires heavy capital investment, which small businessmen cannot afford. In this situation, by paying a nominal amount as rent, they can preserve their raw materials as well as finished products in public warehouses.

(vii) **Creation of employment:** Warehouses create employment opportunities both for skilled and unskilled workers in every part of the country. It is a source of income for the people, to improve their standards of living.

(viii) **Facilitates sale of goods:** Various steps necessary for sale of goods such as inspection of goods by the prospective buyers, grading, branding, packaging and labelling can be carried on by the warehouses. Ownership of goods can be easily transferred to the buyer by transferring the warehousekeeper's warrant.

(ix) **Availability of finance:** Loans can be easily raised from banks and other financial institutions against the security of the warehousekeeper's warrant. In some cases warehouses also provide advance to the depositors of goods on keeping the goods as security.

(x) Reduces risk of loss: Goods in warehouses are well guarded and preserved. The warehouses can economically employ security staff to avoid theft, use insecticides for preservation and provide cold storage facility for perishable items. They can install firefighting equipment to avoid fire. The goods stored can also be insured for compensation in case of loss.

Warehouse Location

The warehouse location selection is a processing of selecting allocation centre in economic region where there are some supply stations and the certain demand point. Generally, the warehouse location selection model follows some principles: adaptable principle, coordinative principle, efficient principle and strategic principle.

FACTORS TO LOOK BEFORE WAREHOUSE LOCATION SELECTION

External Factors

Are your warehouses in the right location to meet the service requirements of customers and internal cost requirements?

Look at—

- supply points
- lead times for supply replenishment to the warehouses
- transportation costs for trailer loads from supply points into the warehouse and for order shipment freight from the warehouses to customers
- time required from order sending by the customer until order delivery receipt at the customer

Internal Factors

- How well inventory placed and managed in warehouses? How well warehouses operate?

Organizational Factors

- Where does the warehouse responsibility appear and rank on logistics and company organization chart?

Factors important in influencing the location of a warehouse include:

Moderate environmental conditions: The environmental conditions that the package or container is exposed to should be considered. A number of factors in environment are not easily controlled, such as humidity, heat, cold.

- Utilities if refrigeration is required
- Security
- Transportation costs

Whether the location is near the city or village, easily accessible or remote, very far from the market or nearby is important in order to decide appropriate means of transport.

- Proximity to markets, especially if frequency of delivery is high
- Customer locality to the proposed new warehouse location
- Supplier's locality to the proposed new warehouse location
- Availability of trained labour
- Cost of the space–Purchase or rent and rates
- Construction and land costs, labour availability, proximity to raw materials, and waste disposal are less important for location of warehouses.

Ideal Warehouse Location

- Protects of stock against moisture, insects, dust, fumes, pests, thieves, fire, etc.
- Provides facilities for ware housing activities like plenty of water for drinking and firefighting.
- Facilitates economics of operation.
- Away from sources of detrimental conditions.
- Easy access from highway, railhead and waterfront. No geographic barriers. There are no natural barriers like river or steep hills
- Proximity to 'A' category customers.

Warehouse Costs

Cost of handling and holding the materials in warehouse and costs of order processing, inventory, and lot quantity are components of warehouse costs.

STORAGE MANAGEMENT

Storage management is meant for minimizing deterioration and spoilage. It is a common practice particularly when dealing with materials that tend to deteriorate or obsolete, to issue old material ahead of new material.

Receiving of Materials: Receiving is essentially a clerical operation. Because man clerical activities are regarded as routine, however, the importance of the receiving function often is underrated.

Most problems or error in a purchasing transaction should come to light during receiving operation. If the problem is not detected and corrected during the receiving operation the cost to correct the mistake later is always higher.

Receiving Procedure: A typical receiving procedure consists of four steps.

- Unloading and checking the shipment.
- Unpacking and inspecting the material.
- Completion of the receiving report.
- Deliver of the material

Identification System

In a broader sense, there are two types of material identification system. These are:

(a) External Systems

The two most commonly used external systems are:

The Harmonized Commodity Description and Coding System: It provides a set of descriptions and six-digit codes for commodity identification, description and reporting. It also contains an option for the addition of 4 more digits to provide more local detail.

The Export Commodity Control Numbers System: Consists of product numbers that take the form of five character alphanumeric code. The system is used primarily for security sensitive materials requiring export control.

(b) Internal system

Most firms follow some type of symbolic approach in designing the system. Symbolic systems can be either numerical or mnemonic. The numerical system typically assigns a 6-10 digit code number to each item. The following example illustrates the concept:

2	137	019	508
General Class	Generic Class	Subclass	Specific item number

Different Types of Storage Systems

Closed System: In this system all materials are stored in a closed or controlled area. Whenever possible, the general practice is to maintain physical control by locking the storage area. Material enters and leaves the area only with the accompaniment of an authorized document.

The system is designed to afford maximum physical security and to ensure tight accounting control of inventory material.

Open System: Storage facilities are completely open, and any worker has access to a storage facility. In plant using this system, no storerooms as such exist; each material is stored as close to its point of use as is physically possible. It places less emphasis on the physical security of materials.

- Materials are stored in bins, on shelves, in racks, on pallets, into the boxes, and so on.
- It also places less emphasis on the accounting control of materials. Materials are usually put into production without the use of requisition or a control document.
- Materials used in this system should not be subject to pilferage, nor should be easily damaged.
- No perpetual inventory records are kept in an open system. To determine the actual usage of a material during a given period, it is necessary to take a physical count of the material at the end of the period and compare this figure with the similar beginning-period figure, adjusted for material receipts during the period. Hence, accounting charges are determined indirectly rather than directly.
- It is most applicable in situation where a repetitive production operation produces standardized products.
- This system is most likely to function successfully if it is not applied to a large no. of items.

Random Access Storage System: It is a unique type of closed stores systems, used by a relatively small no. of large firms. In this system no material has a fixed storage location. When an item enters the storeroom, it is stored in the first available bin or shelf suitable for its storage requirement. When the item is withdrawn from the stores, the storage space is available for another incoming item having similar physical storage requirements. All materials thus stored at random locations throughout the warehouse.

Disadvantage: Tight physical control of materials may be more difficult to achieve. Stores clerks seldom become familiar with the total stock of any item, simply because they lose the close visual contact they have with the materials in a conventional system.

Advantage: The system provides great flexibility. The same storage facilities can easily accommodate different materials, shifts in inventory mix and an unexpected increase in the stock level of an existing material.

Automated Storage/Retrieval System (AS/RS): A combination of the random access storage concept, highly sophisticated storage/retrieval machines, and a computerized control system has produced this system. The storage facility frequently is a 30-80 ft high rise structure constructed of open steel columns. Typically, it is configured into storage cubicles of different sizes and utilizes various types of standardized pallets and containers for storage.

A number of warehouse stock clerks are replaced with automated storage/retrieval machines that are mounted on captive floor rails or on conventional wheels. The tall vehicles normally controlled by computer have a lifting platform with a shuttle that stores and retrieves palletized loads on both sides.

WAREHOUSE DESIGN

While designing warehouse the following criteria needs to be looked into:

- Warehouse design criteria address physical facility characteristics and product movement.
- Three factors to be considered in the design process are:
  - The number of stories in the facility,
  - Height utilization, and
  - Product flow.

Number of stories in the facility: The ideal warehouse design is limited to a single story so that product does not have to be moved up and down. The use of elevators to move product from one floor to the next requires time and energy.

The elevator is also often a bottleneck in product flow since many material handlers are usually competing for a limited number of elevators.

Height utilization: Regardless of facility size, the design should maximize the usage of the available cubic space by allowing for the greatest use of height on each floor. Most warehouses have 20- to 30-foot ceilings (1 foot = 12 inch; 1 inch = 2.54 cm), although modern automated and high-rise facilities can effectively use ceiling heights up to 100 feet.

Through the use of racking or other hardware, it should be possible to store products up to the building's ceiling. Maximum effective warehouse height is limited by the safe lifting capabilities of material-handling equipment, such as forklifts.

Product flow: Warehouse design should also allow for straight product flow through the facility whether items are stored or not. In general, this means that product should be received at one end of the building, stored in the middle, and then shipped from the other end. Straight-line product flow minimizes congestion and confusion.

Storage Plan

A warehouse design should consider product characteristics, particularly those pertaining to volume, weight, and storage. Product volume is the major concern when defining a warehouse storage plan. High-volume sales or throughput product should be stored in a location that minimizes the distance it is moved, such as near primary aisles and in low storage racks. Such a location minimizes travel distance and the need for extended lifting. Conversely, low-volume product can be assigned locations that are distant from primary aisles or higher up in storage racks.

A Sample Storage Area

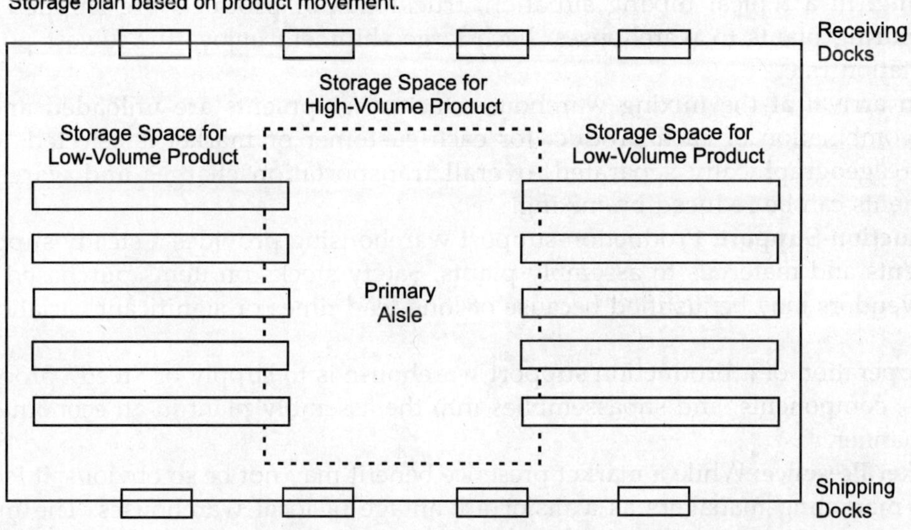

The storage plan should include a specific strategy for products dependent on weight and storage characteristics. Relatively heavy items should be assigned to locations low to the ground to minimize the effort and risk of heavy lifting. Bulky or low-density products require extensive storage volume, so open floor space or high-level racks can be used for them.

On the other hand, smaller items may require storage shelves or drawers. The integrated storage plan must consider and address the specific characteristics of each product.

SERVICE BENEFITS OF WAREHOUSING

Five basic service benefits are achieved through warehousing:

Spot stock: Under spot stocking, a selected amount of a firm's product line is placed or "spot stocked" in a warehouse to fill customer orders during a critical marketing period. In particular, manufacturers with limited or highly seasonal product lines are partial to this service.

Utilizing warehouse facilities for stock spotting allows inventories to be placed in a variety of markets adjacent to key customers just prior to a maximum period of seasonal sales. Suppliers of agricultural products to farmers often use spot stocking to position their products closer to a service-sensitive market during the growing season.

Assortment: An assortment warehouse stocks product combinations in anticipation of customer orders. The assortments may represent multiple products from different manufacturers or special assortments as specified by customers.

In the first case, for example, an athletic wholesaler would stock products from a number of clothing suppliers so that customers can be offered assortments. In the second case, the wholesaler would create a specific team uniform including shirt, pants, and shoes.

Mixing: In a typical mixing situation, truckloads of products are shipped from manufacturing plants to warehouses. Each large shipment enjoys the lowest possible transportation rate.

Upon arrival at the mixing warehouse, factory shipments are unloaded and the desired combination of each product for each customer or market is selected. When plants are geographically separated, overall transportation charges and warehouse requirements can be reduced by mixing.

Production Support: Production support warehousing provides a steady supply of components and materials to assembly plants. Safety stocks on items purchased from outside vendors may be justified because of long lead times or significant variations in usage.

The operation of a production support warehouse is to supply or "feed" processed materials, components, and subassemblies into the assembly plant in an economic and timely manner.

Market Presence: While a market presence benefit may not be so obvious, it is often cited by marketing managers as a major advantage of local warehouses. The market presence factor is based on the perception or belief that local warehouses can be more responsive to customer needs and offer quicker delivery than more distant warehouses.

As a result, it is also thought that a local warehouse will enhance market share and potentially increase profitability.

Stacking and Storage System

In almost any warehouse, forklifts will be used to move materials into, out of and around the warehouse. The largest storage systems are those that are designed for forklift access. They include a wide variety of pallet racks and cantilever racks.

The next down in scale if not importance are the dozens of other types of racks that are needed for warehouse storage. These might be portable racks that can easily move numbers of boxes at a time or be stacked tightly together to save space when needed.

Another versatile storage system is the stackable U-rack. U-racks are designed to be stacked up to 4 units high and can be placed close together when needed for holding heavier loads or further apart for less demanding loads. They can be accessed by forklift or materials can be removed by hand if desired.

Shelving systems are essential warehouse supplies and there are innumerable systems available to suit any specific or general purpose. Some of these may be light duty shelving units for small parts or lightweight goods and others may be heavy-duty and can safely store thousands of pounds of heavy materials. They may have fixed or adjustable steel shelves or they may have wire shelves. Whatever the need, there is a purpose-made steel shelving unit.

Some items need to be stored behind closed doors. Here again, there are innumerable options available that include everything from personal lockers for the staff to small parts cabinets and modular drawer cabinets. They can be as small as a nine plastic drawer cabinet for housing small numbers of screws or as large as a garage, for storing dangerous and restricted use goods.

Then there are the many types of storage bins that will be required in the warehouse. As with the other storage receptacles, these will be designed and constructed according to the purpose they are needed for. They might be made of corrugated fibreboard, plastic or even wire. There will be stackable bins, interlocking bins or stand alone bins. Some bins may be hinged or on wheels. Whatever the storage or handling need, there is an appropriate bin.

Then there are the waste receptacles that need to be considered. There are dozens of types of these, many of which will be needed in the average warehouse. In the office, under-desk wastebaskets will be needed. Outside, large, heavy duty trash containers will be required. Out in the public areas, stone panel trashholders may be required, as well as purpose-designed cigarette butt receptacles.

The number and variety of storage solutions that a warehouse needs is mind-boggling. The catalog of storage containers that a warehouse supplies company will sell is huge. When you look at the storage needs of a single warehouse, it looks as if a warehouse is really an intricate nested system of smaller "warehouses" that work as a unit to ensure maximum efficiency and productivity.

PILFERAGE PROTECTION

Pilferage is the theft of part of the contents of a package. It may also include theft of the contents but leaving the package, perhaps resealed with bogus contents. Small packages can be pilfered from a larger package such as a shipping container. Broader aspects of theft may include taking the entire package, pallet load, truck load, shoplifting, etc.

Solutions may involve all phases of product production, packaging, distribution, logistics, sale, and use. No single solution can be considered as "pilfer proof". Often multiple levels of security need to be addressed to reduce the risk of pilfering.

Some considerations might include:

- Identify who a potential pilferer might be: an internal employee, security guard, truck driver, delivery person, receiver (consignee), organized crime, etc. What level of knowledge, materials, tools, etc. might they have?
- Identify all feasible methods of unauthorized access into a product, package, or system. In addition to the primary means of entry, also consider secondary or "back door" methods.
- Identify available means of resealing, reclosing, or replacing special seals.
- Use extra strong and secure packaging: A weak or damaged package is an invitation to pilferage.
- Consider unique custom seals and labels (change regularly because these are subject to counterfeiting)
- Improve the pilfer resistance to make pilfering more difficult, time-consuming, etc.
- Conceal the identity and value of a pilferable item. Do not bring attention to the item, its package, addresses, names, etc.
- Add pilfer-evident features to help indicate the existence of pilfering.
- Choose a logistics provider who can reduce the risks of pilferage.
- Educate people to watch for evidence of pilfering.
- Use a wider and stronger closure tape, 3 inch or 72 mm, reinforced gummed tape or pressure sensitive tape.
- Use a tamper evident tape or seal that leaves a message or warning if removed.

PRODUCT DETERIORATION

Within the warehouse, a number of factors can reduce a product or material to a non-usable or non-marketable state. The most obvious form of product deterioration is damage from careless transfer or storage. Another major form of deterioration is non-compatibility of products stored in the same facility. The primary concern is deterioration that results from improper warehouse work procedures. A constant concern is the carelessness of warehouse employees. In this respect, the forklift truck may well be management's worst enemy. Regardless of how often operators are warned against carrying overloads, some still attempt such shortcuts when not properly supervised.

In one situation, a stack of four pallets was dropped off a forklift truck at the receiving dock of a food warehouse. Standard procedure was to move two pallets per load. The value of the damaged merchandise exceeded the average daily profit of two supermarkets. Product deterioration from careless handling within the warehouse is a form of loss that cannot be insured against and constitutes a 100 per cent cost with no compensating revenue.

SHRINKAGE

In financial accounting the term **inventory shrinkage** (sometimes truncated to **shrink**) is the loss of products between point of manufacture or purchase from supplier and point of sale. The term **shrink** relates to the difference in the amount of margin or profit a retailer can obtain. If the amount of shrink is large, then profits go down which results in increased costs to the consumer to meet the needs of the retailer. The total shrink percentage of the retail industry in the United States was 1.52% of sales in 2008 according to the University of Florida's, National Retail Security Survey. In Europe shrinkage was about 1.27% of sales and the same figure for Asia Pacific was 1.20% according to the Global Retail Theft Barometer 2008.[2].

Causes of Shrinkage

An estimated 44% of shrinkage in 2008 was due to employee theft, totalling over $15.9 billion. Another 35% was due to shoplifting, totalling over $12.7 billion.[1] The prevention of this type of shrinkage is one reason for security guards, cameras and security tags. Other causes of shrinkage include:

- Damage in transit or in the store.
- Administrative errors such as shipping errors, warehouse discrepancies, and misplaced goods.
- Cashier or price-check errors in the customer's favour.
- Vendor fraud.
- Perishable goods not sold within their shelf life.

PEST CONTROL

Warehouse pest control is an integral part of routine maintenance procedure and is a top requirement to pass business audits for licensing and accreditation. Such huge attention to the sanitation of the warehouse is due to the fact that business products, usually food, are stored here after manufacturing and prior to distribution. Not to mention that final goods stored in these warehouses are very vulnerable to irreversible damage, most notably infestation and contamination.

Warehouse audit: This is one of the main reasons why business put a premium to warehouse pest control. A single sighting of any pest in a factory's storehouse during an audit would spell a lot of damage to the company—financial and reputation-wise. Auditors are very discriminating when it comes to cleanliness and safety of storage facilities, and pests are the number one nemesis they look out for. In their books, pests in warehouses are strong negative indications of a company's negligence to follow proper sanitation procedures. The presence of these pesky creatures in food warehouses spell possible health concerns while in furniture storehouses, these are negative points against the quality of the goods.

Most common culprits : Several pests may be found in warehouses but the common targets of warehouse pest control services can be grouped into three: insects, rodents, and flying birds.

Insect pests are a whole range and may include weevils, several kinds of beetles, and moths. The most common, however, is the warehouse beetle which attacks stored foods. A sign that a warehouse is infested with these beetles are sighting of the adult insects in window sills and in spilled food in crevices and cracks. Their exact location, however, may be quite difficult to pinpoint as they tend to live inside food packages.

Rodents, especially rats, are also a major concern in different warehouses—be it food, clothes, paper, or furniture. This is because rats have the high tendency to gnaw through everything they can rest their teeth on and in food warehouses, they could spell contamination and tons of health concerns.

Lastly are the flying pests such as birds and bats which may make their nests or homes in warehouse window, blocking natural airflow inside the warehouse. Bird and bat droppings are also a huge sanitation problem in warehouses.

INVENTORY MANAGEMENT

"Inventory is an idle material resource of an enterprise awaiting future sales, use, or transformation."

"Inventory is the stock of any item or resource used in an organization and can include: raw materials, finished products, component parts, supplies, and work-in-process".

In accounting language, it may include:

(a) Raw Material: They are required to carry out production activities uninterruptedly.

(b) Work-in-Progress: It is a stage of stocks between raw material and finished goods.

(c) Consumables: These are needed to smoothen the process of production.

(d) Finished Goods: These are the goods which are ready for the consumers.

(e) Spares: Form a part of inventory.

Purposes of Inventory

- To maintain independence of operations
- To meet variation in product demand
- To allow flexibility in production scheduling
- To provide a safeguard for variation in raw material delivery time

Needs of Inventory Management

- To ensure continuous supply of raw material, spares and finished goods.
- To avoid both overstocking and understocking of inventory.
- To maintain investments in inventories at optimum level.
- To keep material cost under control.
- To eliminate duplication in ordering or replenishing stocks.
- To minimize losses through wastage and damages.
- To facilitates finishing of data.

INVENTORY CONTROL

Inventory Control is the process by which inventory is measured and regulated according to predetermined norms such as economic lot size for order or production, safety stock, minimum level, maximum level, order level, etc.

Inventory control pertains primarily to the administration of established policies, systems and procedures in order to reduce the inventory cost.

Objectives of Inventory Control

- To meet unforeseen future demand due to variation in forecast figures and actual figures.
- To average out demand fluctuations due to seasonal or cyclic variations.
- To meet the customer requirement timely, effectively, efficiently, smoothly and satisfactorily.
- To smoothen the production process.
- To facilitate intermittent production of several products on the same facility.
- To gain economy of production or purchase in lots.
- To reduce loss due to changes in prices of inventory items.
- To meet the time lag for transportation of goods.
- To meet the technological constraints of production/process.
- To balance various costs of inventory such as order cost or set-up cost and inventory carrying cost.
- To balance the stock out cost/opportunity cost due to loss of sales against the costs of inventory.
- To minimize losses due to deterioration, obsolescence, damage, pilferage, etc.
- To stabilize employment and improve labour relations by inventory of human resources and machine efforts.

Factors Affecting Inventory Control

- Type of product
- Type of manufacture
- Volume of production

Benefits of Inventory Control

- Ensures an adequate supply of materials
- Minimizes inventory costs
- Facilitates purchasing economies
- Eliminates duplication in ordering
- Better utilization of available stocks
- Provides a check against the loss of materials
- Facilitates cost accounting activities
- Enables management in cost comparison
- Locates and disposes inactive and obsolete store items
- Consistent and reliable basis for financial statements

Inventory Cost

Ordering Costs: It is the cost of ordering the item and securing its supply. It includes:
- Expenses from raising the indent
- Purchase requisition by user department till the execution of order
- Receipt and inspection of material

Inventory Carrying Costs: Costs incurred for holding the volume of inventory and measured as a percentage of unit cost of an item. It includes-
- Capital cost
- Obsolescence cost
- Deterioration cost
- Taxes on inventory
- Insurance cost
- Storage and handling cost

Carrying Cost: It includes
- Capital costs
- Storage space costs
- Inventory service costs
- Handling-equipment costs
- Inventory risk costs

Out-of-Stock Costs: It is the loss which occurs or which may occur due to non-availability of material. It includes:
- Breakdown/delay in production
- Back ordering
- Lost sales
- Loss of service to customers, loss of goodwill, loss due to lagging behind the competitors, etc.

Other Costs

- **Capacity Costs:** Over-time payments, Lay-offs & idle time
- **Set-up Costs:** Machine set-up, Start-up scrap generated from getting a production run started.
- **Overstocking Costs**

Inventory Models

Economic Order Quantity (EOQ): EOQ or Fixed Order Quantity system is the technique of ordering materials whenever stock reaches the reorder point. Economic order quality deals when the cost of procurement and handling of inventory are at optimum level and total cost is minimum. In this technique, the order quantity is larger than a single period's requirement so that ordering costs and holding costs balance out.

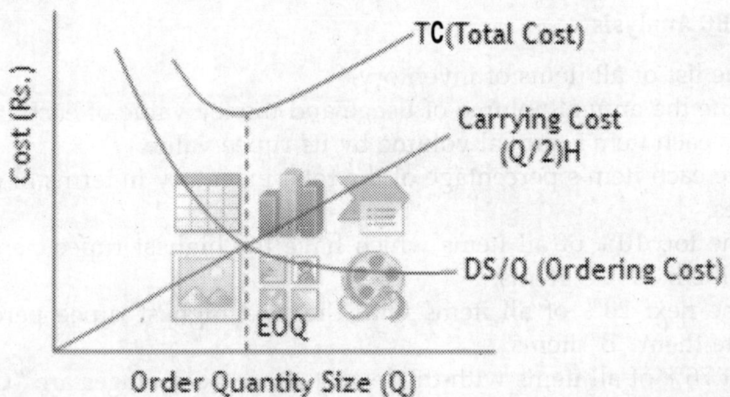

Basic Fixed Order Quantity Model (EOQ)

Total Annual Cost = Annual Purchase Cost + Annual Holding Cost + Annual Ordering Cost

$$TC = DC + \frac{Q}{2}H + \frac{D}{Q}S$$

$$EOQ = \sqrt{\frac{2DS}{H}}$$

TC = Total annual cost
D = Demand
C = Cost per unit
Q = Order quantity
S = Cost of placing order/setup cost
H = Annual holding and storage cost per unit of inventory

Order Points and Service Levels

- Minimum Level – It is the minimum stock to be maintained for smooth production.
- Maximum Level – It is the level of stock, beyond which a firm should not maintain the stock.
- Reorder Level – The stock level at which an order should be placed.
- Safety Stock – Stock for usage at normal rate during the extension of lead time.
- Reserve Stock – Excess usage requirement during normal lead time.
- Buffer Stock – Normal lead time consumption.

Classification of Inventory Control

Always Better Control (ABC) Analysis: This technique divides inventory into three categories A, B & C based on their annual consumption value. It is also known as Selective Inventory Control Method (SIM). This method is a means of categorizing inventory items according to the potential amount to be controlled. ABC analysis has universal application for fields requiring selective control.

Procedure for ABC Analysis

- Make the list of all items of inventory.
- Determine the annual volume of usage and money value of each item.
- Multiply each item's annual volume by its rupee value.
- Compute each item's percentage of the total inventory in terms of annual usage in rupees.
- Select the top 10% of all items which have the highest rupee percentages and classify them as "A" items.
- Select the next 20% of all items with the next highest rupee percentages and designate them "B" items.
- The next 70% of all items with the lowest rupee percentages are "C" items.

Advantages of ABC Analysis

- Helps to exercise selective control.
- Gives rewarding results quickly.
- Helps to point out obsolete stocks easily.
- In case of "A" items careful attention can be paid at every step such as estimate of requirements, purchase, safety stock, receipts, inspections, issues, etc. and close control is maintained.
- In case of "C" items, recording and follow up, etc. may be dispensed with or combined.
- Helps better planning of inventory control
- Provides sound basis for allocation of funds and human resources.

Disadvantages of ABC Analysis

- Proper standardization and codification of inventory items needed.
- Considers only money value of items and neglects the importance of items for the production process or assembly or functioning.
- Periodic review becomes difficult if only ABC analysis is recalled.
- When other important factors make it obligatory to concentrate on "C" items more, the purpose of ABC analysis is defeated.

VED Classification

- VED: Vital, Essential & Desirable classification
- VED classification is based on the criticality of the inventories.
- Vital items – Its shortage may cause havoc and stop the work in organization. They are stocked adequately to ensure smooth operation.
- Essential items–Here, reasonable risk can be taken. If not available, the plant does not stop; but the efficiency of operations is adversely affected due to expediting expenses. They should be sufficiently stocked to ensure regular flow of work.

- Desirable items – Its non-availability does not stop the work because they can be easily purchased from the market as and when needed. They may be stocked very low or not stocked.
- It is useful in capital intensive industries, transport industries, etc.

VED analysis can be better used with ABC analysis in the following pattern:

Category	"V" items	"E" items	"D" items
"A" items	Constant control and regular follow up	Moderate stocks	Nil Stocks
"B" items	Moderate stocks	Moderate stocks	Low Stocks
"C" Items	High stocks	Moderate stocks	Very Low Stocks

FSN Analysis

- FSN: Fast moving, slow moving and non-moving
- Classification is based on the pattern of issues from stores and is useful in controlling obsolescence.
- Date of receipt or last date of issue, whichever is later, is taken to determine the no. of months which have lapsed since the last transaction.
- The items are usually grouped in periods of 12 months.
- It helps to avoid investments in non-moving or slow items. It is also useful in facilitating timely control.
- For analysis, the issues of items in past two or three years are considered.
- If there are no issues of an item during the period, it is "N" item.
- Then up to certain limit, say 10-15 issues in the period, the item is "S" item
- The items exceeding such limit of no. of issues during the period are "F" items.
- The period of consideration and the limiting number of issues vary from organization to organization.

MODERN WAREHOUSE MANAGEMENT

Modern warehouse management can be defined as implementation of computer applications and automated machinery to improve efficiency of warehouse operations.

Parameter	Warehouse	Modern Warehouse
Operations	Manual	Automated
Cost	High	Comparatively Low
Product Placement	Unorganized	Organized
Paper Work	More	Less
Order Processing	Slow	Fast
Time Consumption	More	Less

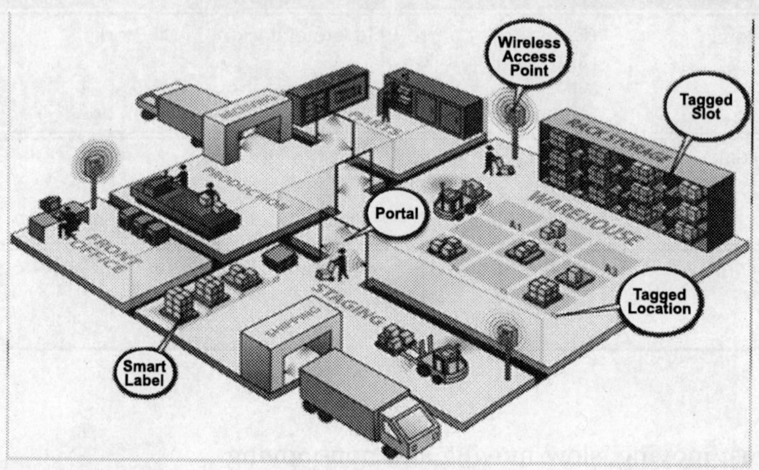

Modern Warehouse Design

Some Automated System

(i) Overhead Conveyor System

(ii) Forklifts

- Horizontal transport of goods with stacking jobs.
- Move goods onto load-carrying devices like pallets, wire-mesh boxes or individual parts.
- Suited for short trips and mid-range transport frequency.

(iii) Automatic Identification and Data Capture

Automatic Identification and Data Capture (AIDC) refers to the methods of automatically identifying objects, collecting data about them, and entering that data directly into computer system.

- The process of obtaining external data, through analysis of images, sounds or videos.
- Getting information and entering that data or feeding it directly into computer systems.
- Modern Warehouse Management often utilizes Auto ID Data Capture (AIDC) technology.

Some AIDC are –

- Radio frequency identification (RFID)
- Bar code scanners
- Mobile computers
- Wireless LANs

(iv) Bar code Scanner

A bar code reader (or bar code scanner) is an electronic device for reading printed bar codes.

(v) Mobile Computers

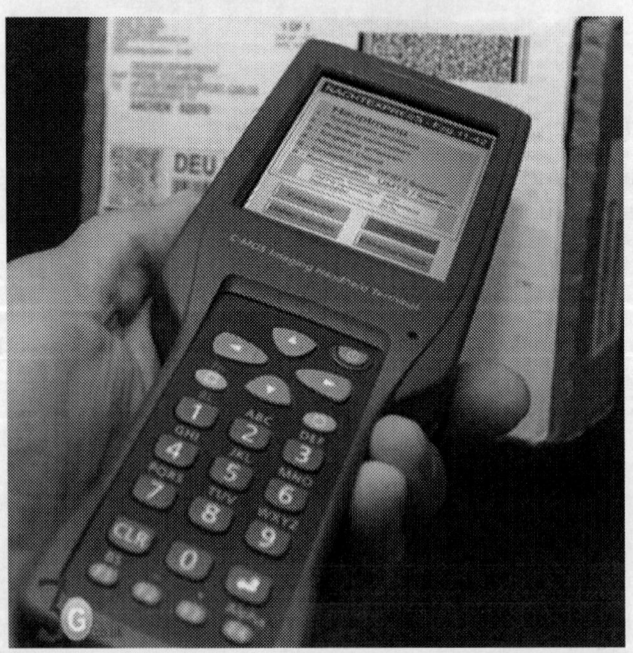

(vi) Radio Frequency Identification – RFID

Radio frequency identification (RFID) is the use of an object (typically referred to as an RFID tag) applied to or incorporated into a product, animal, or person for the purpose of identification and tracking using radio waves.

- Tags can be read from several metres away and beyond the line of sight of the reader
- Provides an accurate knowledge of the current inventory
- Emerged in response to the need for a next generation bar code
- RFID system consists of a tag (transponder) and a reader (interrogator)
- Deals with the remote collection of information (identification number)stored on a tag using radio frequency communications
- Contactless scanning of goods

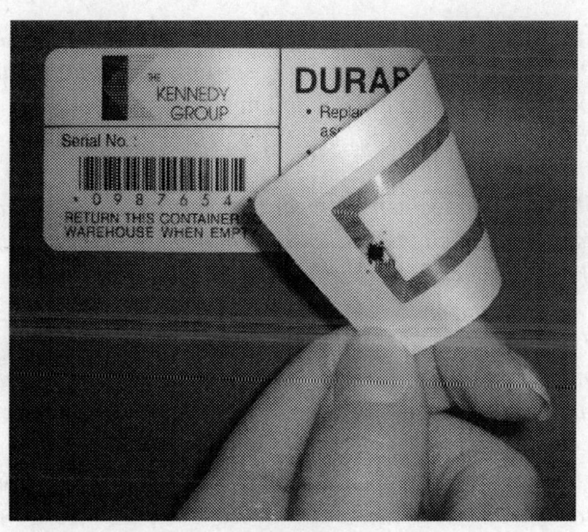

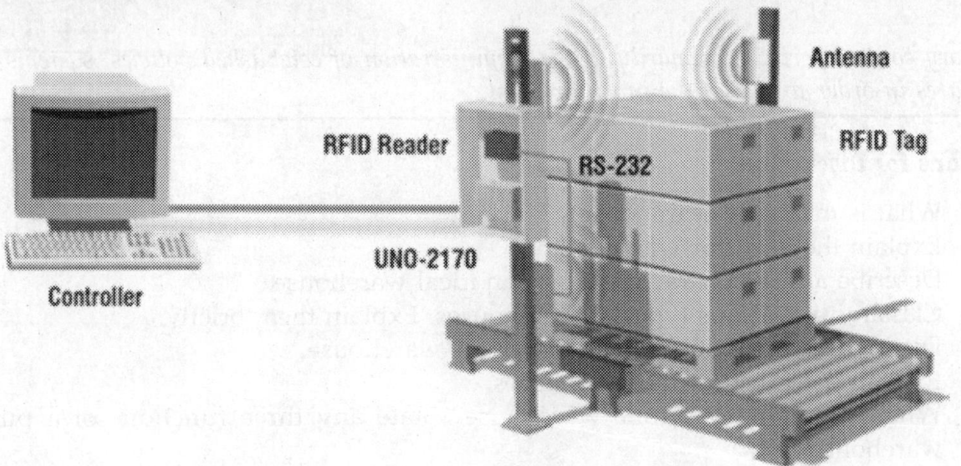

Let Us Sum Up

A warehouse is the centre of any retail distribution organization. The fast and accurate tracking of shipments and organization of those shipments is a vital component to any distribution firm. In order to streamline the warehouse tasks, many companies are turning to upgrade current infrastructures to increase efficiency and speed of various warehousing tasks.

Warehouses preserve goods on a large scale in a systematic and orderly manner. They provide protection to goods against heat, wind, storm, moisture, etc. and also cut down losses due to spoilage, wastage etc. This is the basic function of every warehouse. In addition to this, warehouses nowadays also perform a variety of other functions. In this section, let us learn about the various functions of warehouses.

The warehouse location selection is a processing of selecting allocation centre in economic region where there are some supply stations and the certain demand point. Generally, the warehouse location selection model follows some principles: adaptable principle, coordinative principle, efficient principle and strategic principle.

Storage management is meant for minimizing deterioration and spoilage. It is a common practice particularly when dealing with materials that tend to deteriorate or obsolete, to issue old material ahead of new material.

Inventory is an idle material resource of an enterprise awaiting future sales, use, or transformation. Inventory is the stock of any item or resource used in an organization and can include: raw materials, finished products, component parts, supplies, and work-in-process.

Inventory control is the process by which inventory is measured and regulated according to predetermined norms such as economic lot size for order or production, safety stock, minimum level, maximum level, order level, etc.

Inventory control pertains primarily to the administration of established policies, systems and procedures in order to reduce the inventory cost.

Questions for Discussion

1. What is meant by warehousing?
2. Explain the need for warehousing.
3. Describe any six characteristics of an ideal warehouse.
4. Classify the various types of warehouses. Explain them briefly.
5. Distinguish between public and private warehouse.
6. Explain the functions of warehouses.
7. What is meant by public warehouse? State any three functions of a public warehouse.

8. Describe the advantage of warehouses to the businessmen.
9. How is a bonded warehouse useful for the importers?
10. Warehousing is one of the important auxiliaries to trade. Explain this statement in about 60 words.
11. Write short notes on (i) Private warehouse (ii) Public warehouse (iii) Government warehouse (iv) Bonded warehouse.
12. Explain the factors important in influencing the location of a warehouse.
13. Explain different types of storage system.
14. Write short notes on (i) Stacking (ii) Pilferage protection (iii) Product deterioration (iv) Shrinkage (v) Pest control.
15. Explain the concept of inventory management.
16. Write short notes on (i) EOQ (ii) ABC Analysis (iii) VED Analysis (iv) FSN Analysis.
17. Explain few techniques of modern warehouse management.

9

CHAPTER

Case Studies

Case Study: I

Everyone is Part of the Sales Team

Robin, one of your salespeople, calls the home office of XYZ office supplies, and sounding angry and righteous, blasts the factory and support people for not paying attention to a customer. He claims that they caused late delivery, didn't follow up and shipped the wrong products. The imprudent home-office manager reacts angrily and says to Robin, "Who do you work for anyway? Me (meaning the company) or the customer?"

As tempers flare (as they can in telephone confrontation), the conversation ends with "who the hell do you think you are?"

Questions for Discussion

1. What do you suppose all that was really about?
2. What was Robin's motivation?
3. What emotions did his behaviour disguise, perhaps unconsciously?
4. How should the home-office manager have evaluated the situation?
5. How should we read this whole situation?
6. What would you do as Robin's sales manager?

Case Study: II

Soya Bean Milk Company

Dr S. Chakrabarty was domiciled in Los Angeles, USA for last 8 years. After getting his Masters' in Food Technology from University of California, he had obtained a Ph.D. in the same subject specializing in 'high protein products.' After completing his education, he had joined a company, HyPro Inc., where he was now Director (R&D). The company had developed different types of high protein products, which were marketed through a large number of departmental stores throughout the USA. The company was enjoying a good reputation.

Dr Chakrabarty was seriously thinking of returning to India and settling down in his hometown of Bangalore. He was toying up with the idea for last 2 to 3 years to set up a plant to produce few of such high protein products in India. During his earlier visits, after talking to different people, he had noticed the availability of soya bean in abundance. He had carried out several experiments in his laboratory and has developed what he called as "Soya Bean Milk". He felt that for a poor country, like India, with majority of the children being undernourished, this would be an ideal product.

Soya bean milk would have some percentage of normal milk, water and different other raw materials added to give it a high protein value. It will be pasteurized, so refrigeration would not be essential and will have almost same or better life than average milk. Soya bean milk would cost about 15 per cent more than the regular milk, which he felt, was justified due to its high protein values. To obtain the same proteins, other substitutes or medicines, he felt would be ten times more costly.

As he was 15,000 miles away from his potential market, he first wanted to ascertain the feasibility of this project. He had several questions on which he wanted to get the answers. Some of these were:

(i) Whether the tradition bound Indian population would accept a new concept like Soya bean milk?

(ii) In which town should he set up his plant? And of what capacity?

(iii) In which form should he introduce this soya bean milk–as a substitute to normal milk or by adding different flavours, as a competitive product to already existing soft drinks?

(iv) What sort of distribution arrangement he should have?

Technically he was confident about the production of this soya bean milk. Marketing-wise and commercially whether such a project will be viable or not was his main doubt. His friends had informed him that recently two companies have already introduced soya bean milk in India which was, however, very costly in the market. This did not worry him much as he felt that his product would be superior and that with such large population in India, even a dozen competitors should do reasonably good business.

Questions for Discussion

1. What type of information should Dr Chakrabarty collect to decide on the setting up of this project?
2. What strategy would you recommend for marketing of soya bean milk in India for him?

(AIMA Dec., 1997)

Case Study: III

Nokia Plans to Design Handsets for Disabled

In an effort to take the mobile phone to the next billion worldwide, Nokia has started research to roll out handsets, specifically designed for the disabled. The world's largest handset vendor plans to undertake extensive research in India to understand the consumer behaviour of people with visual or hearing problems, towards the mobile phone.

Nokia is exploring ways to make the mobile phone friendly for such consumers. This could be done through using a different user interface, using icons and pictures in the menu and the phonebook instead of text, using large fonts, louder ringing tones and voice commands.

These phones might have a different design aspect where India will also play a vital role. Talking to ET during his recent visit to India, Nokia global director, product group (entry business unit, mobile phones) Heikki Koivu said the challenge to sustain growth will be to reach out to consumers who do not use a mobile phones.

"We then have to address issues like physical disabilities, low vision, poor hearing and illiteracy. We also need to design phones that can support hearing aids," he said. Mr Koivu said India is a focus market for Nokia to understand consumer behaviour of mobile phones among the disabled.

"It is due to the sheer size of the population in this country. We have started adapting such features in some entry-level handsets like Nokia 1650 shipped to emerging countries like India. But, this will now attain bigger scale," said Mr Koivu.

India and China are two of Nokia's largest markets for entry level phones. The entry-level portfolio includes handsets, which are priced between Rs. 1,500 and Rs. 5,000. Nokia is also planning to bundle its Internet services 'Ovi' in the entry level phones sold in India.

"We are planning to bundle most of the Ovi applications in handsets shipped to India, including the music services Nokia Music Store. All such integration will take place over the next three years for the entry-level handsets. We need to simplify these applications to suit the consumer preferences in emerging markets," said Mr Koivu.

Questions for Discussion

1. "Mobile for disables" – do you like this idea? Explain.
2. What could be the marketing strategy for Nokia to market mobile sets for disables?
3. What could be the additional features can be associated with the mobile set? Explain.

Case Study: IV

What Information is Needed?

When Florida Computer Sales (FCS) opened its doors last year, the lack of information and control became apparent. Customers often wanted to return current requirement and buy new models. This transaction means finding the new equipment in inventory, estimating trade-in value, handling the financing and inserting the used equipment into stock. The record keeping involved phone calls back and forth among customers, salespeople, and FCS; filling out paperwork; reviewing sales slips; searching for inventory; and guessing well. Hiring more bookkeepers to keep track of things did not help. FCS's entrepreneurial business, which was growing rapidly until now, may peak soon. Product sales were increasing so rapidly it was almost impossible to avoid having out-of-stock items. Customers and salespeople were complaining and FCS's business was being hurt.

Questions for Discussion

1. What suggestions do you have for improving information and control at FCS?
2. How would a computer information system help FCS give better service customers?

Case Study: V

Plans Don't Always Work

It all started when the vice president for marketing and sales at ABC limited asked for a special fourth-quarter sales push. He selected you, the sales manager, to design a programme that would enable the company to reach his goal of a significant increase in profits in this quarter over last quarter. You worked on the plan for five days and finally presented your proposal to the vice president: if the company added 8.5 per cent to the promotional budget, your sales team would contribute an extra 17 per cent to the profit.

Your plan would work through the raising of each salesperson's quota by 20 per cent. This additional sales volume would generate enough revenue to increase profits to the goal level desired by the marketing vice president. The additional 8.5 per cent requested for the promotional budget would be sent to motivate the sales forces. Prizes would be awarded based on the percentage each salesperson sold above his or her quota. The prizes were fantastic. The top prize was a luxury-model car, and even the "worst" prize was a deluxe 35 mm camera set. Since this contest was based on percentage of improvement, each salesperson had the opportunity to enhance his or her best sales effort.

You felt your plan could not fail. You had used past sales history to determine projected profits and necessary supporting expenditures. You had even found a way to motivate all the members of your sales team. Unfortunately, the plan didn't work.

Questions for Discussion

1. Why did you go over the expense budget, spending almost 10 per cent more instead of the approved 8.5 per cent increase?
2. Why did sales increase only 7 per cent, instead of the 17 per cent you had promised?
3. Was the plan bad, or was failure caused by poor implementation?
4. Now what are you going to do?

Case Study: VI

THE WILSON COMPANY
Is the Sales Manager's Job Really for Me?

Goy Gresham was still at her desk at 6 p.m. trying to tie up some loose ends with the hope that tomorrow might be a more productive day. Joy is the western regional sales director (a middle management position) in the Wilson Company. Wilson is a manufacturer of a well-known line of sporting goods. As she reads the mail she still has to return, she wonders if being a middle manager is really her kind of job. Selling products, travelling, and meeting with clients seemed much more to her linking than the routine of her present job.

Today is a good example. Joy went to the office early so she could call Lewis Jackson, the eastern regional sales director, to confer on a joint sales forecast they are trying to prepare. Working with Lewis isn't the easiest of tasks. Compromise just isn't a word in Lewis's vocabulary. She also needs to call the production managers of two of the company's eastern plants to find out what is causing the delay in the receipt of the new product lines. Those production people don't seem to realize that a large inventory is needed to keep up sales. The new product lines were promised two weeks ago and still aren't here. The phone calls take longer than expected, but by midmorning Joy is finally able to settle into the major project she has planned for the day. After several days of perusing sales reports of the past several years, she concluded that total sales as well as productivity of individual salespersons, can be improved if the region is redesigned and the territories of each salesperson are adjusted. This is a major project and she must present it to her district sales managers at her monthly meeting tomorrow afternoon.

Joy is away from the office a little longer than expected because of lunch. When she returns she finds a half dozen phone messages, including an urgent call from the corporate vice president of personnel, Wayne McDaniel. She returns Wayne's call, and, much to her dismay, she finds she is going to have to allocate a good portion of tomorrow's sales meeting to presenting the company's new benefits programme. Wayne assures her that all the materials she needs will arrive late this afternoon and stresses the ned for its immediate dissemination and explanation. After tying unsuccessfully to return several of the other phone calls, she returns to the territory redesign project. She finishes that project just before the 3 p.m. appointment she has with a candidate for district sales manager. Joy spends more than an hour with the candidate and is impressed enough with him to immediately make some follow-up phone calls.

Joy looks at her watch and realizes she hasn't enough time to make all the calls she'd planned. The whole day seems to have gotten away from her. She still has the materials from Wayne to review, and she has to prepare the agenda for tomorrow's meeting. She just has to figure a way to motivate better performance from those sales managers. The redesigns of the territory was only a partial solution. Joy wonders what else she can do. "Oh" , she thinks to herself, " I better call and cancel my date of tonight. It has been over three weeks since I've had any life other than work, and it feels like the only time I ever leave this office is to eat lunch."

Questions and Discussion

1. Compare Joy's present job to what you think her previous job as a salesperson was. How are they similar? How are they different?
2. What managerial skills are depicted in the case? Which skill is most important for Joy to possess? Why?
3. Why do you feel Joy might be disenchanted with her present job?

Case Study: VII

Good Packaging can Change Consumer Perception

Good packaging can change consumer perception. Smaller manufacturing companies, that include private labels, have taken to innovative packaging to hit their target consumers. Dadima's Magic mango pickle, ITS fruit tomato ketchup, Mehek Dehradoon Basmati, 24 Letter Mantra and Bread & More are some of the products available in shops with good packaging motifs.

Most of these companies have an advertising budget of Rs 2-5 crore, of which a good amount is invested in packaging the product. "If I am asked to do only packaging and the rest of the communication is outsourced, I'd say give me the entire kitty. Jokes apart, it's prudent to assign 5-7% for packaging alone," said Tarun Das of Oxygen.

Agrees Rajshekhar Reddy of Sresta Bio Products: "Most companies end up spending more in packaging than the product itself as packaging is an important aspect nowadays. Unless the goods stand out from the clutter, it is not sold out. We tend to review our packaging every two years." The company has launched an organic food store chain brand called '24 Letter Mantra' based out of Hyderabad. "We are doubling revenues on a Y-o-Y basis and I think a significant part can be attributed to good packaging," adds Mr Reddy.

This was not so a few years back as packaging was not given much emphasis by the smaller companies. Technology upgradation, awareness and increased competition has helped smaller brands establish themselves in a little time. This, backed by innovative communication ideas, promotions and packaging, has helped these companies grow.

Sresta created innovative packaging for the kids meal segment with a tiffin box. "Packaging has changed in the last few years with innovative technology chipping in. The standards of packing has changed as there are no restrictions in terms of use of colour, shape and even material," adds Mr Das of Oxygen that looks after the entire communication of the company.

The retail boom has also helped these companies as they get a platform to showcase their products in multi-brand outlets. "The consumer buying behaviour is very impulsive and it is the pricing, colour scheme, offers and packaging that attract them to buy a product if that is not an important item," adds Mr Das. Agrees Asheesh Sethi of Noshe Oceanic: "A well-packaged product gives an edge over other products because the consumer might find it attractive if there is not much of a difference in the quality of the product." Groverson's Paris Beauty, a lingerie brand, is a good example of packaging.

While all other brands were concentrating on the same package style, we thought of changing it. Instead of a picture of single women on the packet, we did seven different poses of a single girl wearing different designs of lingerie. This was done to fight back the intrusion of foreign brands in India," added Mr Sethi.

"The consumer can now have a visual impact of the various product lines available at one go. The consumer behaviour has also changed, adds Sethi. Bread & More from the Kwality Group is another example of good packaging. "The recent trend is to constantly evolve the packaging. No one continues with the same look for too long. Most brands that have identified the importance of packaging constantly evolve to cater to the evolving needs of the consumer," says Creativeland Asia MD Sajan Rajkurup.

For Aureole Inspecs' new eyewear brand Mayhem, Innocean has developed key brand visuals and packaging formats to illustrate the brand's cool attitude and appeal. "Sometime, even additions like a branded carrybag help in enlarging the brand idea," says Innocean Worldwide India joint MD Vivek Srivastava.

Questions for Discussion

1. "Good packaging can change consumer perception" – Explain.
2. "Packaging" or "Branding" – Justify.
3. Write short notes on "innovative packaging".

Case Study: VIII

Whole Food Distribution Company

Situation

This company distributes whole foods to small health food stores and large supermarket chains. There is strong demand for the company's products–one product in particular has been recommended by a popular TV chef – and the company has grown to about 50 staff.

Current Initiatives and Concerns

Architecture

The company offices are currently being rebuilt to remove the separation between the levels of the company. Instead of the management sitting upstairs and everyone else downstairs, a mezzanine floor is being constructed, with informal meeting and eating areas. Management hopes that this will improve communications across the firm, and restore the sense of "family" that the company had when it was smaller, in smaller premises.

Balance between small shops and large supermarket chains.

The large supermarkets control a very high share of the total UK market for food. It is essential to distribute via supermarkets if you want your products to reach the majority of the population.

At the same time, the company wants to continue to supply the small shops. However, since the typical order quantities for the small shops are much lower, the costs of delivery and administration are proportionately much greater. Furthermore, some very small shops insist that they cannot afford to buy a whole pack of a single product, and want to buy half a pack. When such demands are met, this incurs further cost and effort.

Thus, smaller shops are seen as less efficient for the company - each one bringing less revenue for the company in return for greater cost and effort. It might be possible to deal with this situation by differential pricing - supplying to supermarkets at a much lower price, in recognition of higher volumes and greater efficiency - but this tactic is understandably unpopular with the small shops.

In any case, excessive dependency on supermarkets carries a commercial risk. There may be arbitrary variation in volumes and strong pressure on prices that can destabilize the other part of the business. Sometimes the popularity of a brand can encourage a supermarket to develop its "own brand", leading to poaching of markets.

Alignment between Company Values and Individual Values

The managing director expressed some envy of the delivery folk. They are at the front line of the company, interacting with the retailers and customers. He likes to do deliveries himself sometimes, as this gives him a chance to escape from the paperwork and talk to people outside the company.

It makes him sad that the delivery folk themselves don't do the job the way he does, with the same attention to the customer. They just want to dump the goods as quickly as possible and push on with the next delivery. When there is a problem, they don't stay to sort it out, and he has to handle the complaints.

Loss of Personal Relationship

Another thing that the managing director misses is the intimacy of a smaller company. At one time, he knew everyone in the company, and understood their strengths and weaknesses, likes and dislikes, ambitions and priorities. Managers and staff mixed socially as well as at work.

Now he has to manage at a higher level of abstraction, making decisions about types rather than individuals.

Other Possible Issues

Positioning – small supplier of unique high value products or sourcing service for important market niche? Warehousing and supply chain inbound. Supply chain assurance, ability to recall product if necessary.

Questions for Discussion

1. Why do you think the company wants to supply to small shops as well as to large supermarkets? How might this be threatened by differential pricing?
2. What do you think would motivate the delivery staff to spend more time on "customer care"?
3. What measures of performance might be appropriate for this company?
4. What are the problems that companies face when they grow beyond a certain size? How can these problems be addressed?
5. What do you think of the leadership style indicated in this case?
6. Are disagreement and conflict (within the management team, between levels) healthy or unhealthy?

Case Study: IX

Apex Electrical Company Ltd.

Mr. Nathan, sales manager of Apex Electrical Co. Ltd, received a proposal from his regional manager at Bangalore for opening a sub-office in Chennai and was considering what the best decision would be the company's short-run as well as long-run interests. The company was in the business of manufacturing and marketing electric motors of a wide range of horsepowers that could be used as a primemover in numerous applications.

The company's factory and head office were situated in Mumbai and it had branch offices at New Delhi, Kolkata and Bangalore: each headed by a regional manager. The regional office at Bangalore was responsible for sales in Karnataka, Tamil Nadu and Kerala. The company also maintained a godown at Bangalore, which, was used as the stocking centre for feeding sales to the entire region. The company's distribution network had grown over several years and as such there was no one rule by which the arrangements could be explained. In Karnataka, due to the proximity of the regional headquarters, the distribution network was closely controlled by the regional office. The company had several dealers covering sales and they all purchased goods directly from the regional office. All the dealers got a fixed discount. The ultimate prices for the customers were fixed by the company. Each dealer covered a specific area, which was generally one to several districts and the company discouraged the interference of one dealer in another's territory. However, in the cities of Bangalore and Mysore, there was more than one dealer. They collectively covered the sales in the city. The company salesmen regularly contacted the dealers and the office maintained good marketing information.

In the states of Tamil Nadu and Kerala, however, the arrangement was quite different. Due to some historical reasons, all the sales in this territory were channelled through one distributor. This distributor in turn had appointed his own dealers to cover the cities of Chennai and Kochi and other districts in these two states. The regional office, therefore, had very little information on the exact marketing set-up in this territory and the distributor operated almost independently. On several occasion, the regional manager had attempted to bring the distributor under closer control. He had the impression that the company was not able to exploit the full potential of the regional due to the authoritarian rule of the distributor.

He occasionally received reports that the distributor was not even aware of certain important tenders floated in the region and that on other occasions he had not bothered to submit quotations in time. There were also complaints from dealers that they did not get a fair deal and would instead prefer to deal with the company directly. The sales and service personnel of the regional office used to visit the states of Tamil Nadu and

Kerala only when requested specifically by the distributor. Their independent visits were generally objected to by the distributor, as it would mean by-passing him. The real problem behind this was that the distributor had, in the initial states, given considerable financial help to the company. He was also an important did not mean, however, that the top management was prepared to sacrifice the company's interests. But at the same time they preferred to leave the distributor undisturbed.

The regional manager felt that the little pieces of negative feedback he had received could be the tip of the iceberg. However, in the absence of any information, he could not put up a convincing case against the distributor. He had always been helpless whenever some dealer working under the distributor complained to him. He felt it would seriously affect their morale if they realized that the company could not control the distributor.

He had discussed this matter at length with the sales manager, Mr Nathan realized that some tightrope waling was needed if he had to steer and clear this problem. Mr. Nathan was, however, anxious to do something about it and one idea was to open an office at Chennai, the headquarters of the distributor. While this would be for the declared purpose of helping the distributor in his marketing effort, it would also put an automatic check on undesirable practices. Moreover, the sub-office could collect more factual information that could be used to put up a convincing case against the distributor, if such a need arose. Accordingly, the regional manager had now submitted a detailed proposal for opening a sub-office at Chennai, which would look after Tamil Nadu to start with.

The company had a strict policy of insisting on the regional office to achieve a fixed ratio of sales per rupee of expense. For the Bangalore office this ratio was 50 in the previous year when the sales were Rs. 2 crore and expenses Rs. 4 lakh. Of this, the sales in Tamil Nadu were Rs. 50 lakh. The proposal stated that a sales forecast of Rs. 60 lakh could be expected in Tamil Nadu next year and estimated expenses of Chennai sub-office at Rs. 1.2 lakh, thus achieving a ratio of Rs. 50 sales per rupee of expense. Among other things, the details of the proposal stated the following splitting up of the expenses–Rs. 40,000 towards salaries and Rs. 30,000 towards travelling expenses of 2 sales personnel who would be transferred from Bangalore to Chennai.

Questions for Discussion

1. What decision would you take if you were in place of Mr. Nathan?
2. Do you feel the proposal of new sub-office is economically justified against the stated policy of the company? If yes, why? If no, then how could it be made justifiable?

Case Study: X

Dilemma in Dividend Payment

A.C. Company Ltd. has improved its profitability in 2003-04, and is on a growth path after poor performance in preceding two years. The following is the summary of the company's operations during preceding three years.

The company's focus in 2003-04 was on cost reduction and funds management rather than growth in sales. Operating and interest cost fell by 3.3% and 60% respectively. According to the company's managing director "The turnover in 2003-04 dipped because of a drop in volumes. However, the sales are not strictly comparable because in the previous year there was a large order worth Rs. 15 crore from a public sector oil company. On the other hand, the net profit growth was higher because of better asset management. This resulted into reduced borrowings and lowered the financial charges". The Company was able to bring down its inventory holding period to 46 days from 81 days and debtors holding period to 95 days from 119 days. The company is changing its debt policy to a conservative policy. The debt equity ratio of 1.8:1 in the 2001-02 has been brought down to 5:1 in 2003-04.

A.C. Company Ltd. operating performance:

Particulars	2001-02, In crore	2002-03, In crore	2003-04, In crore
Sales	53.4	75.6	69.5
Gross profit	3.4	4.5	12.3
Net profit	1.3	1.3	5.9
EPS	1.8	1.8	8.1

The prospects of the company for the increased business in 2004-05 are estimated to be good. According to the managing director "The general industrial activity as such has picked up which should result in a better demand for the company's products from sectors such as automobile, mining and chemicals "Experts think that a compressor industry will grow at 10% in 2004-05. The company's strategy of cost reduction and improving marketing efficiency will continue.

The company operates in the compressor industry and drilling and mining equipment industry. It is number two in the compressor industry after I.S. company. The product profile of the company in the years has shifted in favour of the compressor sector.

In 2003-04 the company's gross block increased to 22 crore from 20 crore. The company has planned for an investment of Rs. 5 crore in its Poona factory. The company's shares enjoys Good Liquidity and its P/E ratio is 32. In the expectation of good performance, the company's share prices started rising since January 2004, and sharply increased to Rs. 285 just before the budget from Rs. 190 in January. The current price is around Rs. 225-35. In the last two years, the company paid a dividend of 10%. The company was wondering should it pay a higher dividend in 2003-04.

Questions for Discussion

1. Analyze its financial conditions.
2. Recommend the dividend to be paid by the company.

References

1. Krishna K. Havaldar, Vasant M. Cavale , Sales & Distribution Management, Tata McGraw-Hill, Latest Edition.
2. Richard R. Still, Edward W. Cundiff, Norman A.P. Govoni, Sales Management: Decisions, Strategies & Cases, Pearson, Latest Edition.
3. Johnson F.M., Kurtz D.L., Scheuing E.E. Sales Management: Concepts, Practice, and Cases, Tata McGraw-Hill, Latest Edition.
4. S.L. Gupta, Sales and Distribution Management, Excel Books, 2010.
5. Cron, Sales Management: Concepts and Cases, 10 Edn, 2010, Wiley.
6. Spiro, Stanton, Management of a Sales Force, 11e, TMH, 2008.
7. Tanner, Sales Management, Pearson, 2010.
8. Still-Sales Management Decisions, Strategies and Cases, 5/e, Pearson, 2010.
9. Cundiff and Govni, "Sales Management–Decisions, Strategy and Cases", Prentice-Hall of India, New Delhi.
10. Laforge, Avila, Schwepker and Williams, "Sales Management", Thomson.
11. Watuba R. Thomas,"Sales Management–Texts and Cases", Business Publication.
12. Johnson, Kurtz and Scheving "Sales Management, Concept Practice & Cases, McGraw-Hill.
13. Simchi Levi (2000). Designing and Managing the Supply Chain, Irwin, McGraw-Hill, IL.
14. Christopher, M., 1992. Logistics and Supply Chain Management: Strategies for Reducing Costs and Improving Services, Pitman, London.
15. Croucher Phil, Rushton Alan and Oxley John, The Handbook of Logistics and Distribution Management.
16. Douglas M. Lambert, 1998. Fundamental of Logistics Management, McGraw-Hill.
17. Sahay B.S., 1998. Supply Chain Management for Global Competitiveness (Macmillan).
18. Chopra Sunil and Meindl P., 2001. Supply Chain Management: Strategy, Planning, and Operation, Prentice Hall.

19. Forrester J.W. 1961. Industrial Dynamics, Cambridge, Massachusetts, The MIT Press.
20. Waters Donald, 2003. Logistics: An Introduction to SCM, Palgrave, McMillan (Indian Edition), NY.
21. Bowersox D. J., Closs D. J. and Helferich O.K. 1986. Logistical Management, Macmillan.
22. Chopra S. and Meindl P. 2001. Supply Chain Management: Strategy, Planning, and Operation, Pearson Education Inc.
23. Christopher M. 1992. Logistics and Supply Chain Management: Strategies for Reducing Costs and Improving Services, Pitman.
24. Lambert D. M. 1998. Fundamental of Logistics Management, McGraw-Hill.
25. Gattorna J. 1995. Handbook of Logistics and Distribution Management, Ashgate Publishing Company.
26. Bowersox Donald J. and Closs David J. "Logistical Management–The Integrated Supply Chain Management", McGraw-Hill International Editions, 1996.
27. Janice H. Hammond and Maura G. Kelly, "Quick Response in the Apparel Industry", Harvard Business School Publishing, Case No. 9-690-038, April 24, 1991, pp. 1-19.
28. Joan Magretta, "Fast, global and entrepreneurial: Supply Chain Management, Hong Kong style An Interview with Victor Fung", Harvard Business Review, September-October 1998, pp. 103-114.
29. Marshall L. Fisher, Janice H. Hammond, Walter R. Obermeyer, and Ananth Raman. "Making supply meet demand in an uncertain world", Harvard Business Review, May-June 1994, pp. 83-93.
30. Marshall L. Fisher. "What is the Right Supply Chain for your Product?" Harvard Business Review, March-April, 1997, pp. 105-116.
31. Rhonda R. Lummus, Robert J. Vokurka and Karen L. Alber., "Strategic Supply Chain Planning", Production and Inventory Management Journal, Third Quarter, 1998, APICS, pp. 49-58.
32. Robert D. Buzzell, "Vanity Fair Mills–Market Response System", Harvard Business School, Case no. 9-593-111, Rev October 12, 1993, pp. 1-31.
33. Satyabir Bhattacharya. "Integrated Supply Chain Management – A key to Effective Manufacturing in the next Millennium", www.indiatoday.com/btoday/200010/plus/.html, 1/1/00, pp. 1-7.
34. Sumantra Sengupta and John Turnbull. "Seamless Optimization of the entire supply chain", IIE Solutions, October 1996, pp. 28-33.
35. Krishnaveni Muthiah (2003). Logistics Management & World Sea-borne Trade, Himalaya Publishing House, Mumbai (for basics of Logistics & marketing interface).
36. Deshmukh & Mohanty (2004). Essentials of SCM, Jaico Publishing House, Mumbai.
37. Simchi-Levi, David Kaminsky, Philipsimchi-Levi, Edith (2004). Designing and Managing the Supply Chain, Tata McGraw-Hill.
38. Mentzer, Fundamentals of Supply Chain Management, Sage India Publishers.

39. Burt, Dobler & Starling, World Class Supply Management, Tata McGraw-Hill.
40. D. Whitney (1988). Manufacturing by Design, Harvard Business Review, July 1988, pp. 83-91.
41. Simchi-Levi, D; Kaminsky, P. and Simchi-Levi, E. (2000). Designing and Managing the Supply Chain: Concepts, Strategies, and Case Studies, Irwin, McGraw-Hill, Singapore.
42. Chopra Sunil, Supply Chain Management: Strategy, Planning and Operations, Peter Meindl, Pearson Education (Singapore) Pte . Ltd.
43. Richard B. Chase, F. Robert Jacobs, Nicholas J. Aquilano, Operations Management for Competitive Advantage, Tata McGraw-Hill Publishing Company Ltd.

INDEX